THE IMAGERY OF INTERIOR SPACES

BEFORE YOU START TO READ THIS BOOK, take this moment to think about making a donation to punctum books, an independent non-profit press,

@ https://punctumbooks.com/support/

If you're reading the e-book, you can click on the image below to go directly to our donations site. Any amount, no matter the size, is appreciated and will help us to keep our ship of fools afloat. Contributions from dedicated readers will also help us to keep our commons open and to cultivate new work that can't find a welcoming port elsewhere. Our adventure is not possible without your support.

Vive la Open Access.

Fig. 1. Hieronymus Bosch, *Ship of Fools* (1490–1500)

THE IMAGERY OF INTERIOR SPACES. Copyright © 2019 by the editors and authors. This work carries a Creative Commons BY-NC-SA 4.0 International license, which means that you are free to copy and redistribute the material in any medium or format, and you may also remix, transform and build upon the material, as long as you clearly attribute the work to the authors (but not in a way that suggests the authors or punctum books endorses you and your work), you do not use this work for commercial gain in any form whatsoever, and that for any remixing and transformation, you distribute your rebuild under the same license. http://creativecommons.org/licenses/by-nc-sa/4.0/

First published in 2019 by punctum books, Earth, Milky Way.
https://punctumbooks.com

ISBN-13: 978-1-950192-19-9 (print)
ISBN-13: 978-1-950192-20-5 (ePDF)

DOI: 10.21983/P3.0248.1.00

LCCN: 2019937173
Library of Congress Cataloging Data is available from the Library of Congress

Book design: Vincent W.J. van Gerven Oei

HIC SVNT MONSTRA

The Imagery of Interior Spaces

Edited by
Dominique Bauer
& Michael J. Kelly

Contents

Michael J. Kelly
Preface:
History and the Interior Space   13

Dominique Bauer
Introduction:
The Imagery of Interior Spaces
and the Hazards of Subjectivity   21

Dominique Bauer
From the Enclosed Individual to Spatial Notions of a
"Beyond": Spatial Imagery in the Work of Jules Romains   35

Marcus Breyer
Sensualizing the "Over There": The Dissolving of Exteriority
and Interiority in "Geo-thoughts" and "Geo-song"   57

Aude Campmas
Evisceration: Exposing Internal Spaces in *La curée*   77

Stijn De Cauwer
The World as Seen through a Window: Interiors and
the Crisis of Morality in the Work of Robert Musil   97

Erin E. Edgington
Artful Arrangements: Interior Space in Edmond de
Goncourt's *La maison d'un artiste*   117

Gabrielle E. Orsi
In Her Chambers: Spaces of Fiction in Elsa Morante   139

Stefanie E. Sobelle
The Inscapability of Dwelling in Yoknapatawpha County   171

Lindsay Starck
"The (Dis)Possessed": Djuna Barnes's *Nightwood*
and the Modern Museum   193

Álvaro Santana-Acuña
Interior Spaces in Literature:
A Sociological and Historical Perspective   219

Contributors   237

Acknowledgments

I would like to express my gratitude to many colleagues and friends, from French studies, literary and cultural history, who supported and encouraged us to edit this volume. I would like to thank them for their enthusiasm, their advice and critical reading, in particular Anne-Françoise Morel of the Faculty of Architecture, Leuven. — Dominique Bauer

Throughout the extended process of writing, editing, revising and reviewing the chapters for this volume, friends and colleagues have provided valuable input and I would like to thank all of them for their support. I would also like to thank the contributors for their participation and, especially, Dominique Bauer for inviting me to be part of this intellectually enriching project. — Michael J. Kelly

PREFACE

History and the Interior Space

Michael J. Kelly

> "Long habit created in me a duty to it."
> — Isidore of Seville, *Synonyms*, 1.45

I would like to preface this volume with a short elicitation and interrogation of a trope quilted throughout its essays: history. From this, I analyze the exposed relationship in modern literature between interior space and history via the encounter with the past, in contrast to the exteriority of the present. The liminal space between these locations is where becoming materializes, where the subjective process formally begins. Interior space, history and subjectivity form the ontological trinity that frames and informs the critical theories and literary problems presented and interrogated in *The Imagery of Interior Spaces*.

As made apparent across the texts analyzed in this volume, interior space represents a desired present ever at risk of being shattered by a subconsciously known exterior reality. The interior is a space without time, the perpetual (present), and, as Bauer says in her Introduction, a "logic of pure presence" that is always in fear of the rupture of historical continuity engendered by the external. In Stijn De Cauwer's "The World as Seen Through a Window: Interiors and the Crisis of Morality in the Work of Robert Musil," it is evident that, in (Western) literature, the concept of interior space, as it relates to the subjective process and history, is inextricably entangled with the development of modernity and its tremendous changes. Interior space offers characters a site for conservative reaction to modernity, a place to hide from it, to ignore it, to occult it, a place to deny the (re-)emergence of politics and to construct an alternate modern history.

We see a diversity of interior spaces functioning in this way. In "In Her Chambers: Spaces of Fiction in Elsa Morante," Gabrielle Orsi discusses how Elisa de Salvi, the protagonist of *Menzogna e sortilegio* (1948), says that her writing "is inextricable from the chamber in which she dwells." In it she will unravel "the enigma of the past" in the pursuit of uncovering "actual history." The interior space serves as the site for Elisa to escape from actualized history. It is the "originating space" of both the novel and of Elisa's subjectivity.

Referring to Morante's late and last novel, Orsi notes that the gardens of *Aracoeli* "combine space and time into a lost unity." In *Aracoeli* (1982) the protagonist, Manuele, imagines the Garden of Eden effectively as an interior space where human *being* was whole. In it was the object allowing the preservation of that being, the perpetual present, the apple. The apple was timeless and could retrieve the past unbound by memory, but its consumption shattered human *being* (humans suffered an ontological break) eliciting human subjectivity. Orsi argues that "the classically Morantian plot is the evasion of an often grim or disappointing reality via a secret dream world of fantasy, memory, and reading." *Aracoeli* plays here on this theme by presenting the cruel and "provocative" divine game in which the interior space and its objects deny the whole of humanity the dream of memory, and the fantasy of the unity of existence.

In "The Inscapability of Dwelling in Yoknapatawpha County," Stefanie Sobelle examines the uses of interior space in a number of works by William Faulkner, including *As I Lay Dying* (1930) and *Absalom, Absalom!* (1936). She demonstrates Faulkner's use of interior space as a way for characters to deal with complex social transformations of the exterior, as a place where selfhood either is or may become, and where past and present can merge. "The past is never dead. It's not even past," Faulkner claims in

Requiem for a Nun (1951). He coalesces time and space into his own literary spatial form, argues Sobelle, who concludes by describing "Faulkner's theory of history as infinitely interiorized."

In "Evisceration: Exposing Internal Spaces in *La curée*," Aude Campmas argues that Émile Zola's *La curée* (1871) "is a tragedy that still deals with dramas of heredity and lineage. The tragic scene is the exposed place where the true origins of the family are revealed." Campmas explores Zola's violation of interior spaces, whether memories, the womb or the household, and shows how interior spaces correlate to artifice, to the attempted preservation of a historical situation and the exotic beyond within a constructed interior. The ensuing metaphor is the nineteenth-century hothouse, a place where what was desired from the external could be cultivated in the interior space. Here amidst the plants the private life of women could flourish, while preserving the illusion of social continuity. The exposure of the woman and the hothouse, of the interior, represent a sacrifice that destroys the illusion.

In "'The (Dis)Possessed': Djuna Barnes's *Nightwood* and the Modern Museum," Lindsay Starck focuses her critical review of Barnes's "novel" *Nightwood* (1937) on the interior space of the museum gallery where time literally is "set aside". She reads the novel as itself a museum, as an interior space uniquely modern. As such it is used to expose and examine the dynamic relation between modern literature, modernity, and history. One of the main characters, Nora, who hopelessly seeks her lover's commitment, desires to be inside the metaphorical (ship in a) bottle. There she can live in the world and its history in a state of being of perpetual present, a continuum in which she can attain immortality. In desiring to be part of the wider metanarrative of history, Nora frames it as a closed interior space.

In "Artful Arrangements: Interior Space in Edmond de Goncourt's *La maison d'un artiste*," Erin E. Edgington elaborates the association between history and interior space through a reading of Goncourt's catalogue volume. In *La maison* (1881), the trinkets and stuff of the house represent an attempt by Edmond, the central (present) character, to conserve the presence of his late brother Jules. They also allow a conservation of the premodern world: nostalgia. Edmond's bedroom is a chamber of the last century, a place that can transport him from the nineteenth century into the previous one. In one scene, in which Edmond kills his hen with a sword, the collected items — here both the sword and the pet hen — show that the interior space can provide not only sustenance, but also better sustenance than the exterior, where people were eating dogs and rats. The possibility of the interior is to protect against exterior reality until the situation "returns to normal"; the interior is the site of repression followed by obsessive habits. And so, despite his gloom, Edmond can find comfort in believing that the nineteenth century has at least brought about one comforting change: "Existence is no longer external." For our character, one of the optimistic alterations of the historical event of modernity is, then, precisely the fact that one can ignore it, and can do so by reverting to the rational and structured interior space for ontological meaning.

Here we encounter an overt correlation with history. History as organized and ordered, as rational, even a duty, is a similarly modernist development. The advent of professional history was equally escapist, or obscurantist. It was a way to make sense of the seeming disorder of the radical breaks from the past engendered by the modern world and its radical new affinities. Museums, homes, galleries, archives, disciplinary departments were interior sites using objects of the past to construct narratives of existence beyond the exterior present. As much as it is an illusion to believe that historical reconstruction could allow one to (re-)experience the past, so deluded are the activities of the collecting characters discussed in this volume. They catalogue, collect and build their interior sanctums, as a monk, to avoid the realities of the world, yet, ironically, do so by way of the methods and by the products that increasing define that modernist, consumerist, capitalist world.

At this point we encounter the subjective ambiguity — as Dominique Bauer discusses below — of the mutual gaze between interior and exterior. In a text not otherwise discussed in this volume, *The Master Builder* (1892), Henrik Ibsen has his characters on stage perform this uncomfortable and almost voyeuristic relationship. In the play, the master builder, Halvard Solness, builds churches until suffering a spiritual crisis that leads him to build only homes, "homes for human beings."[1] The play traverses the relationship between the inner-self, the relationship between outward success and inner happiness, and the master builder as man and the master builder as God. At the beginning of the third act, Aline, Solness's wife, tells Hilda that she sees the people from their little homes staring at her. Aline is an external object of gaze from the interior space of the home which serves as a reflection of her husband's abandonment of the spiritual for the material world, for the modern world, for the benefit of people's physical, external comfort over their inner fulfillment. The interior spaces of the homes seek and judge the external. In the other texts analyzed, we see, in various ways, the characters of the interior using the interior to hide, to rebuild their past world, but these actions require first the judging of the external. In *The Master Builder,* we see exterior space made to feel empty by the gaze of the interior.

By historicizing the interior space as a categorical reaction to modernity we can see its paranoias expand as the literature reaches late modernity, when, ultimately, the interior space will collapse from the pressures of the external. De Cauwer shows, through reading Robert Musil, how the "crisis of the interior" confirmed that the modern city could no longer be kept out. Musil's *The Man Without Qualities* was published in 1940. In it, Musil shows that interior space as a shield is a reactionary position doomed to failure. This is paramount to his criticism of Freud who, Musil thought, provided exactly this interior space as a false hope for maintaining old truths, situations of a different historical situation/moment. Musil described the psychoanalyst's room, De Cauwer explains, as a refuge from the chaos and confusion of modern life. In it, the patient could relax by lying down on the couch of the "soul-improving expert" and no

---

1 Henrik Ibsen, *The Master Builder,* trans. Edmund Gosse and William Archer (Project Gutenberg, 2010), Act II.

longer worry about the outside world: "[I]f the world explodes with all its mechanical energies, here you find the good old time gently flowing."[2] For Musil, we can only create new ontology by embracing the radical changes of society.

We have no knowledge of when we will begin and no knowledge of when we will end. We enter the world agonizing in confusion and pain, crying. We leave the world, and others cry. Existence is a confrontation with ambiguous spaces, boundaries of times, vectors of ontological movement, of interiority and exteriority. For the human mind, claimed Augustine of Hippo, self-consciousness is witnessed by way of the interiority of the corporeal, life cannot be without a body, existence cannot be without a space.[3] In the attempt to preserve and extend life, modern literary figures construct interior spaces to perform the role of the absent body of the desired external reality, the past. In "Sensualizing the 'Over There': The Dissolving of Exteriority and Interiority in 'Geo-thoughts' and 'Geo-song'," Marcus Breyer attempts to reconcile interior and exterior, the modernist crisis, by returning language to body through a comparative encounter with Hugo von Hofmannsthal's "[Lord] Chandos letter" (1902), Peter Waterhouse's "Klangtal" (2003) and the ecological aesthetics of the philosopher Gernot Böhme.

As seen across the essays of this volume, interior and exterior spaces meet at the threshold, the liminal space, where, at the ontological void, being straddles situations and must make the decision to embrace one or the other. In this way, as Álvaro Santana-Acuña notes in his "Postscript: Interior Spaces in Literature: A Sociological and Historical Perspective," the contributors to this volume expose the contrast in modern literature between inside and outside yet avoid "framing literary space in dyadic terms." Interior space is shown as a fundamental position in the subjective process and a crucial aspect of modern literature.

---

[2] Robert Musil, *Posthumous Papers of a Living Author,* trans. Peter Wortsman (Brooklyn: Archipelago Books, 2006), 107.

[3] Augustine, *City of God,* trans. and ed. R.W. Dyson (Cambridge: Cambridge University Press, 2005), 22–29.

Moreover, the interior space appears at the evental moment, at the site where what I call "anti-history" emerges and forces a subjective, historical decision towards fidelity, denial or fetish.[4] Being and anti-history/history are at the core of the struggles encapsulated in modern literature's interior space.

---

4   On the theory of anti-history see Michael J. Kelly, *Speculative Objectivity: A Radical Philosophy of History* (Earth: punctum books, in preparation).

Bibliography

Augustine, *City of God.* Edited and translated by R.W. Dyson (Cambridge: Cambridge University Press, 2005).

Ibsen, Henrik. *The Master Builder.* Translated by Edmund Gosse and William Archer. Project Gutenberg, 2010.

Kelly, Michael J. *Speculative Objectivity: A Radical Philosophy of History.* Earth, punctum books: forthcoming.

Musil, Robert. *Posthumous Papers of a Living Author.* Translated by Peter Wortsman. Brooklyn: Archipelago Books, 2006.

INTRODUCTION

The Imagery of Interior Spaces and the Hazards of Subjectivity

Dominique Bauer

> *In the interior, there were a thousand objects that inspired both curiosity and respect [...]. In the rooms where the three ladies slept, ate and worked, it was almost impossible to walk because of the very old furniture these were crammed with [...] all these heirlooms, a memory of past glories [...]. But the relics, the ruins that impressed most, were the three noble and degraded ladies that lived there.*
> — Benito Pérez Galdós, La fontana de oro[1]

In Benito Pérez Galdós's first and little known novel *La Fontana de oro* (*The Golden Fountain*, 1870), the señoras de Porreño y Venegas, descendants of an illustrious noble family, live in a humble, insignificant and decaying house on the Calle de Belén

---

1 'En el interior [...] había mil objetos que inspiraban a la vez curiosidad y respeto [...] En las habitaciones donde dormían, comían y trabajaban las tres damas, apenas era posible andar a causa de los muebles seculares con que estaban ocupadas [...] Todas estas reliquias, recuerdo de pasadas glorias [...] Pero las reliquias, las ruinas que más impresión producían, eran las tres damas nobles y deterioradas que allí vivían [...]' (Benito Pérez Galdós, *La fontana de oro* [Madrid: Perlado, Páez y Compañía, 1906], 122).

in Madrid.² The exterior does not seem anything much and does not reflect the impressive lineage of its dwellers, as Galdós notes in his typical ironic tone.³ The interior is depressing, dirty and dusty. The walls of the anti-chamber are filled with portraits of five generations of Porreños. Some of these have holes in the ancestors' faces, or have lost their color. All of them are covered in that kind of "classical dust the antiques dealers like so much."⁴ Time stands still in the humble house of the Porreño family. The clock in the house had stopped ticking at midnight on December 31st of the year 1800, and ever since, every moment is that very last moment. The frozen-in-time clock prevents the interior from evolving into the new century and the new political reality

---

2   Galdós's historical novel, *La fontana de oro,* which was largely written before 1868, was first and foremost an ideological and political work, reflecting the tensions between liberals and monarchists at the time of the first liberal constitution. On this, see, for example, Kathleen Ross, "Galdós' 'El audaz": The Role of Reader Response in a Serialized Spanish Novel," *Modern Language Studies* 11, no. 3 (1981): 36. Galdós was influenced by Honoré de Balzac's conception of literature as a means of historical comprehension. On the relationship between political context and events and literature with Galdós, see Stephen Gilman, *Galdós and the Art of the European Novel: 1867–1887* (Princeton: Princeton University Press, 1981), 120; Peter A. Bly, "Galdós, the Madrid Royal Palace and the September 1868 Revolution," *Revista de Estudios Hispánicos* 5, no. 1 (1980): 1–17. In *La fontana de oro,* the characters tend to embody ideas. For this reason, Robert H. Russell articulates the general interpretation that "the figures of La Fontana de oro are little more than drawings in a political cartoon, and most of the characters in the first series of novels (1867–1879) seem to approximate this description. They speak for ideological positions, and Galdós is brutally clear in his own sympathies" ("El Amigo Manso: Galdós with a Mirror," *Modern Language Notes* 78, no. 2 [1963]: 167). However, the multi-layered appearance of the interior space of the Porreño dwelling and its relationship with its inhabitants speaks particularly to other long-nineteenth-century interiors in literature. It explicitly brings forward fundamental aspects of the specific economy of the imagery of interior spaces, like the tension between objectification and the subject/dweller, and the relation between interiority and exteriority, to name the two most salient and overarching features.

3   "Pero si en el exterior ni en la entrada no se encontraba cosa alguna que revelase el altísimo origen de sus habitadores [...]" (Galdós, *La fontana de oro,* 119).

4   "con ese polvo clásico que tanto aman los anticuarios" (ibid, 120).

that is central to the novel. In a sense, since the last tick of the broken clock no further new "moments" in the Porreño house have passed. Everything in the house has become a lengthened here-and-now of a secluded past, long vanished in the turbulent and aversive world outside that opposes the conservative Porreño interior, so distinct from its insignificant exterior.

The dwellers of this timeless bubble of eternal decay, doña Maria de la Paz and her nieces doña Salomé and doña Paulita, seem hybrid creatures that are part and parcel of the architecture, of the furniture and of the paintings on the wall. They are actually the most impressive of all the relics and heirlooms that occupy their home. They are "noble and ruinous," a description that refers as much to their mental and physical state as to the state of the building and the portraits on the wall. Just like their dusty, awkward, spooky ancestors full of holes in their greasy frames, "the three wrecks [*las tres ruinas*]" behave like portrait characters.[5] Symmetrically positioned (*colocadas con simetría*), they offer "a gloomy, glacial and lugubrious spectacle."[6] They are deteriorated like the interior space in which they dwell and the objects that surround them.

Maria de la Paz is depicted in terms of the same symmetry in which a portrait would be described, a similarity that reduces her both to the dwelling in which she lives and to the objects that fill it, and to a formal setting of balances and symmetry. It is as if she is a compositional reality within a pictorial frame, with her earrings like two weights that keep her head in balance. Doña Salomé is skinny like a ghost and is called "a trace" or "remains [*vestigio*]."[7] Her yellow face, marked by an unknown number of years, is "an elongated thing" and would have made "a very beautiful oval" in the days of Carlos IV.[8] The bones, tendons and veins that move underneath her plain collar like a bunch of cords, that "machine [*máquina*]," those "scarcely concealed ana-

---

5   Ibid., 119.
6   "Colocadas con simetría [...] ofrecían un cuadro sombrío, glacial, lúgubre" (ibid., 122).
7   Ibid., 124.
8   Ibid., 123.

tomical pieces," proceed "like the sticks of a loom."[9] The mystical expression, finally, of doña Paulita, with her almost disfigured mouth and glacial gaze, was "due to a habit of contractions and movements, rather than to a natural and innate form."[10]

The Porreño dwelling in La *fontana de oro*, in many respects, represents fundamental aspects of 'the bare bones' of the imagery of interior spaces, as it developed throughout the long nineteenth century and beyond. These features can be found also in other contemporary, iconic literary interiors of the age which are set in the context of bourgeois and (decaying) aristocratic society. For example, Joris-Karl Huysmans's *À rebours* (*Against Nature*, 1894) is highly representative of this society, with its drastically changing (im)balances between the realms of the private and the public, the interior and the exterior.[11] The problematic, often traumatizing relationship between the exterior and interior space, which are sometimes, as in the case of *À rebours*, completely opposite realities, the obsession with objects, the collecting mania, the existential *horror vacui* and the objectification of those who inhabit these interiors, also appear in *La fontana de oro*. These features of literary interior spaces, surrounding subjectivity, the dweller and time, and the complexities of the interior-exterior dichotomies and intertwinements, survive beyond the long nineteenth century as well explored codes. These are constantly remodeled, re-questioned, deconstructed and explored in a wide variety of twentieth- and twenty-first-century literatures, as in the works of William Faulkner, in which space becomes a metaphor of time, of Djuna Barnes or

---

9   "Marcábanse en él los huesos, los tendones y las venas, formando como un manojo de cuerdas […] aquellas mal cubiertas piezas anatómicas se movían […] como las varas de un telar" (ibid., 123).

10 "la expresión mística […] era más bien debida a un hábito de contracciones y movimientos, que a natural y congénita forma" (ibid., 124).

11 On the constitutive elements of these interiors, their historical setting and the way they transcend the long nineteenth century, the particular notion of subjectivity that inheres them, their relation with the exterior that provokes specific notions of the void and of limitlessness and that bear distinctively existential dimensions, see Dominique Bauer, *Beyond the Frame: Case Studies* (Brussels: Academic and Scientific Publishers, 2016).

Elsa Morante on memory, time and space, and throughout the contemporary overcoming of the conceptual-lingual, interior-exterior dichotomy in ecocriticism, environmental humanities or ecological aesthetics.

The dwelling's disintegration, in two separate realities in *La fontana de oro,* represents a salient opposition between the exterior and the interior that reflects back to the interior's inhabitants. One can refer, in this instance, again to the interior in Huysmans's *À rebours,* where the anti-hero, Des Esseintes, locks himself away in splendid isolation in a house that has an interior without an actual exterior. Like Huysmans's anemic dweller, also the "decaying" sisters, the "three wrecks" in Galdós's novel, inhabit a space in which there is no lapse of time, a point that joins together socio-political and existential dimensions. It furthermore integrates the epistemological quality of the image of the interior that may function as a discourse on representation itself, be it literary, architectural or broadly contextual. In the context of the imagery of interior spaces, the interior-exterior opposition is, therefore, never a static situation, and never implies a sterile, un-communicable relation of two dimensions of reality. Rather, the interior space and its subject/inhabitant constitute a coherent literary image that embodies and brings to light the cultural significance of this opposition in its complex variety of layers, ranging from existential to epistemological. As a subtext of representation itself, the interior, in the case of Galdós, connects the anemia of representation with that of the worn, decrepit occupants.

Inhabitants, like those in *La fontana de oro,* seem to find themselves mired in an economy of objectification, to the point of being affected, threatened or even annihilated by it. This economy is nowhere made more explicit than in the stacked interior. In the long nineteenth century, interior spaces became storehouses of loads of often peculiar, bizarre, artistic or simply economically valuable objects. Already the architecturally expanded *cabinets de curiosité,* catalogues, or the later stereographical cabinets, reveal profoundly museological dimensions in this sense. They constitute places where things are seen by voyeuristic or curious spectators. Places, things and the spectator's gaze blend together in a mimetic relation. For this reason, interior spaces sometimes, in a literary way, coincide with the objects they contain, as in the notorious case of Isabella Stewart Gardner's Fenway Court in Boston.[12]

The flexible, liminal and culturally multilayered interior, on the unstable boundaries between "interior" and "exterior," "private" and "public," and always in some way relating to a "beyond," is central to this volume. "Interior space" is in this respect not a randomly chosen subcategory of "space." The wide variety of interior spaces elicited in literature, from the odd room over the womb, secluded parks or train compartments, to the city as a world under a cloth, reveal a common defining feature: these interiors can all be analyzed as codes of a paradoxical, both assertive and fragile, subjectivity in its own unique time and history. They function as subtexts that define subjectivity, time and history as profoundly ambiguous realities, on interchangeable existential, socio-political and epistemological levels.

The purpose of this volume is to critically interrogate fundamental aspects of the interior space in a number of novels of the long nineteenth century, the twentieth century, and of the recent past. Taken together, the various contributions do so in a way that does not argue for or against specific positions within the established and fragmented discourses surrounding the spatial turn.[13] Rather, each contribution, within its own context and

---

12 Now the Isabella Stewart Gardner Museum in Boston, MA.

13 The point of departure of this volume is the interior space as a literary code opening up a field in its own right, against the background of the multifaceted sensitivity for the spatial dimension of cultural meaning, and the varied multidisciplinary setting in the humanities in which this approach has its roots, such as the many spatial turns. Among recent publications surrounding the spatial turn in cultural studies that try to give a comprehensive account of this widespread and fragmented concept, see Jörg Döring and Tristan Thielman, *Spatial Turn: Das Raumparadigm in der Kultur- und Sozialwissenschaften* (Bielefeld: Transcript, 2008), or, more focused on literary theory: Wolfgang Hallet and Birgit Neumann, eds., *Raum und Bewegung in der Literatur: Die Literaturwissenschaften und der Spatial Turn* (Bielefeld: Transcript, 2009). More specifically important to the relation between

from various angles, focuses on interior space as a common denominator. In this way, the volume offers a fresh, coherent literary thesis on interior space as an emerging field in its own right. It is intended for a wide audience of scholars of, or students in, literary studies and the history of literature, cultural philosophy, visual studies, cultural history, the history of ideas, and other related fields of interest across the humanities.

The contributions to *The Imagery of Interior Spaces* can be read in a twofold manner. On the one hand, they exemplify the broader framework of the imagery of the interior space. At this level, the essays can be figured as interventions of the theoretical, ranging in focus from inhabitation and radical intimacy to the tension between interiors and the urbanity that invades them. On the other hand, the essays can be read on a historical level, apart from the shared theoretical paradigm, as short-circuits or critically intense conduits that reveal interior spaces within a contextual unit, such as an author's oeuvre or a novel, and which pertain to a particular socio-cultural and historical setting and language group.

The Chapters

The interior space between radical and intimate subjectivity, caught in its own time, and a dimension of threat and unease, is addressed in a consideration of *la stanza*, the chamber, in the work of Elsa Morante. In "In Her Chambers: Spaces of Fiction

---

space, culture, architecture and literature, also with regards to the various dimensions of interior spaces, is Michel Foucault, *Le corps utopique, les hétérotopies* (Paris: Nouvelles Éditions lignes, 2009). Foucault's "heterotopia" plays a dominant role as a framework for studies on liminal spaces, non-spaces, etc. On the other end of the spectrum, there is Gaston Bachelard, *La poetique de l'espace* (Paris: Presses Universitaires de France, 1957), who, through phenomenological analysis, presents architectural space in terms of a lived, culturally meaningful experience. See finally also Joseph Frank, *The Idea of Spatial Form* (New Brunswick: Rutgers University Press, 1991), a groundbreaking work, first printed in 1945, that introduced the concept of "spatial form" in literary studies, also applying the concept to examples of literary interior spaces.

in Elsa Morante," Gabrielle E. Orsi deals with the chamber as a space of both intimacy and discomfort. In Morante's final novel, *Aracoeli,* the chamber is replaced by the womb, characterized by a unique time that resists capture in memory. Manuele, who wants to return to the womb, eschews representation, for he insists that his memory is physical, direct. He claims to hear his mother's actual voice, rather than her physical voice. Like the chamber, the womb remains, however ambiguous, both a source of suffering and of death. Orsi argues that these iconic Morantian spaces are ultimately ambiguous. The power of fantasy to transform and even usurp reality that occurs in these spaces causes deep unease: in *Il gioco segreto* (*The Secret Game*) the walled garden is a prison, yet the garden and the mansion are, ambiguously, both claustrophobic and "claustrophilic."

One of the salient and reappearing dimensions of the literary interior space throughout its historical development is that of its timelessness or its unique time. In its most radical shape, it constitutes a spatial economy of an eternal present, in which objects and experiences can be frozen in time and in which all otherness and absence in historicity may disturb the fragility of the subject. Memory, contingency, decay or regeneration are therefore central elements of the literary interior space. The cabinet and the subsequent museum exemplify this economy of timelessness to a radical extent, both in their historical development and in their operation as literary images. In her article "'The (Dis)Possessed': Djuna Barnes's *Nightwood* and the Modern Museum," Lindsay Starck focuses on the museum gallery in which time has been "set aside." She proposes understanding *Nightwood* in relation both to the rise of the museum in the early twentieth century and to the modernists' ambiguous relationship with history and contingency, art and life; the latter sheds light on the former, in terms of an economy of exclusion and dispossession. Barnes thus frames the novel as an object that defies possession and which simultaneously reflects our own experience of dispossession in the modern world. *Nightwood* represents dispossession and, through relationships, creates room for subjective perspectives, fragmentation, and the construction of new narratives out of fragments of individual subjectivities.

Nightwood can be read as a museum connected with the museum in the context of modernism. In a similar way, the narrative construction of William Faulker's *Absalom, Absalom!* can be read through the open planning of Frank Lloyd Wright's architecture, without displaying the centrifugal nature of Wrightian architecture. In "The Inscapability of Dwelling in Yoknapatawpha County," Stefanie Sobelle understands Faulkner's multiperspectival narratives in direct connection with the perspectival impact of modernist architecture in the early twentieth century. In a universe of simultaneous, multiple narratives, space becomes a metaphor of time. Events are joined in a synchronic zone and no longer in a sequential framework. In this context, time does not appear to pass and history seems to be a series of repeated, timeless events.

The ambiguities of the interior, with its unstable boundaries, its dystopic relation to the exterior, its interconnections between authenticity and subjectivity, intimacy and unease, creativity and dispossession, history and timelessness, associate an extensive tradition. The process of the objectification of the interior's dweller, which doubles the objectification that the interiors themselves undergo, plays an important part in this tradition. This process is materialized in interiors that constitute spaces to collect and that coincide with the objects/artifacts that fill them. The nineteenth-century bourgeois interior, the stereographical cabinet, the museum, etc., are sophisticated, ambiguous exponents of this development. Their ambiguity resides in the fact that the process of objectification is inherent to the subject's self-representation, matching the interior with the authenticity of its dweller. These interiors are a battlefield between intimacy and exposition, privacy and publicity, authenticity and objectification. In literature, paradigmatic novels such as Huysmans's *À rebours* develop and explore this confrontation to their anemic outcomes.

"She had come to that, being a doll from whose broken chest escaped a thin trickle of sawdust," Zola writes about Renée in *La curée,* Renée who, like the "hothouse" Paris, is transformed into an anatomical Venus (life-sized dolls with removable internal organs). The image of the doll, that embodies various degrees of objectification or annihilation of the interior space's dweller, constitutes a recurring theme in settings where interiors are caught up in a thorough dynamics of invasion, that in Zola's novel *La curée* even becomes literal, corporeal invasion. This radical case of exposure and invasion, of voyeurism and showing what was hidden from view, is studied by Aude Campmas in her contribution "Evisceration: Exposing Internal Spaces in *La curée.*" *La curée* is a novel about the violation, the public exposure of internal spaces, from the female womb to the household. This violation is situated on the symbolic levels of the demolition of the city and the objectification of womanhood, a process that Zola develops through two metaphors for the exposure of internal space: evisceration and the glasshouse. Both are about exposing, invading and destroying something that was formerly internal, and about violently breaking and blurring the boundaries between internal and external.

Objectification affects equally the dweller and the interiors that engage, in this sense, in a mimetic dialogue. A striking example of the "shown" and "catalogued" interior is offered and, at the same time, problematized, in Edmond de Goncourt's *La maison d'un artiste,* which is analyzed by Erin E. Edgington in her contribution "Artful Arrangements: Interior Space in Edmond de Goncourt's *La maison d'un artiste.*" De Goncourt's work, as Edgington demonstrates, effectively straddles the public/private divide. The imagery of the interior space appears here in a work within the Goncourt non-fictional corpus that is hard to classify. It contains long lists of objects and possessions with descriptions that join narrative passages and paragraphs of prose. The anecdotes and reflections, in a more personal tone, complicate *La maison d'un artiste* as a piece of documentary non-fiction and allow for destabilizing the dichotomies between documentary and literary prose, and between reality and art. In this context, a precious, useless bibelot can be rendered utilitarian. Focusing on the blurring boundaries between genres, spaces and catalogue/text, affection and aesthetics, the reader is invited to focus on the ways in which Goncourt disrupts his domestic privacy while simultaneously erecting a textual monument to his artistic and decorative achievements.

The unstable relation between the interior and the exterior and their permeability thus exemplify aspects of the process of exteriorization and objectification of the subject. This process can be understood from the micro-scale of the exteriorized mind, over the dwelling as a spurious source of refuge, to the macro-scale of the city-dweller's rooms that dissolve in the surroundings of the big city. From the point of view of the imagery of interior spaces, the mind and the home are subjected to the same processes of exteriorization, often radicalized in various forms of alienation and in the incapability of matching, identifying the subject's authenticity with the interior it inhabits.

In this context, the advent of the modern big city, perhaps *par excellence,* stages a problematic interior, amidst the velocity of modern life and the fundamental changes that established frameworks of life and knowledge underwent. In the words of Georg Simmel, in his 1903 *Die Großstädte und das Geistesleben,* the modern city was characterized by the "speedy compaction of shifting images" and by the fragmentation "within what one can grasp in one glimpse."[14] The cultural and mental impact of this context on individuals was tremendous. In "The World as Seen Through a Window: Interiors and the Crisis of Morality in the Work of Robert Musil," Stijn De Cauwer addresses Musil's analysis of the destructive nature of the culture of his day as a reaction to the complexities and vast challenges of modern life, a reaction that he conceives of as a crisis of morality. De Cauwer shows how Musil goes against reactions of seclusion and instead strives towards the creation of new ways of understanding. He does so by embracing the fragmentation of various domains in modernity and combining them. Musil stages his critical analysis repeatedly in spatial terms, through the introduction

---

14 Georg Simmel, *Die Großstädte und das Geistesleben* (Frankfurt am Main: Suhrkamp Verlag, 2006), 35.

of interior-space settings, for example, the psychiatric asylum, the little château of Ulrich's father in *Der Mann ohne Eigenschaften,* or the military boarding school in *Die Verwirrungen des Zöglings Törleß*. In Ulrich's father's house, the interiority of a home is connected to the outdated form of morality it embodies as a building of a bygone era. Otherwise, Musil plays with the contrast between inside and outside. From behind the fixed window frames of his father's house, the modern world outside remains incomprehensible.

Responding to the same challenges of modern city life after the second industrial revolution, Jules Romains's take on Paris, analyzed by Dominique Bauer in "From the Enclosed Individual to Spatial Notions of a 'Beyond': Spatial Imagery in the Work of Jules Romains," presents the crisis of the interior in the modern city as a crisis of the contingent subject, socially disconnected and isolated "in a room where one is alone." When the city exists as a collective being, an *unanime,* and breaks through the walls of the interior, the alienated subject finds itself in surroundings where nothing ceases to be "interior." The subject is everywhere at once, thinking, experiencing what others think. The price for this simultaneity is the ultimate dissolution in death. The absolute interior matches the subject's self-destruction and again underlines, in a very programmatic way, the paradox of subjectivity. Romains's work is more complex than this radical outcome may seem to suggest. For, at the same time, Romains's emerging notion of totality that gradually overtakes that of the original unanime also opens up to an ontology of absence, to a new kind of nostalgia that seems to break away from the logic of pure presence in which Romains's interiors are caught.

Although it cannot be reduced to this, Romains's work, to a great extent, marks the aporetic, even self-destructive, outcome of a discourse on interior/exterior dimensions that was closely intertwined with the overblown spectator in rationalism, Enlightenment, the nineteenth-century bourgeois culture and the culture of modernist architecture. Partly expanding the German and Austrian criticism that arose in the latter context (e.g., Hofmannsthal), Marcus Breyer problematizes, in "Sensualizing the 'Over There': The Dissolving of Exteriority and Interiority in 'Geo-thoughts' and 'Geo-song'," conceptual language as a traditional means to dissociate the modern subject from its natural environs and to draw a sharp division between interior and supposed exterior space. Drawing on an analysis of Peter Waterhouse's *Klangtal* and responding to Goodbody's "dual crisis" of modernity, he argues, against the interiority/exteriority divide, for an ecocritical approach that enables us to experience the sensuality of language and pleads for a context in which literature can become a medium to educate our corporeal responsiveness to our own naturalness.

Bibliography

Bachelard, Gaston. *La poétique de l'espace*. Paris: Presses Universitaires de France, 1957.

Bauer, Dominique. *Beyond the Frame: Case Studies*. Brussels: Academic and Scientific Publishers, 2016.

Bly, Peter A. "Galdós, the Madrid Royal Palace and the September 1868 Revolution." *Revista de Estudios Hispánicos* 5, no. 1 (1980): 1–17.

Döring, Jörg, and Tristan Thielman. *Spatial Turn: Das Raumparadigm in der Kultur- und Sozialwissenschaften*. Bielefeld: Transcript, 2008.

Foucault, Michel. *Le corps utopique, les hétérotopies*. Paris: Nouvelles Éditions lignes, 2009.

Faulkner, William. *Absalom, Absalom!* London: Vintage, 2005.

Frank, Joseph. *The Idea of Spatial Form*. New Brunswick: Rutgers University Press, 1991.

Galdós, Benito Pérez. *La fontana de oro*. Madrid: Perlado, Páez y Compañía, 1906.

Gilman, Stephen. *Galdós and the Art of the European Novel: 1867–1887*. Princeton: Princeton University Press, 1981.

Hallet, Wolfgang, and Birgit Neumann, eds. *Raum und Bewegung in der Literatur: Die Literaturwissenschaften und der Spatial Turn*. Bielefeld: Transcript, 2009.

Ross, Kathleen. "Galdós' 'El audaz': The Role of Reader Response in a Serialized Spanish Novel." *Modern Language Studies* 11, no. 3 (1981): 33–43. DOI: 10.2307/3194377.

Russell, Robert H. "El Amigo Manso: Galdós with a Mirror." *Modern Language Notes* 78, no. 2 (1963): 161–68. DOI: 10.2307/3042882.

Simmel, Georg. *Die Großstädte und das Geistesleben*. Frankfurt am Main: Suhrkamp Verlag, 2006.

1

From the Enclosed Individual to Spatial Notions of a "Beyond": Spatial Imagery in the Work of Jules Romains

Dominique Bauer

In this essay, the spatial imagery in the work of Jules Romains is analyzed in relation to the central philosophical concept that underlies it, the *unanime*. The unanime is a collective being that suddenly emerges when, for example, people come together in theater halls, gather around a kiosk, or form a funeral procession.[1] As a post-Second-Industrial-Revolution phenomenon, the unanime typically applies to the big city and the "actual realities" of modern life, to use the words of Romains's travelling

---

1   Alain Cuisinier, *Jules Romains et l'unanimisme* (Paris: Flammarion, 1935), esp. 21–75, and Peter J. Norrish, *Drama of the Group: A Study of Unanimism in the Plays of Jules Romains* (Cambridge: Cambridge University Press, 1958), 3–45. Already prepared in his first poem, *La ville consciente* (1904), in *L'âme des hommes* (1904), or in the novel *Le bourg régénéré* (1906), unanimism finds its programmatic expression in *La vie unanime* (1908), "la pierre angulaire de tout l'édifice romainien" (André Figueras, *Poètes d'aujourd'hui: Jules Romains* [Paris: Éditions Seghers, 1967], 24, quoted in Peter Norrish, *Drama of the Group*, 3).

companion towards unanimism, Georges Chennevière, in the article "Le frisson nouveau," which he published in *Vox* in July 1905.[2] As a group entity, formally composed of movements of points, bundles and plains, the unanime incarnates a panoptic consciousness. As the spatial form of a simultaneity of points of view, it accomplishes the comprehensive perspective of the immediate, exhaustive presence of consciousness with all of reality. In that sense, the panoptic unanime opposes the deformed perspective of the monoscopic, subjectivist point of view. Immediacy implies a comprehensive simultaneity here, and, on this basis, moves towards the ideal of a total image, calling all possible views into an eternal present.

To understand the connection between Romains's multifaceted spatial imagery, the cultural content it communicates and the indicated intrinsic link between immediacy, simultaneity and the sense of an eternal present, Romains's unanimism is read against the background of other expressions of simultaneity in literature and the plastic arts at the beginning of the twentieth century, above all in Futurist art. Romains shares with futurist artists, like Giacomo Balla, a sense of reality as a radical, irreducible present averse to any plausible absence in representation. This notion of reality pervades Romains's vision of poetry and the role of the poet and poetic representation. However, the following analysis shows that Romains's *unanimes* also come to bear a liminal dimension, a dimension of a beyond, of invisibility and ineffability that precisely detracts from the concept of reality as a pure present that marks Romains's ideal panoptic ontology.

---

2   Cited in Michel Décaudin, *La crise des valeurs symbolistes: Vingt ans de poésie française, 1895–1914* (Rome: Bulzoni, 1978), 240.

Simultaneity, Pure Presence and the Nascent Globalization of the Unanime

In Romains's *La vie unanime*, the "surrounding immensity"[3] of the city breaks through the seemingly "impenetrable"[4] walls of the narrator's room. From then on, the latter becomes a being that has "something total and [something] ephemeral,"[5] that is interior to the passers-by as they are to him: "Nothing stops being interior."[6] In Romains's unanimism, the city becomes an organic, unified consciousness that derives self-awareness from the poet-prophet and protagonists-subjects drawn out of their various cloisons, their interior spaces of isolation. Freed from their thoughts and the relative frontiers of their bodies, individuals are endowed with an immediate and simultaneous consciousness, chased as they are from the isolated room in which they were alone.[7] If not, they remain absorbed in self-contained reading in the *Galeries de l'Odéon*, where the group only "lives a bit; [but] has no unity."[8] They participate in the literary salon with its "illusory center"[9] or the Sorbonne library where "everybody is closed into their isolated destiny."[10] However, freed from "the room where one is alone" the individual temporarily "evaporates," as Romains writes in *Le poème du métropolitain*. In the metro entrance, individual beings are, for an instant, no longer thinking about themselves but rather all want the same thing, before they each regain their "autonomy" and "let the collective soul vanish."[11]

---

3   "l'immensité d'alentour" (Jules Romains, *La vie unanime* [Paris: Gallimard, 1983], 49).
4   "les murs [...] imperméables" (ibid.).
5   "J'ai quelque chose de total et d'éphémère" (ibid., 53).
6   "Rien ne cesse d'être intérieur" (ibid., 47).
7   "Dans ma chambre où l'on est seul" (ibid., 18).
8   "Il vit peu; il n'a pas d'unité [...]" (Jules Romains, *Puissance de Paris* [Paris: Gallimard, 2000], 113).
9   "un centre illusoire" (ibid., 106).
10 "Chacune est close dans un destin isolé [...]" (ibid., 115).
11 Jules Romains, "Le poème du métropolitain," in *Deux poèmes: Le poème du métropolitain. À la foule qui est ici*, i–xi (Paris: Mercure de France, 1910), x.

Romains's unanimism remains an interesting witness to the changes that spatial imageries in literature underwent in large Western cities after the Second Industrial Revolution, with their industries and technological development, their speed, global interconnections and the masses of people that populated them. In this respect, Romains's model metropolis, Paris, differs fundamentally from the countryside and the sleepy towns of la province, like the one in his novel *Le bourg régénéré*. In contrast to Paris, these towns are inert, lifeless, isolated from the rest of the world. In the same way, as *Le bourg régénéré* shows, their inhabitants live secluded, unnoticed lives behind the façades of their houses, in rooms that are reminiscent of the solitary *chambre* in *La vie unanime,* with its initially impenetrable walls. They are completely disconnected from one another and unaware of the greater dynamics and full consciousness of reality that is taking shape in the modern city. Gradually these provincial towns are, however, integrated in Romains's unanimist logic. This process takes place as his system moves from the "small" unanimes that he describes in *La vie unanime, Puissances de Paris* (1911) or *Mort de quelqu'un* (1911), such as the theater hall or the Rue Montmartre, towards a greater European and even global unanimism.

A number of Romains's earlier works already illustrate this transition.[12] In the epic poem, *Un être en marche* (1910), a group of schoolgirls marches out of town into the countryside which subsequently mixes with the unanimist shape and the balances and rhythms of the group that passes through it. In *Les copains* (1913) the two friends Broudier and Bénin cycle through the country in perfect balance while dedicating themselves to the shape of the circle, that is, the principle of their movement. In *Mort de quelqu'un,* the village of father Godard is no longer absorbed in its traditional ancestral autarky in which people did not have children living in Paris and which was unconnected

---

12 Romains's project to establish the European space as a unanimist universe is first and foremost embodied in his *Les hommes de bonne volonté,* a cycle of twenty-seven novels that he published between 1932 and 1946.

to the big city by telegraph. Now however, the rhythmic succession of telegraph poles ties together the village, the city and the landscape in which "one felt the surroundings become" and in which father Godard finds himself when he travels by train to Paris and glares out of the window.[13]

This is not to say that the distinction between Paris, the provincial town and the remote village is absolute. On the contrary, the small village may very well have furnished a model for the unanime, the antecedents of which go back to primitive times, as Cuisinier suggests.[14] The interior dimension that defines the autarkic nature of the village seems to have been transferred to the unanime in the context of modern life. In Romains's conservative play, *Cromedeyre-le-Vieil* (1920), the radically isolated village is presented as such an interior.[15] The village is "one single house;"[16] its being closed to the exterior world is expressed by the fact that one can only perceive a small line of sky in between the roofs, and that streets are rather hallways than streets. One can hear people sleep in their houses and see them eat. One is only really outside when outside the last wall of the village, because the whole of the village is an interior.[17] The presentation of Cromedeyre resembles the idea, expressed in *La vie unanime*, that once the individual has broken out of her isolation, the entire city becomes an interior space.[18]

Romains's unanimism responded in this sense — on the basis of a peculiar mixture of anti-modernist elements and the em-

---

13 "On sentait l'alentour devenir" (Jules Romains, *Mort de quelqu'un* [Paris: Gallimard, 1923], 92).
14 Cuisinier, *Jules Romains et l'unanimisme*, 50.
15 The houses of the hilltop village of Cromedeyre are internally interconnected; the "internal walls" that separate the house are only very relative. The village, as such, is, however, completely socially and racially sealed off from the outside world, disconnected from the villages in the valley against which the proud race of Cromedeyre behaves in a very hostile and demeaning way in order to safeguard their traditions and customs.
16 Jules Romains, *Cromedeyre-le-Vieil* (Paris: Éditions de la Nouvelle Revue de France, 1920), 68.
17 "C'est Cromedeyre entier qui est son intérieur" (ibid., 69).
18 See note 6.

bracing of industrial times — to the shifting boundaries between the individual and the collective, the private, and the public.[19] Romains was among those authors who, like Emile Verhaeren, Paul Adam, Chennevière, Camille Claudel, and Guillaume Apollinaire, embraced, at the beginning of the twentieth century, that new world as a positive force.[20] This energy, or rather, the spatial movement of the city in which it materialized, forms a body of which the individual/poet may become the instantaneous consciousness. In this way, the "individual" loses his subjective isolation and becomes a simultaneous consciousness, in terms of an assembly of all points of view.[21] As a panoptic consciousness, the "individual" is able to dilate to all sides, a movement that finds its ultimate completion, as Romains's novel *Mort de quelqu'un* demonstrates, in death: "my death will be nothing but the courage to expand to the limit."[22]

The simultaneity of points of view, meant to overstep the shortcomings of the merely subjective, deformed, monoscopic perspective, guaranteed an immediate presence with reality. This position is articulated in "the simplicity of one desire"[23] that opposes the "external sparkles" by which "individual minds can grasp the city"[24] and that are on the level of "impulses" rather

---

19 Michel Décaudin, *La crise des valeurs symbolistes* (Toulouse: Privat Éditeur, 1958), 238.
20 Marie-Claire Bancquart, "Langage du corps, language de la ville dans la poésie de Jules Romains avant 1914," in *Actes du colloque Jules Romains* (Paris: Flammarion, 1979), 42–55.
21 In Cuisinier's *Jules Romains et l'unanimisme,* the first exhaustive in-depth analysis of Romains's work before *Les hommes de bonne volonté* (1932–1947), this is explicitly stated where Cuisinier describes Romains's famous moment of unanimist intuition in the *Rue d'Amsterdam* in 1903: "Il eut subitement l'intuition d'un être vaste et élémentaire, dont les rues, les voitures et les passants formaient le corps et dont lui-même, en ce moment privilégié, pouvait se dire conscience" (17).
22 "Ma mort ne serait que le courage de me dilater jusqu'à la limite" (Romains, *Mort de quelqu'un,* 152).
23 "la simplicité d'un désir" (Romains, *Le poème du métropolitain,* x).
24 "les esprits individuels […] ce petit groupe […] il n'en [de la ville] prendra que le poudroiement extérieur […]" (Romains, *Puissances de Paris,* 114).

than on that of "thoughts."25 The immediate presence with reality that characterizes Romains's total consciousness is intimately connected with the fact that this consciousness expresses a simultaneity of plural moments/points of consciousness. The latter derives precisely from the fact that this consciousness testifies to a radical presence that allows for no absence with reality, no restriction. Romains's unanimism, in this sense, shares distinctive aspects of simultaneity as an aesthetic strategy in the plastic arts at the beginning of the twentieth century.

Within this logic, unanimism seems to leave no room for absence, absent-mindedness or the contingency of the individual en cloison, as, for example, some passages in *Puissances de Paris* will show. This does not mean that Romains's underlying notion of a subject, an artist or consciousness of simultaneous points of view does not produce moments of absence. The subtle and diaphanous grid of spatial images in many of Romains's poems and novels show an underlying tension between the contingent individual and the panoptic ideal. This is evident in, for example, *Ode génoise* (1925), in which the play of the accordion crosses a "happy distance" that is at the same time "present and far away [*lointain*]," or the world "at the horizon of the *terroir*," "a rampart of mysteries."26

The Radical Present, Infinity, and Becoming as a Formal Dynamics

The individual that occurs in *La vie unanime,* isolated in his room and fighting the emerging unanime outside, is present already in *Le bourg régenéré.* Published two years prior to *La vie unanime, Le bourg régenéré* evolves along familiar lines. In this novel, a young postal worker arrives at his new town without great ambition, with the sole intention of abstracting "himself from the whole, to surround himself with a membrane impene-

---

25 "guerre plus d'impulsions que de pensées" (ibid., 115).
26 Jules Romains, "Ode Génoise," *Chants des dix années* (Paris: Gallimard, 1928), 127–61, at 141, 132.

trable by influxes, [to] be the heterogeneous thing, the little grain of stone that the total life would embrace and not permeate."[27] This description captures the initial individual *en cloison*. The latter individual finds himself in an unreal, delusional situation, with his merely subjectivist perceptions and his thoughts that are "abstract" or "external,"[28] an individual that is barely alive. However, as in *La vie unanime* and *Mort de quelqu'un*, the individual breaks free from its state of unawareness and enters a situation of immediate presence and interconnection with the consciousness, the experiences and thoughts of those that are integrated, absorbed into the unanime. As a result, the city becomes real and turns into an autonomous entity, a living being in its own right. The event that triggers the mechanism leading to this unanimist metamorphosis is a rather peculiar and comical one. While entering the municipal urinal, he decides, for no particular reason, to write the following words on a piece of slate: "He who possesses lives at the expense of he who works; whoever does not produce what he consumes, is a social parasite."[29] From that moment onward, all of a sudden, something starts happening in the village. A friend of the old inn-keeper reads the postal worker's words in the urinal and talks about it with him, while he realizes that he has retired too soon. Somewhere

---

27 Jules Romains, *Le bourg régénéré: Petite légende* (Paris: Éditions de la Nouvelle Revue Française, 1920), 11. When the city starts awakening from its lethargy to become an unanime, a rentier in his apartment looks suddenly with very different eyes to the surrounding walls. They are no longer a limit, but rather go-betweens that connect the place with a "vaster thing" and that "transmit the pressure of all that lays behind them," a scene which is highly reminiscent of the part in *La vie unanime* where the walls of the "room where one is alone eventually" let through a "tepid drizzle" (Romains, *La vie unanime*, 49).

28 The word "abstract" (*abstrait*) is used often to contrast the immediate presence with reality of the unanimist consciousness. When the unanimist part of the postal worker awakes, his "abstract ideas [*idées abstraites*]" go to sleep (Romains, *Le bourg régénéré*, 14). When he feels, during his walk through the town, the inner connections between a window, a cake shop, a gas lamp, and the façade of a public building, he has "a kind of immediate perception" that opposes "abstract formula" (ibid., 20).

29 Ibid., 17.

else in town a person of independent means suddenly becomes aware of the fact that he has had no life and that the walls that surround him are, in fact, not limits, but intermediary connections with an immensity beyond. People become aware of the fact that they behaved like social parasites and change attitudes, turning the sleepy, unreal town into a lively, coherent, interconnected unanime.

The basic image of an isolated interior that gradually dissolves into a liminal space before disappearing entirely, presents itself primarily as the dissolution of the monoscopic and contingent point of view. These dynamics, as in the case of Futurism, only spuriously consist of "moments" and "points." They establish an eternal present that is conceived of in terms of a simultaneity of points of view. Romains's notion of the unanime should, in this sense, be understood as pure movement against the shared background of other applications of simultaneity at the beginning of the century. The unanime as an interior, closed space (*espace clos*), a *space without place,* without demarcation, follows the logic of simultaneity and the imperative of an immediate presence with reality and reality as an immediate presence.[30] Reality conceived of as an uninterrupted flow can, without contradiction, be depicted as a succession of (spurious) moments.[31] Marie-Hélène Boblet-Viart and Dominique Viart

---

30 This spatial image of infinity, that within the work of Romains results in a sort of secondary effect of the simultaneity of points of view, may point toward notions in contemporary literature of infinity as "un espace sans lieu," for which the work of Alessandro Baricco is representative. For a more extensive treatment of this issue see Dominique Bauer, "Le présent et l'absence dans l'imaginaire des espaces intérieurs," in *L'espace, les phénomènes, l'existence: De l'architectonique phénoménologique à l'architecture,* eds. Alexander Robert and Guy Van Kerckhoven (Leuven: Peeters, 2017), 147–61.

31 This does not mean that other applications of simultaneity in art would not be relevant. In addition to Futurism, there is the simultaneity of points of view in the work of Robert Delaunay, for example, in his various studies of the Eiffel Tower, looked at simultaneously from various angles (see Sherry A. Buckberrough, *Robert Delaunay: The Discovery of Simultaneity* [Ann Arbor: University of Michigan Press, 1982], 57). Also, one of the aspects of the simultaneous view with Romains is the fading away of the corporeal limits between interior and exterior, the individual's inner body and the world be-

suggest that, in Futurism, "the moment is fixed in its current, present being [*actualité*], and at the same time eternalized," calling the Futurist dialects of moment and duration "the instantaneism [*l'instantanéisme*] of an eternal present which is absolute" — speed may "abolish the present that is however immediately re-actualized."[32] The various moments that constitute, for example, Giacomo Balla's *Girl Running on Balcony* (1912) are not contingent moments, but rather depict an enduring presence.[33] Because Romains's total consciousness effectuates the establishment of a timeless present, conceived of as a dynamic flow, the individual *en cloison* contrasts with it precisely in terms of temporal particularity and deformation. The radical presence with reality is communicated and determines the spatial imagery in Romains's work in various ways:

a. the poetic strategy, the role of the poet and the initial position of the isolated individual;
b. the unanime as a formal dynamics revolving around a center;
c. infinity beyond.

---

yond his bodily confinement. On the connection between simultaneity and the interpenetration of individuals, objects and surroundings see Pär Bergman, *"Modernolatria" et "Simultaneità": Recherches sur deux tendances dans l'avant-garde littéraire en Italie et en France à la veille de la première guerre mondiale* (Stockholm: Svenska Bokförl, 1962), esp. 147–57. In painting, one can find traces of this latter transgression in the work of Fernand Léger (see Judy Sund, "Fernand Léger and Unanimism: Where There's Smoke…," *Oxford Art Journal* 7, no. 1 [1984]: 49–56).

32 Marie-Hélène Boblet-Viart and Dominique Viart, "Esthétiques de la simultanéité," in *Jules Romains et les écritures de la simultanéité: Galsworthy, Musil, Döblin, Dos Passos, Valéry, Simon, Butor, Peeters, Plissart*, ed. Dominique Viart (Lille: Presses universitaires du Septentrion, 1996), 26–27.

33 This analysis of a body in action is based "on the instantaneous and simultaneous persistence of the images in the retina" (see Marzio Pinottini, "L'unanimismo e l'estetica del futurismo," in *Unanimismo: Jules Romains*, ed. Pasquale A. Jannini and Sergio Zoppi [Roma: Bulzoni, 1978], 106).

a. Poetic Strategies

> *Unanimism is not a literary movement;*
> *it is a conscience that comes into being.*[34]

In his 1929 article "La conscience créatrice chez Jules Romains," Jean Prévost draws an interesting distinction between the sociologist Émile Durkheim and Romains. Durkheim explains present society as a "consequence [*un effet*]" or as a "temporary result [*un résultat passager*]" of its origins, and a "kind of abstract history [*une sorte d'histoire abstraite*]." Romains, on the contrary, approaches modern life through intuition, "that kind of intuition that joins best intelligence" through a process in which the vibrations of the group are enlightened by those of the poet, as the poet changes and adapts to "ever extending groups," an approach that the author prefers to call "poetic induction [*induction poétique*]" rather than "intuition."[35] In contrast with the study of modern life as an object, as something already accomplished, something with an 'origin' from whence it resulted, no such temporal fissure exists between the poet and modern life in Romains's unanimism.[36] Romains's "poetic induction," his "immediate poetry [*poesia immediata*]," or "immediate literature [*letteratura immediata*]," opposes symbolism.[37] Romains wanted

---

34 "L'unanimisme n'est pas un mouvement littéraire, c'est une conscience qui devient" (Jules Romains, "L'unanimisme et Paul Adam," *Revue Littéraire de Paris et de Champagne* 42 [1906]: 285).
35 Jean Prévost, "La conscience créatrice chez Jules Romains," *Nouvelle Revue Française* 16 (1929): 477–78.
36 In that sense, unanimism has never been a "theory": Olivier Rony underlines that "Si philosophique, au fond, que soit l'intuition théorisée qui réside dans les profondeurs de l'unanimisme, Jules Romains ne cessera de le présenter comme une experience sensible et indépendant, pour tout dire, d'une recherche intellectuelle organisée" (Olivier Rony, *Jules Romains ou l'appel au monde* [Paris: Robert Laffont, 1993], 58). Michel Décaudin stresses that "unanimism was neither a 'system' nor the outcome of abstract speculation, it was 'a way of sensing' [...] and organizing one's perceptions [...]" (Michel Décaudin, "Documents pour l'unanimisme," in *Unanimismo*, eds. Jannini and Zoppi, 20–21).
37 Pinottini, "L' unanimiso e l'estetica del futurismo," 97–98.

to bridge the gap that symbolism had created between poetry and life. Romains's poetry embodies an economy of movement, of becoming, of the instantaneous present or the eternal point where things becoming enter the poet's consciousness. As Cerenza Orlandi states, "unanimism presents itself as the lyrical form that connotes the present."[38]

It has been mentioned in a number of studies that Romains tried to seize reality, not in terms of a historical development, an accomplished fact to be contemplated or a future prospect, but in terms of "an actual presence."[39] In his classic study on the crisis of symbolist values, Michel Décaudin shows how the connection with the present and with "life" not only marks the difference with symbolism, but also with other authors who cheered the big city and modern life, such as Verhaeren or the inner-core representatives of the Abbaye de Créteil, to whose *external adherents* Romains belonged. Romains regarded poetry as an economy of becoming, a process that is not the development of a historical narrative and not a reference to the future. While establishing an enduring present, Romains's unanime constitutes an entity in terms of duration. As a fundamental feature of the unanime, duration constitutes the temporal pendant of the unanime's spatial building blocks, e.g., "center," "circle," "circular movement," "balance," "rhythm," and "undulation," and its appearance as an interior or a liminal space moving towards a *beyond*.[40]

b. *The unanime as a formal dynamics*

The temporal elements of presence and duration that express temporal simultaneity find their counterparts in an imagery

---

38 Cerenza Orlandi, "La nozione di Dynamis nella Vie Unanime," in *Unanimismo,* eds. Jannini and Zoppi, 131.

39 Decaudin, *La crise des valeurs symbolistes,* 240.

40 At 10 p.m., the Rue Montmartre "has almost no recollection of itself, she does not last" (Romains, *Puissances de Paris,* 26). The group of people reading in the Galeries de l'Odéon is only a poor group, without memory and in which nothing continues (*Rien en lui de continu*) (*La crise des valeurs symbolistes,* 114).

that expresses spatial simultaneity. The requisite of pure presence finds its counterpart, respectively, in the panoptic view and the ubiquity of its subject, as expressed in *Mort de quelqu'un*. The young man at the end of the novel is absorbed in the spatial extension of a being that seems to be everywhere. He experiences the simultaneity that characterizes the unanime's omnipresence: he finds himself transcending his corporeal limits, feeling that "he is not only *there* where he says 'I,'" but also wants to go in various directions at once.[41] Duration finds its basic spatial metaphor in the circle, with its spatial balance, and in the recurring nature of undulations and rhythms. Together with duration, these spatial characteristics give an outspoken formal outlook to the unanime. This outlook underlines the impossibility of reflecting on the unanime in terms of a fixed content, for the latter would provide the unanime with a past or a future dimension, or turn it into a "finalized" object of reflection.

Every moving being or object, thought or memory, can be expressed in terms of forms and spatial relationships. Examples abound. The bourg of *Le bourg régénéré* "was full of analogous curves [*courbes analogues*]; every inhabitant had his own." All these curves had formal similarities [*une parenté de forme*]. In a passage that highlights the panoptic structure of the unanime, "various points [*plusieurs points*]" and "sometimes extended parts [*parties étendues*]" coincide, and "multiple lines" form "one bundle [*un faisceau*]." Referring to the recurring theme of the indispensable aspect of balance, "delicate symmetries [*des symmétries delicates*]" allow them to harmonize and to form a unanimist city.[42]

Having a center, being balanced, not only demarcates the unanime, it also supplies it with a strength that transcends and breaches the cloisons, the membranes of the isolated individu-

---

[41] "Il sentit avec une sorte d'évidence que son âme n'était pas seulement là où il disait 'Moi'" (Romains, *Mort de quelqu'un,* 150). Spatial simultaneity is expressed explicitly where the young man "wants to go in all directions at once [*dans tous les sens à la fois*]" (140), while "a need for ubiquity inflates his heart [*un besoin d'ubiquité lui gonflait le cœur*]" (140).

[42] Romains, *Le bourg régénéré,* 13.

als, towards a beyond. In *Puissances de Paris,* the military band on the Square Parmentier gives the shapeless public "circular shivers [*frissons circulaires*]."[43] They are two "concentric lives [*deux vies concentriques*]," "where the one results from the other by undulation [*ondulation*]."[44] Losing themselves in the rhythm of the band, the membranes that surround the individuals lose their purpose and no longer "isolate the little internal meanders [*les petits tourbillons intérieurs*]."[45] When the band stops, the group spreads out and runs thin. Cracks appear in the balance, and some "fragments are happier than the group"; however, the group "exists a lot" where its soul is best placed, "there where the circles of chairs surround the kiosk."[46] In *Bal du Quatorze Juillet,* the street knows that she will live for as long as the rhythm of the waltz reaches. What does not transform the sounds into circular movements is the nebula, the "*chose mal réelle* that has not yet decided between the universe and its own being."[47] This background explains the awkward relationship between the absent-minded individual, "abstract" and "external," and the collective beings that emerge, dilate and withdraw in the modern city. They celebrate a spatial imagery of the fading existence of subjects and of the emergence of collective beings.

Pertinent in this respect are three radioscopies of part VI, *Les vies intermittentes* (Intermittent Lives] of *Puissances de Paris,* namely, *Un salon littéraire, Les galeries de l'Odéon,* and *La bibliothèque de la Sorbonne.* The postal worker in *Le bourg régénéré* initially wants to shield himself with an impenetrable membrane. The same seems to go for the Bibliothèque Nationale's visitors, whose isolation is under attack while their membranes begin to dissolve, simply because there are many of them in the library. Other than that, their discontinuous structure provides

---

43 Romains, *Puissances de Paris,* 57.
44 Ibid.
45 Ibid., 58.
46 "des fragments plus heureux que l'ensemble" and "là où les cercles de chaises entourent le kiosque sonore" (ibid., 59).
47 "la chose mal réelle, qui n'a pas choisi entre l'univers et son être, et qui hésite" (ibid., 94–95).

them the illusion of unity. In this respect, the library shares many features with two other intermittent lives. The literary salon that "holds [*renferme*]" a number of people is marked by an illusory center that is "a great void [*un grand vide*]," an "abandoned space [*un espace désert*]."[48] The *Galeries de l'Odéon*, where the aligned readers are "pinned [*piqués*]" on the books and occasionally somebody tears himself out of the line, has no unity, no center and lacks continuity. Readers remain isolated in their individual meditations, living off the books that keep them alive but prevent them from "existing highly [exister hautement]."[49] As a group, the readers in the *Galeries de l'Odéon* do not have a memory and only absorb the "external sparkles [*le poudroiement extérieur*]" of the city's thought.[50]

In *La Bibliotèque Nationale*, the isolated destiny in which the readers are trapped disposes of a "special time [*un temps spécial*]," which hurries, condenses or moves slowly depending on the reader.[51] It is a kind of subjectivist time that matches both the deformed image of the monoscopic point of view and the clock that fixes time and is therefore an "illusion creating machine [*des machines à illusion*]."[52] The only total view is that of the unanime. This opposition between the time of the unanime and that of the isolated, subjectivist individual revolves around the contrast between a contingent reality and the needs of an immediate presence and a radical present.

The spatial metaphors of the unanime and the unanime as either a closed interior or a liminal space embody a reality that is pure movement filling space. In Romains's universe, there is no real ontological difference between things that seem more fixed and things that seem more fluid. Realities that are hard to grasp and petrify materially, such as sounds, feelings, memories or reminiscences, are, in an almost filmic way, turned into spatially

---

48 Ibid., 105–6.
49 Ibid., 113.
50 Ibid., 114.
51 "Chez certaines il se hâte, se condense; chez d'autres il bat lentement" (Romains, *Puissances de Paris*, 115).
52 Romains, *Mort de quelqu'un*, 11.

moving things.⁵³ With Romains, the world becomes paradoxically a world of spatialized things because reality has become floating, organic, unstable and unfixed. Things may seem fixed, but fixation is an illusion.

One of the most complex aspects of Romains's world is precisely this relation between fixation and elasticity. Romains himself notes this tension. In a notable passage, he relates that things can at once seem fixed and yet also on the move. True to the origins of unanimism, he exemplifies this tension by referring to one of the symbols of the new age that precisely produced this complexity, the factory:

> Things seemed at the same time to remain and to move. Nothing could be more fixed and more solidly planted into the soil than the chimneys of factories; but the smoke they disperse is mobile in such a natural way that one might regard this as the effusion of pure movement.⁵⁴

The elasticity of things and people seamlessly matches the elasticity of the modern world and the elasticity of its visual images. The retired train conductor Jacques Godard, in *Mort de quelqu'un,* had never really been able to appreciate Paris. When he "fixed [*fixait*]" the city, "measured it for a moment [*la mesurait un instant*]" from within his fast-moving train, it only looked like "a heap of muddy snow that the machine was going to chase away."⁵⁵ This type of perspectival elasticity and its subjectivity apply to time as well. To Jacques Godard, "time seems to be something arbitrary, elastic [quelque chose d'arbitraire,

---

53 *Mort de quelqu'un* offers a number of interesting examples of such spatialization of ephemeral things like sounds "vibrations tièdes du timbre" (12). "Timbre" is a word that occurs relatively often throughout the novel and is always described as a spatial reality on the move.
54 "Les choses semblaient à la fois demeurer et bouger. Rien ne pouvait être plus fixe, plus solidement cloué au sol que ces cheminées d'usines; mais les fumées qu'elles faisaient étaient mobiles avec tant de naturel qu'on eût dit une effusion de mouvement pur" (Romains, *Mort de quelqu'un,* 154).
55 "un tas de neige boueuse que la machine allait chasser" (ibid., 8).

d'élastique]" to the point of making him lose faith in objectively fixed, and thus non-subjective, time: watches are "illusion-creating machines."[56] As there is no fixed time there is no fixed single appearance for any given object. Godard has seen too many things "heap up, twist, get stuck on each other according to the velocity of the train" in order to still believe in that. [57]

Amidst a world on the move, in which physical, corporeal and mental boundaries are breached, the unity, the lifespan and the extent in which the unanime remains a closed interior or becomes a liminal space, are determined by duration and spatial balances. When, in *Mort de quelqu'un,* father Godard gets on the coach that will take him to the train to Paris, he enters a small and secluded universe of passengers that is subsequently sealed off from the outside. The opposition between the interior space of the coach and the exterior constitutes a kind of mental connection between the members of the company in the coach.[58] The balance between the exterior and the interior comprises the coherence of the members of the company, and the existence of this unity as a separate reality having its own soul. The soul of the company transcends the individuality of the people precisely by being spatial balance. Although there is not really "a center [*un centre*]" in the coach and the soul oscillates between the various bodies, thoughts align, "a little above the heads, under the grooved ceiling."[59] This formal spatial equilibrium is de-

---

56 Ibid., 11.

57 Ibid.

58 The balance that allows for the group to exist as an unanime, despite the fact that there was not really a center, also disappears when the interior–exterior opposition is breached. This happens when the coach stops in front of a tavern. Both the coach and the tavern are interiors that are brought out of balance because literal doors are opened: the passengers have to leave the coach in order to enter the tavern and the inn-keeper has to leave the family table in order to open the door to his clients. Opening the coach is again described in terms of breaking an equilibrium: "The interior [...] was no longer in balance and leaned over like a boat run aground [*L'intérieur* [...] *n'avait plus d'équilibre et s'inclinait comme un bateau échoué sur le sable*]" (ibid., 69).

59 "un peu plus haut que les têtes, sous le plafond de bois à rainures" (ibid., 58).

scribed very explicitly through the image of the two opposite sides of the coach "as jaws joined together in a closed mouth."[60]

c. Notions of Infinity and the Void as "A Space without Place"

"The circle is the principle of our movement."[61] The formal dynamics of the unanime defined by rhythms and balances, by the circle, the globe, the center, the circular movement, serve as metaphorical translations of a pure presence. In *Les copains,* when the two friends Bénin and Broudier cycle through the countryside, they ponder the infinity of the earth and their own limitlessness. They consider the earth's roundness, a globe that equals infinity because it does not end, whereas other things do. The horizon in front of them is inexhaustible. They become aware of what the "world is for two men in movement [*deux hommes en mouvement*]," the two of them dividing the planet in two parts, one on the left and one on the right.[62] They constitute a small universe between them, outside of the world. When they move, they limit and possess an uncontested space. The principle of their movement is the circle that will nurture their strength. Their thought takes the shape of a circle, the village that of a disc "and the planet never had more reasons to be a globe."[63] The difference between the two friends as isolated individuals and the unanime is very explicitly expressed in the language of a present that is stripped of past and future dimensions. The present Bénin carries when he is alone is "only small and compressed by a dense past and a voluminous future."[64] Broken out of their isolation an "enormous present [*un présent énorme*] now swings between them."[65]

---

60 "une bouche fermée dont les mâchoires se rejoignent" (ibid., 58).
61 "Le cercle est le principe de notre movement" (Jules Romains, *Les copains* [Paris: Gallimard, 1972], 74).
62 Ibid.
63 "et la planète, eut jamais autant de raisons d'être un globe" (ibid.).
64 "ne porte qu'un présent tout petit que compriment à la fois le passé dense et l'avenir volumineux" (ibid., 64).
65 Ibid.

Conclusion

The requisite of pure presence implied in the immediate consciousness of reality and the simultaneity of all points of view is intimately connected with a sense of space as demarcation, demarcation of the contingent subject and of its absolute pendant in the poet-prophet, with his panoptic aspirations. As distinctive passages in *Le poème du métropolitain, Mort de quelqu'un, Puissances de Paris,* and *Les copains* show, the subject's contingency evaporates in the panoptic consciousness of the unanime. Yet, outside this spatial discourse, centered on space as demarcation, notions of an elusive infinity, as a space without points and place(s), and a corresponding contingent subject subtly arise in the margins of liminal spaces and dissolving boundaries.

Moving from a notion of immediacy towards a notion of totality against which "the present sensation is never satisfied with itself," as Cuisinier notes, emerges the ineffability of a reality of infinite dimensions, a beyond that allows for a new kind of nostalgia.[66] *Les quatre saisons* offers an example in which the breached cloison, infinity, movement, and the void blend. *Automne* initially brings the reader to fading boundaries between the individual *en cloison* and what the latter initially fears as an abyss: "Every limit is steam; every prison is smoke." From the abyss, he initially doubts, another human being is pushed towards him. This breach of isolation, that has put "the house and the road in power of a new dawn," constitutes a unanime, and makes human beings into "new creatures [*créatures neuves*]." However, undulating movements [*des mouvements ondoient*] that represent the continuous present of the unanimist consciousness remain on the side of things that disappear before they can be named [*avant que tu les nommes*]. The solitude that is lifted elsewhere in the panoptic context of the unanime, when the membrane of isolation no longer serves a purpose, remains: "movements undulate on the edge of your solitude." In the last

---

66 Cuisinier, *Jules Romains,* 150–51.

strophe, these movements, before they can be named, "plunge back into the eternal silt."[67] They remain elusive and out of reach.

In passing from immediacy to totality, a transition that results from the very logic of simultaneity itself, notions of space appear which bear a distinctive dimension of elusiveness, of a beyond, of absence, and that hereof derive their nostalgic nature. Although produced within the totalitarian aspirations of the unanime, these dimensions fall outside and even run counter to the requisite of a pure present. The new nostalgia in the context of the big cities joins a subject that has not evaporated into a panoptic consciousness, but that has preserved its loneliness and its contingency.

---

67 "Toute limite est vapeur/Toute prison est fumée;" "par l'abîme dont tu doutes/Un homme est poussé vers toi;" "La demeure et le chemin/Sont au pouvoir d'une aurore;" "Et des mouvements ondoient au bord de ta solitude;" and, "replongent [...] dans le limon éternel" (Jules Romains, "Les quatre saisons," in *Amour couleur de Paris, suivi de plusieurs autres poèmes* [Paris: Éditions de la Nouvelle Revue Française, 1921], 19–35, at 21–23).

Bibliography

Bauer, Dominique. "Le présent et l'absence dans l'imaginaire des espaces intérieurs." In *L'espace, les phénomènes, l'existence: De l'architectonique phénoménologique à l'architecture*, edited by Robert Alexander and Guy Van Kerckhoven, 147–61. Leuven: Peeters, 2017.

Blancquart, Marie-Claire. "Langage du corps, langage de la ville dans la poésie de Jules Romains avant 1914." In *Actes du colloque Jules Romains. Bibliothèque nationale 17–18 février 1978. Avec une présentation de André Boudin*, 42–54. Paris: Flammarion, 1979.

Bergman, Pär. *"Modernolatria" et "Simultaneità": Recherches sur deux tendances dans l'avant-garde littéraire en Italie et en France à la veille de la première guerre mondiale*. Stockholm: Svenska Bokförl, 1962.

Boblet-Viart, Marie-Hélène, and Dominique Viart. "Esthétiques de la simultanéité." In *Jules Romains et les écritures de la simultanéité: Galsworthy, Musil, Döblin, Dos Passos, Valéry, Simon, Butor, Peeters, Plissart*, edited by Dominique Viart, 19–43. Lille: Presses Universitaires du Septentrion, 1996.

Buckberrough, Sherry A. *Robert Delaunay: The Discovery of Simultaneity*. Ann Arbor: University of Michigan Press, 1982.

Cerenza Orlandi, G. "La nozione di *dynamis* nella *Vie unanime*." In *Unanimismo: Jules Romains*, edited by Pasquale A. Jannini and Sergio Zoppi, 125–55. Roma: Bulzoni, 1978.

Cuisinier, Alain. *Jules Romains et l'unanimisme*. Paris: Flammarion, 1935.

Décaudin, Michel. "Documents pour l'unanimisme." In *Unanimismo: Jules Romains*, edited by Pasquale A. Jannini and Sergio Zoppi, 13–28. Roma: Bulzoni, 1978.

———. *La crise des valeurs symbolistes: Vingt ans de poésie française 1895–1014*. Toulouse: Privat Éditeur, 1960.

Figueras, André. *Poètes d'aujourd'hui: Jules Romains*. Paris: Éditions Seghers, 1967.

Norrish, Peter. *Drama of the Group: A Study of Unanimism in the Plays of Jules Romains.* Cambridge: Cambridge University Press, 1958.

Pinottini, Marzio. "L'Unanimismo e l'estetica del futurismo." *Unanimismo: Jules Romains,* edited by Pasquale A. Jannini and Sergio Zoppi, 95–111. Roma: Bulzoni, 1978.

Prévost, Jean. "La conscience créatrice chez Jules Romains." *Nouvelle Revue Française* 16 (1929): 473–92.

Romains, Jules. *Cromedeyre-Le-Vieil.* Paris: Éditions de la Nouvelle Revue Française, 1920.

———. "Les quatre saisons." In *Amour couleur de Paris, suivi de plusieurs autres poèmes,* 19–35. Paris: Éditions de la Nouvelle Revue Française, 1921.

———. *Le bourg régénéré: Petite légende.* Paris: Éditions de la Nouvelle Revue Française, 1920.

———. *Les copains.* Paris: Gallimard, 1972.

———. "Le poème du métropolitain." In *Deux poèmes: Le poème du métropolitain. À la foule qui est ici,* i–xi. Paris: Mercure de France, 1910.

———. *La vie unanime.* Paris: Gallimard, 1983.

———. *Mort de quelqu'un.* Paris: Gallimard, 1923.

———. "Ode génoise." In *Chants des dix années,* 127–61. Paris: Gallimard, 1928.

———. *Puissances de Paris.* Paris: Gallimard, 2000.

———. *Un être en marche: Poème.* Paris: Mercure de France, 1910.

Rony, Olivier. *Jules Romains ou l'appel au monde.* Paris: Robert Laffont, 1993.

Sund, Judy. "Fernand Léger and Unanimism: Where There's Smoke…" *Oxford Art Journal* 7, no. 1 (1984): 49–56. DOI: 10.1093/oxartj/7.1.49

2

Sensualizing the "Over There": The Dissolving of Exteriority and Interiority in "Geo-thoughts" and "Geo-song"

Marcus Breyer

This essay shows how the "dual crisis" of modernity and its accompanying twofold topology of interiority and exteriority have been reflected upon and tackled in modern literature. In my reading of Peter Waterhouse's "Das Klangtal" ("The Sound Valley," 2003), I show that modern literature can be a medium through which we can re-sensualize our language and educate our corporeal responsiveness to our own naturalness. Based on a conversation between Waterhouse's "Klangtal," Hugo von Hofmannsthal's "[Lord] Chandos letter" (1902) and Gernot Böhme's ecological aesthetics, I argue for an ecocritical approach that helps us experience and intensify the sensuality of language. This approach also calls on us to educate our senses to the effect that we learn to be responsive to the nature that we ourselves are.

Ecocritical attempts to problematize the separation of the human sphere from nature have most famously been made by Timothy Morton's book *Ecology without Nature*, which argues that the ecocritical preoccupation with "ambience poetics" has put "something called Nature on a pedestal and admir[ed] it from afar."[1] Morton reveals how environmentalist thought has been predicated upon assumptions that are ultimately corrosive to its agenda by pointing to nature as something "over there," thereby reinforcing its exteriority to our being human. In fact, the assumption that nature is something exterior permeates ecocritical thought. P. Wesley Schultz speaks of "the notion of being connected with nature [as] a psychological one," which excludes the corporeal dimension of our existence as a means by which we are always already situated in naturalness.[2] Similarly, Lisa Gerber's article on the aesthetics of humility argues that "part of being humble is coming into contact with and finally appreciating an external reality" and standing "before something that inspires awe."[3] Despite being sympathetic to Schultz's and Gerber's concerns and motivations, I cannot help but wonder: why is it that oneness and connectedness with nature tend to be treated as theoretical, epistemological or psychological terms — sometimes tacitly reinforcing or openly perpetuating the divide between an interiority of the human self and an exterior nature? And how can we as environmentalists, ecocritics, and as scholars of the humanities guard ourselves against the interiority/exteriority divide that dissociates us as humans from the nature that we ourselves are?

A fruitful point of departure in this endeavor is Axel Goodbody's assertion that modernity is marked by a "dual crisis," that is, a crisis of language as well as a crisis of the human relationship with nature: the subject's experience of nature shapes language, and vice versa, language affects the experience of nature

---

[1] Timothy Morton, *Ecology without Nature: Rethinking Environmental Aesthetics* (Cambridge: Harvard University Press, 2007), 5.

[2] P. Wesley Schultz, "Inclusion With Nature: The Psychology of Human-Nature Relations," in *Psychology of Sustainable Development*, eds. Peter Schmuck and P. Wesley Schultz (New York: Springer, 2002), 62.

[3] Lisa Gerber, "Standing Humbly before Nature," *Ethics and the Environment* 7, no. 1 (2002): 42, 43.

(which includes our human naturalness).⁴ Language therefore is not primarily a tool that helps the human mind map their environs, but it also opens up and constitutes human environments. In his meditations on "Heidegger, Language, and Ecology," Charles Taylor situates this claim in a philosophical tradition that he coins "expressive-constitutive" thinking: in this line of thinking, language makes possible "new purposes, new levels of behavior, new meanings" and thus helps constitute our human environments and shapes our perception as well as our practices and attitudes towards our environs.⁵ Accordingly, as I will illustrate, a conceptual language that is taken for granted, or, in fact, as something natural, perpetuates abstraction from the senses and is ultimately corrosive to any immediacy of experience. If a de-sensualized language opens up the arena in which we as moderns attain knowledge of ourselves, a re-sensualized or re-enchanted language itself could be a promising way to re-situate ourselves in and as nature. And, accordingly, if sensual experience in modernity is instrumentalized and reduced to the "detection of signals [*Feststellen von Signalen*]," as Böhme argues, the re-exploration of the body and its responsiveness would have to complement the re-enchantment of our language.⁶ Likewise, Maurice Merleau-Ponty's phenomenology is based on the idea that we as humans must overcome the primacy of the body as an "information machine" and rehabilitate our "actual body."⁷ Merleau-Ponty argues that we must re-instate this "actual" bodily dimension of our existence and its reciprocity in its relationship

---

4   Axel Goodbody, *Nature, Technology and Cultural Change in Twentieth-Century German Literature: The Challenge of Ecocriticism* (Basingstoke: Palgrave Macmillan, 2007), 146.
5   Charles Taylor, *Philosophical Arguments* (Cambridge: Harvard University Press, 1995), 102. According to Taylor, this line inquiry spans from Herder to Nietzsche and Heidegger, but it should also include e.g., Hans Blumenberg's metaphorology and Niklas Luhmann's systems theory.
6   Gernot Böhme, *Für eine ökologische Naturästhetik* (Frankfurt am Main: Suhrkamp, 1989), 32.
7   Maurice Merleau-Ponty, "Eye and Mind," in *The Merleau-Ponty Aesthetics Reader: Philosophy and Painting,* eds. Galen A. Johnson and Michael B. Smith (Evanston Northwestern University Press, 1993), 122.

with its environs as the body is always already integrated with its environs as "the world is made of the very stuff of the body."[8]

One of the most intriguing ideas in this regard can be found in Gernot Böhme's ecological aesthetics of nature. Böhme seeks to respond to the ecological crisis and the human place within by drawing attention to the human body, which he claims has been suppressed in and largely absent from Western thought. He therefore seeks to promote a refamiliarization with the body in a revised practice of bodiliness (*Leiblichkeit*), which can be best described by differentiating the two German words *Leib* and *Körper*. Even though both words can be translated as "body," they form a distinction that lacks an equivalent in the English vocabulary. The body as *Körper* refers to the alterable and modifiable object which we *have* and which we can use and govern, decorate and display, improve and optimize. The body as *Körper* entails an instrumental relationship in which the body serves as mere object that is acted upon to attain various ends. It is this instrumental and detached relationship that distinguishes it from the body as *Leib*, which refers to the body that we are and that is identical to the self. The body as *Leib* is always already responding to and interacting with its environs and thereby transcends the borders of the mere physical body as *Körper*. Its permeability dissolves the split between interior mind and exterior matter and gives rise to a transformative ethics in which the self is freed from its isolated interiority and recognizes its corporeal existence and its joyful and sensual unification with the exterior.[9] A practice that familiarizes ourselves with a permeable and responsive natural body that we *are*, so Böhme's argument goes, helps us as humans embrace and cherish our corporeal oneness with nature. This identity of the self and a responsive and resonating body reassures us of our own naturalness and ultimately calls upon us to become humble, empathetic, and compassion-

---

8   Ibid., 125.
9   For *Leib* and *Körper* see also Kate Rigby, "Gernot Böhme's Ecological Aesthetics of Atmosphere," in *Ecocritical Theory*, eds. Axel Goodbody and Kate Rigby (Charlottesville: University of Virginia Press, 2011), 141–42.

ate participants and 'experiencers' in the intricate conversation of all beings and things natural.

Lord Chandos's Narcissist Ecology

Peter Waterhouse's "Klangtal," and Hofmannsthal's "Chandos letter" as its intertextual reference point in intellectual and literary history, are the central sources of this essay since they can be situated in the discursive field sketched out above. Hofmannsthal's letter has become a commonplace reference in the discourse on language skepticism around the turn of the twentieth century.[10] Even though these readings have proved to be fruitful, placing and re-placing the text in the discourse on language skepticism alone may also have prevented scholars from recognizing the wide range of implications that lay elsewhere in the letter.[11] This is not to deny that Lord Chandos's crisis is a crisis of language, but it is also a crisis of sensual experience and thus the human body. As I shall illustrate, Hofmannsthal's letter is situated at the heart of this "dual crisis" of modernity theorized by Goodbody.

Lord Chandos's relationship to language can be described in two stages: while his poetic aspirations initially impel him to break free from stylistic conventions and limitations, the unsatisfiable nature of these aspirations and his narcissism ultimately debar him from language altogether. In the beginning, Chandos's poetic language allows him to exist in a state of oneness with all entities and to conceive of "the whole of existence as

---

10 Cf. Tobias Heinz, *Hofmannsthals Sprachgeschichte: Linguistisch-literarische Studien zur lyrischen Stimme* (Tübingen: Niemeyer, 2009), 221ff.; or Christopher Ebner, *Sprachskepsis und Sprachkrise: Fritz Mauthners Sprachphilosophie im Kontext der Moderne* (Hamburg: Diplomica, 2014), 85ff, which argues that Hofmannsthal's crisis of language is in fact a crisis of abstract/social rather than poetic language.
11 Cf. Rudolf Helmstetter, "Entwendet: Hofmannsthals Chandos-Brief, die Rezeptionsgeschichte und die Sprachkrise," *Deutsche Vierteljahrsschrift für Literaturwissenschaft und Geistesgeschichte* 77, no. 3 (2003): 450.

one large unit."[12] Boundaries are constantly crossed and interior as well as exterior space blend into each other as "the spiritual world and the physical world did not seem to be in opposition."[13] Chandos's inspirational and poetic guide in this great unifying plan is the Roman stylist Sallust,[14] whose *varietas* (i.e., his linguistic ingenuity and innovation), challenged the primacy of clarity and precision among rhetors and writers of his time.[15] From Sallust's asyndetic and paratactic structures one can infer a poetic agenda that strives for a poetic harmonization and a "creative union of old and new."[16] Sallust and the early Chandos are united in their attempt to emancipate themselves from the confinement of linguistic conventions in order to find a language from which this harmonizing practice would emerge. As long as Chandos remains a writer he devotes himself to a language that can penetrate all entities and become a medium of cognition. Once poetic language is no longer reduced to an ornamental extra, once it has left "the confined space of rhetorical tricks," it articulates and constitutes Chandos's oneness with all entities.[17]

As Chandos's poetics allows him to transcend linguistic conventions, it also reveals the artifice of conventionalized and conceptual language, thus drawing attention to the limitations of the human experience of nature. He exposes the human-nature relationship as a context of self-delusion, insofar as experience is led by a language that is mistaken for something natural. When he recognizes the human origins and cultural technique of an abstract and conceptual language, Chandos ventures into a language that no longer treats nature as an abstract "over there" and

---

12 "das ganze Dasein als eine große Einheit" (Hugo von Hofmannsthal, "Ein Brief," in *Sämtliche Werke XXXI* [Frankfurt a.M.: Fischer, 1991], 47). All English translations of Hofmannsthal are mine.
13 "geistige und körperliche Welt schien mir keinen Gegensatz zu bilden" (ibid.).
14 Cf. ibid., 46.
15 Cf. Michael von Albrecht, *A History of Roman Literature: From Livius Andronicus to Boethius* 1 (Leiden: E.J. Brill, 1997), 445.
16 Ibid..
17 "Geheg[e] der rhetorischen Kunststücke Hofmannsthal" (Hofmannsthal, "Ein Brief," 46).

gives rise to a joyful oneness with nature: he feels a "wordless and infinite delight" as interiority and exteriority become inseparably intertwined.[18] It is "limitless" or "infinite," as Helmstetter argues, precisely because of the transgression of the bounds of the symbolic order.[19] He dissolves the symbolic order that separates the interiority of the self from the sensual seductions of an exterior nature.

The oneness of all entities is more than just a mere poetic equivalent filling in the gap left by a conceptually framed modern topology of interiority vs. exteriority. This oneness is not just a phenomenon in language, but also is inspired by "sensual and spiritual pleasure."[20] An oft-quoted example of this spiritual and sensual intensification of oneness is Chandos's identification with the rats, for whose death he himself is responsible.[21] This identification not only serves to illustrate his oneness with nature, it also hints at an inherent narcissism and limitations that ultimately lead to his failure. Chandos describes this identification with the rats as a sensual experience and a synaesthetic coalescence of himself with the sensual experience of the rats' bodies. He associates tactile, acoustic and olfactory senses when he speaks of the "cool-musty air in the cellar filled with a sweet and poignant smell" and joins tactile and visual senses in the "cold gaze of rage."[22] The oneness that articulates itself in the intertwining of several senses and intense bodily perception is not "pity [*Mitleid*],"[23] not a vicarious suffering with the rats, not a oneness of compassion. Rather, the pleasure is in the elevating aesthetic experience of "the fullest and most sublime present."[24]

This oneness is not inspired by a sense of humility but founded upon a poetic narcissism and an increasingly instrumental

---

18 "wortlose[s], schrankenlose[s] Entzücken" (ibid., 54).
19 Cf. Helmstetter, "Entwendet," 466.
20 "sinnliche und geistige Lust" (Hofmannsthal, "Ein Brief," 47).
21 Cf. ibid., 50–51.
22 "süßlich scharfen Geruch [...] angefüllte kühl-dumpfe Kellerluft"; "kalte Blick der Wut" (ibid., 51).
23 Ibid.
24 "vollste erhabenste Gegenwart" (ibid., 51).

relationship to nature. The encyclopedia, for which he wants to utilize one creature after the other, further illustrates the narcissism to which Chandos has fallen victim.[25] Chandos's narcissism is far from being the productive kind of self-love as an integrative force and condition for love altogether, of which Fromm speaks, but it is clearly marked as a selfish and destructive narcissism.[26] This harmful kind of narcissism creates a sharp distinction between the self and the world that is exterior to it. For a destructive narcissist, this limiting of the self entails that he or she is incapable of recognizing and affirming anything exterior to the self in a non-instrumental and non-manipulative manner: "The world outside is looked at only from the standpoint of what he can get out of it […] He can see nothing but himself."[27] Despite his insights into the artifice and constructedness of the separation of interiority and exteriority, Chandos's joyful moments of oneness with nature remain short-lived and delusive. The spiritual and sensual oneness lapses back into self-centeredness that allows for oneness only insofar as the world exterior to the self can be incorporated into the elevation and empowerment of the self. Chandos does not strive to attain a sense of oneness for the sake of nature itself, but instrumentalizes this oneness for the sake of his poetic ambitions to exalt himself in a magnum opus that would ensure him a place in the literary canon.[28] All entities remain means to this end, and the oneness with them is only answerable to his poetic narcissism.

Chandos's role as a poet also brings about a different aspect that contributes to his failure to achieve a more successful and sustainable dissolution of the interiority/exteriority divide. His relation to language is limited by his obsession with the written word.[29] Chandos's experience of sensual and spiritual oneness with nature and his sensualizing of the exterior come at a high price: the de-sensualization of language, as well as ultimately its

---

25 Cf. ibid., 48.
26 Cf. Erich Fromm, *The Art of Loving* (New York: Harper & Row, 1956), 57–63.
27 Ibid., 60.
28 Cf. Hofmannsthal, "Ein Brief," 47.
29 Cf. Helmstetter, "Entwendet," 469.

reduction to an inward-looking medium, re-intensify the interiority/exteriority divide. His obsession with written language removes him from interpersonal interaction and further isolates him from the outside world. His attempts to engage in oral conversation fail and leave him speechless, with his words disintegrating "in the mouth like moldy fungi."[30] After one such failed conversation with his daughter, he is able to find comfort only in loneliness and restoring himself by galloping "on the lonely pasture."[31] Neither the dissolving of the precariousness of the interiority/exteriority divide nor the revision of language and sensual experience from within language can continue to exist as ways to achieve an affirmative and fruitful oneness with a supposedly outside world.

Towards an Aesthetics of 'Geo-thoughts' and 'Geo-song'

About one hundred years later, Waterhouse's "Klangtal" revisits the speechless Lord Chandos and embarks on another quest to rehabilitate poetic language and to revitalize its sensualizing potential. "Klangtal" presents a very different response to the problems mentioned above and does not entrap itself in destructive narcissistic fantasies. "Klangtal" is a literary meditation on the problem of interiority and exteriority in the experience and recognition of nature. In Waterhouse's story, the entanglement of language and the senses permeate these boundaries and exemplify how a poetics of corporeality (*Leiblichkeit*) can reinforce a poetic practice that re-sensualizes the human experience of nature. "Klangtal" illustrates how language itself shapes, constitutes, and transforms the human-nature relationship, and it helps us picture how we can challenge and undermine the separation of what is presumably interior and exterior in the human experience of nature. "Klangtal" responds to this separation by means of provocative imagery, metaphors, sound associations, resonances, and fluctuations of sound, image, and

---

30 "im Munde wie modrige Pilze" (Hofmannsthal, "Ein Brief," 49).
31 "auf der einsamen Hutweide" (ibid., 49).

meaning, all of which make for a conceivably challenging task for translators.[32]

In "Klangtal," a narrator reminisces about anecdotes and conversations with his parents during his childhood in Malaysia. These anecdotes are interspersed with reflections on language and sensual perception. In order to grasp the significance of these reflections and the language being spoken, it can be helpful to go back to Nietzsche''s theory of language as depicted in "Über Wahrheit und Lüge im aussermoralischen Sinn" ("On Truth and Lies In a Nonmoral Sense").[33] According to Nietzsche, each word is derived from a double transposition: first, a sensory stimulus is transposed into an image before the image is transposed into a sound.[34]

Nietzsche uses this double transposition to uncover the arbitrariness and the metaphorical nature of language, but he also claims that language, even if it seems as detached from the senses as abstract concepts and terms, is founded upon physiological processes. These physiological processes, though, seem all too remote considering our modern preoccupation with conceptual language, a language that consists of ossified metaphors.[35] Only by pointing to human forgetfulness can Nietzsche explain how language has come to be taken for granted, as something natural, and as something that is related to truth.[36]

---

[32] Thanks to the excellent work done by David Gramling and his students at the University of Arizona, "Klangtal" is now also available to the English-speaking world. All translated quotes from "Klangtal" will be from their translation published in *Transit* 9, no. 2 (2014).

[33] Here, I am only focusing on the Nietzschean idea of the metaphoricity of language. For a more exhaustive analysis of Nietzsche's theory of language in relation to Hofmannsthal, please see Joel Westerdale, *Nietzsche's Aphoristic Challenge* (Berlin: de Gruyter: 2013), 67–71.

[34] Cf. Friedrich Nietzsche, "Über Wahrheit und Lüge im aussermoralischen Sinne," in *Der Streit um die Metapher: Poetologische Texte von Nietzsche bis Handke*, ed. Klaus Müller-Richter and Arturo Larcati (Darmstadt: Wissenschaftliche Buchgesellschaft, 1998), 33.

[35] Cf. ibid., 35.

[36] Cf. ibid., 33.

Waterhouse's "Klangtal" revives the physiological origins of language and brings them back to our senses. When "Klick" becomes "Glück" ("the click was like happiness") and when "the words 'tears' and 'eels' became sounds," the reader participates in successful attempts to excavate layers of abundant sensuality in language and to make these rediscovered riches fruitful for a revision of language and sensual experience.[37] Waterhouse's "Klangtal" penetrates the surface level and explores the seductive sensuality of language. The disintegration of words that leaves Chandos speechless becomes part and parcel of an exploration into verbal sensuality and into the possibility of a perceptual language. In his analyses of Waterhouse's language, Dittberner argues that Waterhouse adds details to general terms so that the reader is not only informed but also animated.[38] While this may be a precise observation for many of Waterhouse's other writings, the situation is quite different with respect to "Klangtal." Adding detail as a conscious and creative transformation of language is not its most remarkable poetic strategy. Rather than adding an animating extra to conceptual language, "Klangtal" divests words of the strings that hold them in their place in the semantic web and draws the reader's attention to their acoustic quality. As a poetic strategy, this requires restraint and a responsiveness to these sounds rather than creativity. Accordingly, "Klangtal" does not present a world centered on a subject. In contrast to Hofmannsthal's Chandos, to whom the act of perceiving is most important, Waterhouse foregrounds the being-perceived of nature.[39] This gives rise to a radical relativist stance on linguistic truth claims. If truth is in any way related to language, this relation must be predicated on the primacy of the perceived entities themselves as "they need to be real always."[40]

---

37 Peter Waterhouse, "Das Klangtal," *Neue deutsche Literatur* 51 (2003): 66; "The Sound Valley," trans. Andrew Ziesig et al., *Transit* 9, no. 2 (2014): n.p.

38 Cf. Hugo Dittberner, "Peter Waterhouse, unterwegs zu den Namen," Text+Kritik 137 (1998): 3.

39 Cf. Luigi Reitani, "Durchlässige Textlandschaften: Zu einer poetischen Konstante im Werk von Peter Waterhouse," *Text+Kritik* 137 (1998): 71.

40 Waterhouse, "Sound Valley," n.p.

The speaker and their environs do not enter into a hierarchical relationship, but rather coexist in a decentered and dynamic cosmos. Kubaczek goes so far as to suggest a "scatteredness [*Gestreutheit*]" of entities.[41] In this dynamic relationship, in which the subject must always be responsive to nature as well as the sensual layers and associations in language, the borders between subject and nature, interior and exterior, and different modes of sensual perception are constantly challenged:

> His nose was fruit — that is, a bud, fruit: his nose [*Nase*] traced the fruit [...], but his nose was itself the fruit. Pineapple [*Ananas*], Malayan nanas, wafted out, and his nose was pineanose [*Ananase*]. The child tickled his nose, the tickling was like tasting, it was a tickling "tasten" [*touching*]; it was like the English "to taste." In German, the child swept [*abtasten*] his nose with a handkerchief corner, or "touchcloth," but in English it touchclothed ["it tasted"] also.[42]

And shortly after that:

> "And now we are driving over the Johore Strait" [...] In this instant, everything was a strait; the sky a blue strait, a tree a vertical strait [...] the fluidity of the Johore Strait had a changeling power, a kinship strength. I thought about how ants built ant straits [...] and snakes snaked as the straits and roads snaked; on all sides, snake-like, moving. The land we were driving into began to snake like a country road, stretching heaven- and Himalaya-ward.[43]

The first of the two passages quoted above intertwines haptic and gustatory senses in language and experience to the effect that the narrator partially identifies with the pineapple. By vir-

---

41 Martin Kubaczek, "Sprachliche Topographie: Zur Konzeption des poetischen Raums bei Peter Waterhouse," *Text+Kritik* 137 (1998): 57.
42 Waterhouse, "Sound Valley," n.p.; "Das Klangtal," 66–67.
43 Waterhouse, "Das Klangtal," 68.

tue of sound association across three different languages — German, English, and Malayan — the perception of a pineapple unfolds in a multisensual and compassionate appreciation of the fruit. As sensual and verbal association bleed into one another, the synaesthetic chain of associations offers a holistic challenge to mono-sensuality and sensual merism. The second passage illustrates the merging of language and landscape into a verbal landscape (*Sprachlandschaft*).[44]

This verbal landscape is a landscape insofar as its emergence from a perceiving subject is still present as it is inscribed into the list of verbal and sound associations. This landscape, however, unfolds without a center that governs and organizes it. The subject that is still inscribed into this landscape does not impose its creative potential upon the landscape but responds to the sounds and associations. Consequently, the entities in this landscape coexist in "structureless simultaneity [*strukturlose Gleichzeitigkeit*]."[45] Subject, nature, and language are entangled in this verbal landscape to such an extent that any attempt at separation would inevitably destroy the landscape as well as the "changeling power" and "kinship strength" by which subject, nature, and language enrich each other. This humility in nature and language transcends Chandos's destructive narcissism by tying a sense of space to an attentive and humble responsiveness to nature and language. Waterhouse's neologism for this practice of thinking and speaking is "not thoughts; but geo-thoughts" ("nicht Gedanke, [...] Geodanke") and "not song; but geo-song" ("nicht Gesang, [...] Geosang").[46] "Geo-thoughts" and "geo-song" call for a corporeal, responsive, and affirmative existence in nature rather than before it. On the part of the subject, they require a sense of humility that guards against perceiving nature as something exterior to the subject and something 'over there'. This kind of humility is not a humility *before* nature, but rather humility *in* and *as* nature.

---

44 Kubaczek, "Sprachliche Topographie," 60.
45 Ibid., 57.
46 Waterhouse, "Sound Valley," n.p.; "Das Klangtal," 78.

Waterhouse's "geo-thoughts" and "geo-song" complement Böhme's ecological aesthetics of nature as they represent literary elaborations on Böhme's concept of *Befindlichkeit*. Böhme's concept is a nominalization derived from the German verb *sich befinden,* which means "to be situated/located" and "to feel." Böhme uses this concept in its full variety of meanings, thus drawing attention to the unity of affective responsiveness and sense of space.[47] In merging the "how" and "where" in the experience of nature, Böhme attempts to dissolve the interiority/ exteriority divide. Instead of cultivating and reinforcing the subject's retreat into the interior vis-à-vis nature exterior, Böhme seeks to establish a practice that re-situates the human subject in nature. This requires the subject to be humble, so as to accept its own naturalness and heteronomy. Waterhouse's "geo-thoughts" and "geo-song" complement Böhme's ecological aesthetics as they represent literary practices from which a genuine responsiveness to nature can emerge. "Geo-thoughts" and "geo-song" bind the subject to a very corporeal communication with nature and prevent the retreat into mere interiority. Language and responsiveness to nature and space are tied together and they inspire and enhance one another as language becomes "alive, physical, you yourself will be physical and experienced and you will resound, your body educates itself linguistically […] an education of living arms and hands and eyes and ears."[48] With this in mind, there can be no doubt about Dittberner's claim that every reading of Waterhouse is a provocation of sensual perception as well as of a playful manner of speaking.[49] Waterhouse's "Klangtal" intensifies our sensual experience of nature and revises a conceptual and abstract language that would serve to reinforce the interiority/exteriority divide. He entangles language and sensual perception into a "body language."[50] In this way, "Klangtal" presents a literary practice that fruitfully engag-

---

47 Cf. Böhme, *Für eine ökologische Naturästhetik,* 47.
48 Waterhouse, "Sound Valley," n.p.; "Das Klangtal," 80.
49 Cf. Hugo Dittberner, "Peter Waterhouse," 4.
50 Waterhouse, "Sound Valley," n.p.; "Das Klangtal," 74.

es with Böhme's ecological aesthetics and helps us to re-situate ourselves within nature.

Conclusion: Challenging the "Dual Crisis"

Waterhouse's "Klangtal" can therefore be read as Chandos's more optimistic ecological counterpart as it largely succeeds in offering an inspiring literary and sensual re-enchantment of our human experience of nature. The major contribution in resolving the dual crisis of modernity and its interiority/exteriority divide is the sense of humility that it retains. This sense of humility does not degrade the subject, but rather guards against inherent destructive narcissistic tendencies. Chandos fails to cultivate this humble sense of responsiveness to nature once he has cut the Gordian Knot of de-sensualized experience and conceptual language. His destructive narcissism debars him from maintaining a fruitful way of engaging with the joyful experience of oneness. The experience of oneness lapses back into a divide between interiority, into which he retreats, and exteriority, which he fails to master.

The sense of humility in "Klangtal" emerges from its revision of both conceptual language and a manipulating relationship to the senses. Waterhouse's "Klangtal" promotes a perceptual language that not only unfolds from the subject's inherent creative potential but that emerges from the being-perceived of nature. In the ecological aesthetics of Böhme, this emphasis on the being-perceived is predicated upon a mimetic potential, i.e., our human potential to enter into a non-manipulating relationship with nature.[51] The perceptual language of "Klangtal" speaks to our human senses and enables us to discover our corporeal naturalness in the sensuality of language.

The synaesthetic nature of this perceptual language illustrates the significance of the body as *Leib* and the rehabilitation of corporeal experience. The crucial role of the body is also evident in a very explicit way: "I traveled here into pain, out of the

---

51 Cf. Gernot Böhme, *Für eine ökologische Naturästhetik*, 29.

world, disembodiment, Austria, culture [...] In fish pain, animal pain, pained screams, tiny pain, body pain, sadness glows and wafts and rings. Not Weltschmerz."[52] The voyage into the "sound valley" is thus described as a refusal to continue to be complicit in a cultural tradition that debars us from discovering our corporeal experience and heteronomy and that dissociates us from our naturalness. The "sound valley" is the very corporeal yet hypothetical space of otherness that emerges from the dissolving of interiority and exteriority and in which the "world" and its defining systems of signification and meaning-making are suspended: "All the sounds are true" as long as they can be perceived, be they "singing, squeaking, scratching, croaking, knocking, shouting, bellowing."[53] The "sound valley" is the space of an empathetic and responsive *Leib* that is answerable only to its *Befindlichkeit* that situates it *as* nature *in* nature. The "pain" that it feels is not a "Weltschmerz," which implicates that the suffering that inspires its refusal to participate in disembodied practices, is not a suffering with the state of society or culture.[54] Rather, its "animal pain [...] body pain" suggest that it is a suffering with nature.[55] In situating corporeal experience in a communicative relationship with the naturalness of the self, the subject is guarded against retreating into interiority.

The "dual crisis" of modernity, once it is recognized as such, can be treated and overcome from within, as "Klangtal" suggests, if language and sensual experience educate each other mimetically: holistic and corporeal experience push the symbolic order of language to its limits and transcend it, always alert to synaesthetic experience and expression as well as to the enchanting power of language and senses that guide each other. This kind of

---

52 Waterhouse, "Sound Valley," n.p.
53 Ibid.
54 Ibid..
55 The suffering with nature, the "Leiden an der Natur," (24) is the starting point for Böhme's ecological aesthetics that also sets him apart from his intellectual precursors of the Frankfurt School, most notably Theodor W. Adorno, who portrays nature as an idealized Other of enlightenment, e.g., in his reflections on the idyllic Ammorbach.

synaesthetic language, temporarily spoken by Chandos, permanently spoken by the characters of "Klangtal," is at once a provocation and seduction. As readers, we become participants who need to respond to the sensual and verbal provocations, to that which beckons to our senses and our understanding of language.

The perceptual language prompts us to respond to the sensuality of language and its inherent sound associations. If literature cultivates this perceptual language, it challenges the detached third-person perspective, from which we speak about nature as an exterior "over there" or "out there." Instead, it calls for a relation based on communication with nature — as a communicative co-emergence of an "I" and a "thou." If the ecological crisis demands that we become responsive to our environs, it entails more than just describing its colors, flavors, and sounds in what Morton describes as "ambient poetics."[56] A true and genuine responsiveness to nature requires that we explore and humbly accept our own naturalness. It entails above all that we no longer conceive of ourselves as being separated from an exterior nature. And it asks us to explore all possibilities to re-enchant a supposedly disenchanted modernity:

> The theories [...] say that this modern world — of logical consistency, of empirical verifiability, and technological sobriety — destroys spirituality; but that is wrong. The enchantment and transformation of the self has never occurred before an altar or a throne, but before the dust und oily water in the harbor basin or before the scratch in car paint.[57]

Finally, if the ecological crisis is as severe as environmentalists think it is, the oily water is already overspilling the edge of the harbor basin and is becoming an oil spill on a planetary scale. What a convenient — and high — time for an enchantment of ourselves. Rather than continuing to admire nature as an 'over

---

56 Morton, *Ecology without Nature*, 32–35.
57 Peter Waterhouse, *Die Geheimnislosigkeit: Ein Spazier- und Lesebuch* (Salzburg: Residenz, 1996), 115.

there,' we need to recognize the entanglement of language and sensual experience. We must attempt to cultivate an awareness for the corporeal and sensual implications of language as well as for the ways in which sensual experience shapes, transforms, challenges, and "enchants" language. Waterhouse's "Klangtal" can be a fruitful text for the ecocritical discourse as it illustrates how we can cultivate and engage with new and sensual vocabularies — and also, of course, how we can revisit canonical texts of our Western traditions, such as the "Chandos letter," in relation to its assumptions on language and sensual experience.

Bibliography

Albrecht, Michael von. *A History of Roman Literature: From Livius Andronicus to Boethius.* Leiden: Brill, 1997.

Böhme, *Gernot: Für eine ökologische Naturästhetik.* Frankfurt a.M.: Suhrkamp, 1989.

Dittberner, Hugo. "Peter Waterhouse, unterwegs zu den Namen." *Text+Kritik* 137 (1998): 3–5.

Ebner, Christopher. *Sprachskepsis und Sprachkrise: Fritz Mauthners Sprachphilosophie im Kontext der Moderne.* Hamburg: Diplomica, 2009.

Fromm, Erich. *The Art of Loving.* New York: Harper & Row, 1956.

Gerber, Lisa. "Standing Humbly before Nature." *Ethics and the Environment* 7, no. 1 (2002): 39–53. DOI: 10.1353/een.2002.0005.

Goodbody, Axel. *Nature, Technology and Cultural Change in Twentieth-Century German Literature: The Challenge of Ecocriticism.* Basingstoke: Palgrave Macmillan, 2007.

Heinz, Tobias. *Hofmannsthals Sprachgeschichte: Linguistisch-literarische Studien zur lyrischen Stimme.* Tübingen: de Gruyter, 2009.

Helmstetter, Rudolf. "Entwendet: Hofmannsthals Chandos-Brief, die Rezeptionsgeschichte und die Sprachkrise." *Deutsche Vierteljahrsschrift für Literaturwissenschaft und Geistesgeschichte* 77, no. 3 (2003): 446–80.

Hofmannsthal, Hugo von. "Ein Brief." *Sämtliche Werke XXXI*, 45–55. Frankfurt a.M.: Fischer, 1991.

Kubaczek, Martin. "Sprachliche Topographie: Zur Konzeption des poetischen Raums bei Peter Waterhouse." *Text+Kritik* 137 (1998): 53–67.

Merleau-Ponty, Maurice. "Eye and Mind." In *The Merleau-Ponty Aesthetics Reader: Philosophy and Painting,* edited by Galen A. Johnson and Michael B. Smith, 121–49. Evanston: Northwestern University Press, 1993.

Morton, Timothy. *Ecology without Nature: Rethinking Environmental Aesthetics.* Cambridge: Harvard University Press, 2007.

Nietzsche, Friedrich. "Über Wahrheit und Lüge im aussermoralischen Sinne." In *Der Streit um die Metapher: Poetologische Texte von Nietzsche bis Handke,* edited by Klaus Müller-Richter und Arturo Larcati, 31–42. Darmstadt: Wissenschafliche Buchgesellschaft, 1998.

Reitani, Luigi. "Durchlässige Textlandschaften: Zu einer poetischen Konstante im Werk von Peter Waterhouse." *Text+Kritik* 137 (1998): 68–76.

Rigby, Kate. "Gernot Böhme's Ecological Aesthetics of Atmosphere." In *Ecocritical Theory,* edited by Axel Goodbody and Kate Rigby, 139–52. Charlottesville: University of Virginia Press, 2011.

Schultz, P. Wesley. "Inclusion With Nature: The Psychology of Human-Nature Relations." In *Psychology of Sustainable Development,* edited by Peter Schmuck and P. Wesley Schultz, 61–78. New York: Springer, 2002.

Taylor, Charles. *Philosophical Arguments.* Cambridge: Harvard University Press, 1995.

Waterhouse, Peter. "Das Klangtal." *Neue deutsche Literatur* 51 (2003): 66–80.

———. Die Geheimnislosigkeit: Ein Spazier- und Lesebuch. Salzburg: Residenz, 1996.

——— "The Sound Valley." Translated by Andrew Ziesig et al. *Transit* 9, no. 2 (2014): n.p. https://transit.berkeley.edu/2014/gramling-et-al/,

Westerdale, Joel. *Nietzsche's Aphoristic Challenge.* Berlin: de Gruyter, 2013.

3

Evisceration: Exposing Internal Spaces in *La curée*

Aude Campmas
Translated by Lesley Lawn

Émile Zola's novel *La curée* (published in 1871 and commonly translated as *The Kill*) denounces the commercialism of the French Second Empire through the character of Aristide Saccard, who gained significant wealth as a result of his financial speculation of Haussmann's renovation of Paris. The novel is also a criticism of social manners, as it follows the decline of Saccard's wife Renée, who, like a modern Phaedra, has an affair with her stepson. As Zola notes in his preface to *La curée*, it "resounds with gold and flesh."[1] However, the constant references to the destruction of Paris also extend the significance of the novel and, as Jann Matlock notes, the Commune is a haunting presence throughout.[2]

This chapter will explore the way in which Zola integrates his condemnation of the defeat of the Franco-Prussian War and the subsequent civil war (the Commune) — which in his view

---

1 "la note de l'or et de la chair." Zola's preface to the first edition cited by Jean Borie, Émile Zola, *La curée* (Paris: Gallimard, Folio classique, 1999), 7.
2 Jann Matlock, "Everyday Ghosts: Zola's *La curée* in the Shadow of the Commune, 1871–72," *Romanic Review* 102, nos. 3–4 (2011): 321–47.

were a result of the politics of the Second Empire — with his reflections on family, womanhood and, more importantly, on sterility.³ *La curée* is a novel about the violation of internal spaces, from the female womb to the household. Saccard's fortune is based firstly on the rape of Renée, since it is because of her ensuing pregnancy that she is given to him in marriage, and secondly on the back of Paris's symbolic pillage (*sac*) by the speculators. The initial violation recurs incessantly throughout the novel in symbolic form: on the level of the nation (invasion), the city (demolition), the family unit (destruction via incest), and motherhood (negated via sterility). To illustrate this, Zola develops two metaphors for the public exposure of private/internal space: the glasshouse and evisceration. In both cases, something that was formerly internal has been exposed as a criticism of the Second Empire's transgression of family values.

Whether through the feminized descriptions of disemboweled buildings or the flowers in a glasshouse depicted as sex organs — *La curée* extracts the female entrails and puts them on display.⁴ These entrails represent both the internal parts of the belly and the reproductive organs, and, by metonymy, children (in French, children are referred to as the "fruits of entrails"). Torn from the body, exposed entrails become the symbol of aborted pregnancies.⁵ In this context, the word "exposure" is understood in the sense of sacrifice.

---

3   Although a direct consequence of the Franco-Prussian war, the Commune, which took place from March 18 to May 28, 1871, was an armed conflict amongst the French.

4   Flowers are sexual organs. This is emphasized in *La curée*'s fourth chapter ,when the plants are the screens into which the lovers are projecting their desire. Zola concludes this highly suggestive scene by saying that "It was the boundless copulation of the Hothouse" (Émile Zola, *The Kill*, trans. Brian Nelson [Oxford: Oxford University Press, 2008], 159).

5   While in *La curée* the image of the eviscerated woman is hinted at, the theme of the "flanc troué dans sa fécondité" is given full rein in *La terre*. The pregnant Françoise is killed by her sister by the blow of a scythe to her belly. See Émile Zola, *Les Rougon-Macquart: Histoire naturelle et sociale d'une famille sous le second Empire, vol. 4, La terre* (Paris: Robert Laffont, 1992), 1043.

In this chapter, a brief description of the figure of the bad mother and of women as exotic, sterile flowers is followed by an analysis of the way in which, by transforming Paris and Renée into "anatomical Venuses" (life-sized dolls with removable internal organs), the metaphor of evisceration is integral to the dialectic of violence and defiance, vis-à-vis the corrupted intimacy of the female body during the Second Empire.

In *La curée,* Zola condemns those Parisian women who leave their homes for the pleasures of public life. This movement of private life towards the public arena is a transgression of family values that leads to the increase in the number of bad mothers. The figure of the bad mother is typically outlined in three ways: the woman who neglects the education of her children; the woman who refuses to have children; and, the mother who aborts or gives birth to physically or mentally deformed children.[6] All these women, the potential mothers of the future nation, are considered by the nation to be sterile, in real or metaphorical terms, since a child who is raised poorly, sick, disabled or not born at all is of no social value.[7] These anxieties are embodied in the character of Renée, whose main crime is being the representative of aborted motherhood (another form of transgression because she does not fulfill her destiny of becoming a

---

6   This corruption of the notion of motherhood was certainly considered to be the worst. Since 1865, the ruling classes had been concerned about the declining birth rate in France. "The nation is in danger!" (Catherine Rollet-Echalier, *La politique à l'égard de la petite enfance sous la IIIe République* [Paris: PUF, 1990], 109) exclaimed Doctor Boudet, echoing the Legislative Assembly's declaration in July 1792 in the face of the Austro-Prussian invasion. The concept of the nation, the fatherland, links the political community with its genealogy. The decline in the birth rate has ideological, political and demographic consequences, since the survival of the nation is at stake. During the Third Republic, the public authorities intervened much more in the private domain, as testified by numerous legal texts, parliamentary reports and works on social welfare (for a study into the birth rate in France during this period see ibid., 27–67). Zola's work represents such concerns, which were exacerbated by the debacle of 1871. Zola's anxiety was mingled with another fear, that of the degeneration of the species, hence his concern with the mother that aborts.
7   See ibid., 122.

good mother). The act of rape to which she is victim and which leads to a miscarriage corresponds to the symbolic rape, at the end of the novel, which destroys the figure of woman as nature incarnate, that is, the mother, thus leading to the miscarriage of society.[8] Sterile, Renée is defiled and an agent of corruption: she is a monster.

In *La curée,* the woman as monster takes an apparently unexpected form — a horticultural hybrid of an exotic hothouse flower. However, at the time, it was a common metaphor. Just a few years after *La curée* was published, Edmond Texier summed up the anxieties of the period with regards to maternity and the female body by saying that the human species is becoming corrupted, metamorphosed, and losing its qualities.[9] Texier then compares women's appearances to a greenhouse and women's rotten intimacy (sex, womb) to a clinic (i.e., a disease).[10] The environment stigmatized by Texier is that of the great industrial town, constructed and directed by a bourgeoisie obsessed with money and appearances, and of which the greenhouse has become the symbol. By extension, the greenhouse becomes a common metaphor for describing an unhealthy artificial environment, a transparent environment that negates the possibility of intimacy.

There are numerous expressions during the Second Empire based on the image of the "hothouse." A "hothouse atmosphere" is used to evoke an intense and sensual atmosphere. An emotion that was "raised in a hothouse" is one that had developed in an exaggerated and over-indulgent way. "Living in a hothouse" implied someone living the life of a recluse. Women described as

---

8 Chapter 6, Renée has an epiphany about her condition and what happened to her. She realizes how her husband, Maxime and society have used her, have stripped her of everything. She looks at herself in a mirror and repeatedly asks herself the rhetorical question "who, then, has stripped her naked?" (Zola, *The Kill,* 240).

9 Edmond-Auguste Texier, *Les femmes et la fin du monde* (Paris: Calmann Lévy, 1877), iii.

10 "Ce monde féminin qui par ces côtés superficiels a l'air d'une serre chaude, par son intimité profonde et gangrenée est une clinique" (ibid.).

"hothouse flowers" and "hothouse atmosphere" were the most commonly used expressions. For Texier, the main problem is the destruction of the private, protected from the outside, household. Paris and the urban environment do not escape the comparison. The greenhouse is culture against nature, town against countryside. Paris appears as a greenhouse whose greenspaces are now little more than an artificial nature. Such an artificial space can only render unnatural the beings who live and grow there. Here, the fear of the species' degeneration is symbolized by a system founded on botanical metaphors: the greenhouse is the corrupting environment while the hybrid exotic flower represents the degenerated, denatured species. The greenhouse, a corrupted society, women as sterile flowers — Texier continues to develop in his essay a network of metaphors around the figure of the bad mother already in bloom in Zola's novel.

Indeed, in order to portray the desertion of the domestic setting for the public arena, Zola makes use of these horticultural metaphors. The emphasis on flowers as sexual organs and as a metonymy for women's sexuality grew with Linnaeus openly discussing the sexuality of plants. It continued to develop due to the passion for exotic flowers during the Second Empire. Those horticultural hybrids, which are paradoxically sterile, resemble enlarged genitals (natural plants are often at lot smaller and less colorful) and therefore make the sexual analogy even more ostensible.[11] During the same period, as demonstrated by Naomi Schor, post-revolutionary literature reveals a fear of the female body and of the sexual energy that it generates.[12] To ward off this energy, the author either has to make the female body disincarnate, Chateaubriand's allegorical woman, or make it hyper-

---

11 For more details see Aude Campmas, "Les fleurs de serre: entre science et littérature à la fin du dix-neuvième siècle," in *Visions/Revisions: Essays on Nineteenth-Century French Culture,* eds. N. Harkness, P. Rowe, T. Unwin and J. Yee (Oxford: Peter Lang, 2003), 49–61.
12 Naomi Schor, "Triste Amérique: Atala and the Postrevolutionary Construction of Woman," in *Rebel Daughters: Women and the French Revolution,* eds. Sara E. Melzer and Leslie W. Rabine (Oxford: Oxford University Press, 1992), 139–56.

incarnate, as with Zola's woman as animal (for example Nana). In both cases, there is a sort of "de-corporalization" that neutralizes the woman's body.

The post-Linnaean floral metaphor also contributes to the disembodiment of the female. It allows sexuality to be referred to in the form of euphemism: the young girl waiting for marriage in the same way as the flower awaits the bee. Towards the end of the century, with a sort of metaphorical zeal, the flower-sex becomes almost pornographic, loses its innocence and this over-sexualization is related to the loss of fertility, which has almost certainly to be considered as a denunciation of the dissolute morals of certain women in society, and as fear of the degeneration, or ultimate extinction, of the human race, a fear exacerbated by the debacle of 1870. In this period, there was a flowering of plant life which can be read as a metonymy of the woman reduced to a deadly sexual organ. The prime example is the vegetal *vagina dentata* of Huysmans's *À rebours* (*Against Nature*, 1884). An obvious pastiche of the descriptions in *La curée*, it reveals something that was merely embryonic in Zola's novel. In Chapter VIII of *À rebours*, the main character, Des Esseintes, having just contemplated an abundance of exotic plants bought from local horticulturists, succumbs to a nightmare, a hallucinatory vision of a woman as flower and virus:

> He made a superhuman effort to free himself from the embrace, but with an irresistible gesture she held him in her arms, seizing hold of him, and he saw, his face haggard, the wild Nidularium blossoming between her upraised thighs, opening wide its sword-shaped petals above the bloody interior.[13]

---

13 Joris-Karl Huysmans, *Against Nature*, trans. Margaret Mauldon (Oxford: Oxford University Press, 1998), 81.

Although the center of the Nidularium looks generally like a flower, it is in fact a rosette of red bracts reminiscent of a vulva.[14] The Latin name given to this false flower, *nidularium* (from *nidus,* nest), implicitly emphasizes this shape. The scarlet leaves, rigid and serrated, add the final touch to the analogy of the vagina armed with teeth — all the more so since the word bract is borrowed from the Latin *bractea* meaning "metal leaf." The reference to "sabre blades [*lames de sabre*]," a military paraphrase of *bractea,* reveals that Huysmans was in fact aware that this flower was not a flower at all, and therefore could not bear fruit. This real yet false exotic and aggressive flower is the grotesque archetype of the monstrous woman-flower that can be found in the literature of the Second Empire. For Zola, the dracaenas with their shiny blade-like leaves, the caladiums' bloody caresses and the hibiscus flowers all foreshadow Huysmans's Nidularium: "They resembled, it might have been imagined, the eager, sensual mouths of women, the red lips, soft and moist, of some colossal Messalina, bruised by kisses, and constantly renewed, with their hungry, bleeding smiles."[15]

There are two other plants with which Renée is associated and which exemplify this fear of (unfertile) female sexuality. The first is the Chinese hibiscus, a sterile hybrid. The second is the poisonous tanghin of Madagascar (*Tanghinia venenifera*), which had an infamous reputation at the time. In 1872, the year of the publication of *La curée,* Blanchard described it in the *Revue des Deux Mondes.*[16] The tree was used to "establish" the guilt of a person when there were not enough proofs to condemn her/him. For this purpose, the poisonous seeds of the tree were absorbed by the accused. If he/she died, he/she was pronounced guilty; if he/she resisted the poison, he/she was considered innocent. When understanding her desire for Maxime, Renée absorbs some of the tree's leaves, establishing a form of transcen-

---

14 A bract is an intermediary between leaf and petal, differing generally from the leaf in both form and color.
15 Zola, *The Kill,* 38.
16 Émile Blanchard, "L'Ile de Madagascar," *Revue des Deux Mondes* 101, Second Period, 42nd Year (Sep. 1, 1872): 204–20.

dental guilt. "Renée, her mind wandering, her mouth dry and parched, took between her lips a sprig of the tanghin tree that was level with her mouth, and sank her teeth into one of its bitter leaves."[17] As a degenerate, sterile woman, Renée is culpable in the eyes of society.

The flower is also considered monstrous because, like the anatomical Venus, it hides nothing and therefore denies the possibility of a reassuring interior. Dagonet reminds us that, according to the Ancients, the flowers exhibit their sexuality. Furthermore, no parts or organs are enveloped by other parts.[18] This image of the "indecent" flower fits with the idea of the exotic vegetation that channels all the fears and fantasies linked to the unknown, the untamed wildness of virgin forests, which at that time were considered places of unfettered primitive energy.

The environment in which these flowers develop is of fundamental importance. The hothouse, like the glass coffins and the eviscerated buildings leaves the interior on show. Worse still, the distinction between the outside and inside is blurred and with it the natural order. The glasshouse enables nature to invade domestic spaces. The phenomenon becomes noticeable from the beginning of the nineteenth century, reaching its height during the Second Empire. In 1805, during a visit to the house of an aristocrat, a naturalist returning from Vienna with Napoleon's army was surprised to find some non-native species normally too tender to survive the European climate. Until then, he had only seen such plants in hothouses in botanical gardens, or in their natural habitat.

Bory de Saint-Vincent's account is one of first descriptions of private, urban hothouses. It is contemporaneous with the first sales of glasshouses for domestic use and is therefore a useful point of reference. From an ecological point of view, these collections represent groups of plants that would be impossible in the wild. For an amateur botanist, the flowerbeds in the hothouse combine, in defiance of lines of longitude, elements

---

17 Zola, *The Kill*, 40.
18 François Dagognet, *Le catalogue de la vie* (Paris: PUF, 1970), 30.

that in nature would be separated by thousands of miles. Bory de Saint-Vincent describes this artificial "other-world" to his friend Leon Dufour, saying that he plans to sketch the "enchanted land" and then send a report of it to the botanical institute and the Jardin des Plantes.[19] For the naturalist, the greenhouse is an "enchanted land" reminiscent of the foreign places he has visited in the past, although Bory de Saint-Vincent does not refer to any specific geographical location. The reproduction of a generic tropical climate, rather than a defined place, is sufficient to ensure the survival of species originating from geographical areas that, in reality, are very far apart.

The originality of this environment, which lacks any definition, since it aims to create an average tropical climate, produces a strange impression; it defies geographical differences, but also rejects the distinction between internal and external space. The greenhouse is elsewhere, "other-worldly," both here and now, and yet nowhere in particular. The plants in this artificial habitat look natural: e.g., the coconut palms grow as in the Tropics. The greenhouse seems to be a place that is utopian yet real, and in which — although it is possible to distinguish between the here and there, the native from the non-native — the distinction between nature and culture is necessarily blurred.[20] However, glasshouses are not so much homes for flowers as hospitals for exotic plants. The routine of daily care protects a plant life that is both artificial and fragile, since it depends on this environment, and yet vivid and flamboyant because it has been forced, it is "a true work of art."[21]

---

19 Jean Baptiste Bory de Saint-Vincent, "Lettre à Léon Dufour, Vienne décembre 1805," in *Correspondance de Bory de Saint-Vincent*, ed. Philippe Lauzun (Agen: Maison d'édition et d'imprimerie moderne, 1908), 93.

20 See Michel Serres, *Jouvences sur Jules Verne* (Paris: Les Éditions de Minuit, 1974), 151.

21 John Claudius Loudon and Charles Joseph Hullmandel, *The Green-house Companion: Comprising a General Course of Green-house and Conservatory Practice throughout the Year: A Natural Arrangement of all the Green-house Plants in Cultivation: With a Descriptive Catalogue of the Most Desirable to Form a Collection, Their Proper Soils, Modes of Propagation, Management, and References to Botanical Works in Which They Are Figured: Also, the*

During the early years of the century, this aspect had not been truly recognized, although the seeds were there. What Bory de Saint-Vincent observes, and which would be substantiated throughout the nineteenth century, is the osmosis between exotic vegetation and women in the private space:

> Among others, I remember the boudoir of the countess C […] whose sofa was surrounded by jasmine twining around daturas planted in soil, all on the first floor. It was reached from the bedroom by passing through thickets of African heathers, hydrangeas, camellias, then quite uncommon, and other prized shrubs, planted in beds bordered with violets, all colors of crocus, hyacinths and other flowers edged with grass. On the other side was the bathroom, elegantly placed under glass where papyrus and iris grew around the marble basin and the water pipes.[22]

The private life of women flourished amongst the plants. Since the Napoleonic Code was established (1804), women, like hothouse flowers, were beings that had to be protected and confined within interior spaces. Since public spaces were out of bounds, it is not surprising that the glasshouse, a controlled environment to thrive in, became the ultimate feminine space. Woman is nature: the glasshouse is nature controlled by man. Throughout the century, glasshouses became increasingly common and reached the height of popularity during Napoleon III's reign. The number of horticultural magazines, specialized dictionaries, and horticultural and glasshouse catalogues are evidence of this great public enthusiasm.[23] Monique Eleb-Vidal

---

Proper Treatment of Flowers in Rooms, and Bulbs in Water Glasses (London: Printed for Harding, Triphook, and Lepard and John Harding, 1824), 3.

22 Arthur Mangin, *Histoire des jardins chez tous les peuples, depuis l'Antiquité jusqu'à nos jours* (Tours: Alfred Mame et fils, 1883), 422.

23 Glasshouses were erected in private houses. According the catalogue of the Musée Nationale d'Histoire Naturelle, forty or so works were published between 1845 and 1900, for example, G. Delchevalerie, *Plantes de serre chaude et tempérée, constructions des serres, cultures, multiplications, etc.* (Paris: Li-

and Anne Debarre-Blanchard observe how the conservatory is as important for women as the drawing room or the boudoir. It is also a sign of upper-class status.[24]

The conservatory where Princess Mathilde, Napoleon III's cousin, held her famous *salon-serre,* was considered one of the high places of the Second Empire. The Goncourts described it thus: "With her somewhat barbaric taste, the Princess has scattered, amidst the most beautiful exotic plants in her *serre,* all sorts of furniture from every country, every period, every color and shape. It has the strangest appearance of a bric-à- brac in a rainforest."[25] It is not surprising then that, in *La curée,* the glasshouse, frequented mostly by women, should become a metaphor for female intimacy, an unexplored, wild space.

Woman, flowers and botany are therefore at the heart of a network of associations leading towards a reflection on the hybrid, whose uncertain nature connects science and literature in texts that are themselves an amalgam. A composite monster, but also alive and very real, the sterile hybrid becomes the sign that foreshadows the decadence of modern society. In a context in which the culture of plant hybrids is seen as a perversion of the laws of nature (the sterility of the created species being proof in-

---

brairie agricole de la Maison rustique, 1869); Jean-Baptiste-Louis Letellier, *Flore universelle: Plantes d'orangerie, de serres froide et tempérée* (Paris: 108 rue du faubourg Saint-Martin, 1851); Édouard Morren, *Plantes de serres: Exposition universelle, 1867, Paris* (Paris: Imprimerie et Librairie Administratives de Paul Dupont, 1867); and, Paul-Émile de Puydt, *Traité théorique et pratique de la culture des plantes de serre froide, orangerie et serre tempérées des jardiniers, précédé de notions pratiques de physiologie végétale et de physique horticole, et de conseils pour la construction des différentes serres* (Brussels: E. Tarlier, 1860). For more on this phenomenon see Monique Eleb-Vidal and Anne Debarre-Blanchard, *Architectures de la vie privée, maisons et mentalités, XVIIe–XIXe siècles.* Brussels: Archives d'architecture moderne éditions, 1989.

24 Eleb-Vidal and Debarre-Blanchard, *Architectures de la vie privée,* 270–71. They quote Léonce Reynaud, *Traité d'architecture* (Paris: Dunod, 1863), 530–32.

25 Edmond et Jules de Goncourt, *Journal: Mémoires de la vie littéraire, Vol. 2, 25 décembre 1867* (Paris: Fasquelle et Flammarion, 1956). 391.

deed that hybridization goes against nature), the woman/flower is the ideal vehicle for anxieties about safeguarding heredity.

From the beginning of the nineteenth century, man was considered an evolving species. Realization of this led to new ways of imagining man and woman, and reinforcing others. Built on the legacy of Christian tradition, woman was still the mother of all evils and thought to pass on these evils to future generations, but also now in a biological sense. She was responsible for the degradation of the species, either by passing on degenerate traits or because she refused to have children at all. The fear that the human species would fall into decline is symbolized by a system based on botanical metaphor. The greenhouse is the corrupting environment, while the exotic flower hybrid represents a degenerate and altered species. This monstrosity in plant form plays on the distinctions between external and internal spaces. This distinction is also consubstantial to the anatomical Venuses, which are the second metaphor about the anxiety generated by reproduction and the female body.[26]

In *La curée,* this criticism of the sterile woman and the desertion of family values and its consequences for the nation extends to the whole city, and the symbolic evisceration of women corresponds to the very real destruction of the buildings during Haussmann's public works program. The title of the novel is already an indication as to the significance of the notion of evisceration. In hunting, when the stag is killed, the *curée* is the moment when the intestines are given to the hunting dogs. According to tradition, the spoils are covered with a cloth before being revealed to the pack. This ritual is of primordial importance since it celebrates the act of evisceration, when that which was hidden inside the animal is exposed to view. *La curée* is founded on this violent act of exposure and appropriation.[27] In

---

[26] These flowers in the form of sexual organs form part of the fantasy of nature revealing itself before the scientist.

[27] Note that, during the Third Republic, the term is used to describe the Prussian invasion, the siege of Paris and the Commune. See, for example, Catulle Mendès, *Les 73 journées de la Commune (du 18 mars au 29 mai 1871)* (Paris: Lachaud, 1871), 284.

the very beginning of the novel, Saccard uses hunting terms in a powerful evocation of the violence suffered by the city: "There lay his fortune, in the cuts that his hand had made in the heart of Paris, and he had resolved to keep his plans to himself, knowing very well that when the spoils were divided there would be enough crows hovering over the disemboweled city."[28] His vision of the city as a body to be conquered, but also cut open, is close to that of Baron Haussmann, who says in his memoirs that he wanted to eviscerate the older quarters of Paris.[29] The choice of the term emphasizes the fact that the desire to explore the interior of the buildings is akin to the desire to explore inside the human body.

The evisceration that allows the internal spaces, that until then had been hidden from view, to be seen, draws on an erotic and morbid curiosity, similar to that which led to the foundation of museums of anatomy during the same period. In Chapter VII, the Board of Inquiry, which was inspecting the demolition site near the Place du Château d'eau (now Place de la République), included, amongst others, a doctor and a manufacturer of surgical instruments. The group is very excited by the sight of the "pallid entrails" or "pale insides" (*entrailles blafardes*).[30] During the inspection, which has all the appearance of a bawdy day out, the first anecdote to be told by one of the members is of his romantic memories on seeing the walls of his old bedroom. The eviscerated building immediately triggers the memory of a woman's belly. Then there is mention of Louis XV and his private parties, causing titillation among the visitors as they stand amidst the ruins of the "follies [*petites maisons*]."[31] During the visit, Saccard says that "You can look as long as you like, the ladies are gone," but for these gentlemen, in the midst of these vast eviscerated buildings, such women are their sole preoccu-

---

28 Zola, *The Kill*, 70.
29 Georges Eugène Haussmann, *Mémoires du Baron Haussmann*, Vol. 1 (Paris: V. Havard, 1890), 257.
30 Zola, *The Kill*, 247; *La curée*, 319.
31 In Louis XV's reign these "petites maisons" were places where private parties were held.

pation.³² Their pleasure in observing the innards of the buildings is connected to the pleasure of opening up or penetrating the body. A whole set of connections — the doctor, the eviscerated city/body, the surgical instruments, sexuality and, above all, the second part of the chapter which, after the demolition, centers on the "the 'end' of a woman [*la fin d'une femme*], Renée"³³ — all point to the city being seen as an anatomical Venus, a wax model of the female form with removable parts, thus allowing the anatomical secrets of a woman's abdomen to be explored.

Although the first wax anatomical models appeared in the eighteenth century — the most famous being those of Clemente Susini and Giuseppe Fusini — they were at the height of their popularity at fairs and in anatomical museums during the second part of the nineteenth century.³⁴ These human-sized dolls usually lay in large glass coffins. Their fixed and languid pose amid satin sheets emphasized the erotico-morbid nature of the scene. It should be noted that after 1856, Place du Château d'eau was dominated by Pierre Spitzner's famous Musée anatomique et ethnologique. Spitzner's collection included a Venus that was 'undressed', one organ at a time, by a demonstrator in a white coat.³⁵ Around the model's abdomen, there were four replica male hands cut off at the wrists. Together with those of the demonstrator, these hands, representative of the doctors, created the impression that a curée was being carried out on the woman's body. The spoils were being literally handed out of this woman's body: "to touch a woman has become, in ordinary parlance, a euphemism for her use as a sexual object [...]."³⁶ For the male

---

32 Zola, *The Kill*, 252.
33 Zola, *La curée*, 327. In the English translation, "She was breaking down" (Zola, *The Kill*, 254).
34 Kathryn A. Hoffmann, "Sleeping Beauties in the Fairground: The Spitzner, Pedley and Chemisé Exhibits," *Early Popular Visual Culture* 4, no. 2 (2006): 139–59.
35 Michel Lemire, "Fortunes et infortunes de l'anatomie et des préparations anatomiques, naturelles et artificielles," in *L'âme au corps: arts et sciences 1793-1993*, ed. Jean Clair (Paris: Gallimard, 1993), 95.
36 Sigmund Freud, *Inhibition, symptôme et angoisse*, trans. Michel Tort (Paris: PUF, 1978), 45.

spectator, the symbolic touching of these disembodied hands added a certain pleasure to the evisceration, which in this case is close to an act of rape.[37]

The chapter preceding the visit to the demolition sites is part and parcel of this sub-text about the anatomical Venuses. Renée is herself described as a toy, a doll that is violently stripped naked for the pleasure of men: "She had come to that, being a big doll from whose broken chest escaped a thin trickle of sawdust."[38] The novel operates on these levels of equivalence. Renée's death in Chapter VIII corresponds to a description of Paris aflame with the setting sun. In the context of the novel, the violation of the female body is inseparable from that of the moral values of the nation. The civil war is the negation of the family of which the patriarchal metonymy is the woman. The objectification of Renée as an eviscerated doll contributes to this twofold loss of interiority (spiritual and domestic), since the spiritual interiority of the woman is integral to the notion of the home (interior and family). The evisceration of the woman and the city eventually merge into one another:

> On either side, great pieces of wall burst open by pickaxes, remained standing; tall, gutted buildings, displaying their pale insides, opened to the sky their wells stripped of stairs, their gaping rooms suspended in mid-air like the broken drawers of a big, ugly piece of furniture [...] On the bare walls, ribbons of flues rose side by side, lugubriously black and with sharp bends.[39]

In this description, Zola mixes architectural terms and those referring to clothing and the human body with a discourse on emptiness and violence. The female body, the spiritual and do-

---

37 In *Ouvrir Vénus*, Didi-Huberman devotes a chapter to anatomical Venuses in which he analyses how they functioned in the nineteenth century. Georges Didi-Huberman, *Ouvrir Vénus: Nudité, rêve, cruauté* (Paris: Gallimard, 1999).
38 Zola, *The Kill*, 240.
39 Ibid., 247–48.

mestic spaces are destroyed in the same motion. However, the act of rape in *La curée* is polymorphous: it is hubris, which also means insult and excessiveness, as reflected by the reign of Napoleon III.

Basing his argument on the comparison between Second-Empire women and artificial, sterile hybrids, Zola makes *La curée* the beginning of a reflection on (in)fertility. The desertion of home and family and the rejection of motherhood in the hothouse that is Paris, and in which the distinction between the external and the internal is destroyed, give structure to this novel that was written when France was still occupied by Prussian troops, an occupation that was also seen as the rape of the nation. If *La curée* has been seen as a modern Phaedra, it is because it is a tragedy that still deals with dramas of heredity and lineage. The tragic scene is the exposed place where the true origins of the family are revealed.[40] In *La curée,* for those involved, it is a double revelation of original relationships with civil war and family being two sides of the same coin. *La curée* operates on the level of the tragic model: the evisceration of internal spaces (both sacrifice and revelation) allows recognition of the original relationships and their sins. At the end of the novel, when the sun is setting on Paris while Napoleon III disappears into the distance, Zola's final revelation is this: that the Commune was the *enfant maudit,* the accursed child of the Second Empire.

---

40 On the family as a tragic setting see André Green, *Un œil en trop: Le complexe d'Œdipe dans la tragédie* (Paris: Editions de Minuit, 1969), 18.

Bibliography

Blanchard, Émile. "L'Ile de Madagascar." *Revue des Deux Mondes* 101, Second Period, 42nd Year (Sep. 1, 1872): 204–20.
Bory de Saint-Vincent, Jean Baptiste. "Lettre à Léon Dufour, Vienne décembre 1805." In *Correspondance de Bory de Saint-Vincent*, edited by Philippe Lauzun, 92-94. Agen: Maison d'édition et d'imprimerie moderne, 1908.
Aude Campmas, "Les fleurs de serre: Entre science et littérature à la fin du dix-neuvième siècle." In *Visions/Revisions: Essays on Nineteenth-Century French Culture*, edited by N. Harkness, P. Rowe, T. Unwin & J. Yee, 49–61. Oxford: Peter Lang, 2003.
Dagognet, François. *Le catalogue de la vie*. Paris: PUF, 1970.
Delchevalerie, G. *Plantes de serre chaude et tempérée, constructions des serres, cultures, multiplications, etc.* Paris: Librairie agricole de la Maison rustique, 1869.
Didi-Huberman, Georges. *Ouvrir Vénus: Nudité, rêve, cruauté*. Paris: Gallimard, 1999.
Eleb-Vidal, Monique, and Anne Debarre-Blanchard. *Architectures de la vie privée, maisons et mentalités, XVIIe–XIXe siècles*. Brussels: Archives d'architecture moderne éditions, 1989.
Freud, Sigmund. *Inhibition, symptôme et angoisse*. Translated by Michel Tort. Paris: PUF, 1978.
Goncourt, Edmond and Jules de. *Journal: Mémoires de la vie littéraire*. Vol. 2. Paris: Fasquelle et Flammarion, 1956.
Green, André. *Un œil en trop: Le complexe d'Œdipe dans la tragédie*. Paris: Editions de Minuit, 1969.
Grimard, Édouard. *L'esprit des plantes, silhouettes végétales*. Tours: Alfred Mame et fils, 1869.
Haussmann, Georges Eugène. *Mémoires du Baron Haussmann*. Vol. 1. Paris: Victor Havard, 1890.
Hoffmann, Kathryn A. "Sleeping Beauties in the Fairground: The Spitzner, Pedley and Chemisé Exhibits." *Early Popular Visual Culture* 4, no. 2 (2011): 139–59. DOI: 10.1080/17460650600793557.

Huysmans, Joris-Karl. *Against Nature*. Translated by Margaret Mauldon. Oxford: Oxford University Press, 1998.

Lemire, Michel. "Fortunes et infortunes de l'anatomie et des préparations anatomiques, naturelles et artificielles." In *L'âme au corps: Arts et sciences 1793–1993*, edited by Jean Clair, 70–101. Paris: Gallimard, 1993.

Letellier, Jean-Baptiste-Louis. *Flore universelle: Plantes d'orangerie, de serres froide et tempérée*. Paris: 108 rue du faubourg Saint-Martin, 1851.

Loudon, John Claudius, and Charles Joseph Hullmandel. *The Green-house Companion: Comprising a General Course of Green-house and Conservatory Practice throughout the Year: a Natural Arrangement of all the Green-house Plants in Cultivation: With a Descriptive Catalogue of the Most Desirable to Form a Collection, Their Proper Soils, Modes of Propagation, Management, and References to Botanical Works in Which They Are Figured: Also, the Proper Treatment of Flowers in Rooms, and Bulbs in Water Glasses*. London: Harding, Triphook, and Lepard and John Harding, 1824.

Mangin, Arthur. *Histoire des jardins chez tous les peuples, depuis l'Antiquité jusqu'à nos jours*. Tours: Alfred Mame et fils, 1883.

Matlock, Jann. "Everyday Ghosts: Zola's *La curée* in the Shadow of the Commune, 1871–72." *Romanic Review* 102, nos. 3–4 (2011): 321–47.

Mendès, Catulle. *Les 73 journées de la Commune (du 18 mars au 29 mai 1871)*. Paris: Lachaud, 1871.

Mirbeau, Octave. *Le jardin des supplices*. Paris: Le Livre de poche, 1957.

Morren, Édouard. *Plantes de serres: Exposition universelle, 1867, Paris*. Paris: Imprimerie et Librairie Administratives de Paul Dupont, 1867.

Puydt, Paul-Émile de. *Traité théorique et pratique de la culture des plantes de serre froide, orangerie et serre tempérées des jardiniers, précédé de notions pratiques de physiologie végétale et de physique horticole, et de conseils pour la construction des différentes serres*. Brussels: E. Tarlier, 1860.

Reynaud, Léonce. *Traité d'architecture*. Paris: Dunod, 1863.
Rollet-Echalier, Catherine. *La politique à l'égard de la petite enfance sous la IIIe République*. Paris: PUF, 1990.
Schor, Naomi. "Triste Amérique: Atala and the Postrevolutionary Construction of Woman." In *Rebel Daughters: Women and the French Revolution,* edited by Sara E. Melzer and Leslie W. Rabine, 139–56. Oxford: Oxford University Press, 1992.
Serres, Michel. *Jouvences sur Jules Verne*. Paris: Les Éditions de Minuit, 1974.
Texier, Edmond-Auguste. *Les femmes et la fin du monde*. Paris: Calmann Lévy, 1877.
Zola, Émile. *La curée*. Paris: Gallimard, 1996.
———. *Les Rougon-Macquart: Histoire naturelle et sociale d'une famille sous le second Empire, Volume 4: La terre*. Paris: Robert Laffont, 1992.
———. *The Kill*. Translated by Brian Nelson. Oxford: Oxford University Press, 2008.

4

The World as Seen through a Window: Interiors and the Crisis of Morality in the Work of Robert Musil

Stijn De Cauwer

In the opening pages of Robert Musil's unfinished masterpiece *The Man without Qualities* (1930–1943), the overwhelming and dizzying experience of life in the modern city is evoked. The novel is set in Vienna in 1913, on the brink of world war on a scale that defies comprehension. Musil powerfully describes the rhythms, motions, energies and movements that make up the modern city. This vertigo-inducing activity belittles the urban-dwelling human being who no longer knows what their place is amongst these inhuman and mechanical forces. The different dynamics that constitute the city are too complex for a person to grasp in a comprehensive overview. The constant flow of stimuli, opinions and conflicting theories leave one's mind reeling. Even doing nothing within this frantic activity requires a huge amount of energy:

> If all those leaps of attention, flexing of eye muscles, fluctuations of the psyche, if all the efforts it takes for a man to just

hold himself upright within the flow of traffic on a busy street could be measured, he thought — as he toyed with calculating the incalculable — the grand total would surely dwarf the energy needed by Atlas to hold up the world, and one could then estimate the enormous undertaking it is nowadays merely to be a person who does nothing at all.[1]

These are the thoughts of Ulrich, the main protagonist of *The Man without Qualities*, as he is first introduced in the novel. Ulrich is looking at the motion on the street, ironically trying to measure the flow of traffic with a stopwatch, though he knows that it is futile to try to grasp the bustling activity in that way. He wonders how the activities of one individual could have any impact at all on this complex mass of motion. A person could only stare passively at all these activities that are beyond her or his comprehension, and be subjected to it or withdraw from society. This is the impasse staged by Musil in the opening pages of the novel.

A significant part of the staging, Ulrich is first introduced standing behind a window looking at life on the street. From behind the rigid frame of the window, standing inside the little chateau of Ulrich's father, the hustle and bustle on the street, all the motion of the traffic, can only appear as incomprehensible chaos. This specific framing reveals a key feature of Musil's theoretical analysis of a fundamental crisis that was causing havoc in Austria and Germany during the entire first half of the twentieth century. Throughout his life, from his essays to his novels, Musil developed a theoretical diagnosis of why his times were so inclined towards destruction. According to him, this was due to a problematic, and even pathological, reaction to the complexity and vast challenges of modern life. In Musil's view, people reacted to the overwhelming challenges of the present by turning to inadequate and outdated theoretical and moral frameworks, but these frameworks only increased the incomprehension and

---

[1] Robert Musil, *The Man without Qualities*, trans. Sophie Wilkins and Burton Pike (London, New York: Vintage International, 1995), 7.

frustration, bringing the prevailing tensions to a boiling point. Ulrich cannot comprehend the chaos on the street because he is looking at it through the too-rigid framework of the window. According to Musil, a much more flexible and creative approach was needed to make the most of the possibilities modernity offered. Trying to "shield off" the effects of modernity by secluding oneself in a closed space would only increase the confusion. In this essay, I show how Musil staged this critical analysis repeatedly in spatial terms, whether by means of a particular building or by playing with the contrast between inside and outside.

In a tongue-in-cheek piece from *Posthumous Papers of a Living Author* (1936) — a collection with short miniatures that Musil released when he realized that it took him a long time to publish the continuation of *The Man without Qualities* — he mocks Freudian psychoanalysis.[2] Musil did not have a high opinion of the theories of his Viennese contemporary, who was the talk of the town. For him, Freudian theory was steeped in an outdated view on the family, and especially the mother, that no longer corresponded to rapidly changing gender roles.[3] Musil describes the psychoanalyst's room as a refuge from the chaos and confusion of modern life. The patient can relax, lay down on the couch of the "soul-improving expert" and no longer worry about the outside world: "[…] if the world explodes with all its mechanical energies, here you find the good old time gently flowing."[4] While the world "outside" had become incomprehensible, chaotic and overwhelming, a world in which people no longer knew what

---

2 Andreas Huyssen has coined the phrase "modernist miniatures" to describe the short texts such as those collected in *Posthumous Papers of a Living Author*. See Andreas Huyssen, *Miniature Metropolis: Literature in an Age of Photography and Film* (Cambridge: Harvard University Press, 2015).

3 The rapid changes to gendered customs at the end of the nineteenth century — for example, women becoming allowed to register at certain faculties for the first time — was perceived by some as a threat. For more on the changing gender roles see Agatha Schwartz, *Gender and Modernity in Central Europe: The Austro-Hungarian Monarchy and its Legacy* (Ottawa: University of Ottawa Press, 2010).

4 Robert Musil, *Posthumous Papers of a Living Author*, trans. Peter Wortsman (Brooklyn: Archipelago Books, 2006), 107.

their place was, on the psychoanalyst's couch, life "as it used to be" is restored, and everybody has a clear role and place in the sheltered structure of the family. What is important to notice is that Musil makes a connection between what he considers to be the outdated morality of psychoanalysis and the enclosed space of the therapist's office, functioning as a shelter from the threats of modern urban life. This is a constellation — a critique of outdated moral guidelines and a spatial framing — that recurs repeatedly in Musil's work.

In the early twenties, Musil analyzed the crisis of the time and the role of morality plays within it. He wrote a series of rich essays in which he scrutinized the situation in Germany and Austria in the years following the First World War. In the long, but unfinished, essay "The German as Symptom" (1923), he provides a general theory of the role of morality in our life and why this general human condition has turned into a state of crisis around the turn of the century. In his view, human beings are essentially shapeless, yet formed in the smallest details by the prevailing moral guidelines, customs and institutional apparatuses of that society. Without the roles, shapes and patterns provided by society, people would drown in existential angst and insecurity.[5]

To avoid the constant existential insecurity over our life choices, people adopt pre-existing moral models. The prevailing moral codes, including social roles, symbols and hierarchies, serve as firm guidelines for people to feel like they belong to a meaningful and ordered society in which they have a specific role and place. Several characters in *The Man without Qualities* defend the view that we should unquestionably and firmly adhere to the prevailing moral norms because they provide the best and most certain guidelines for life. Early in the novel, Ulrich's father is described as adhering to the principle that in order to pass freely through a door one must respect that

---

5 Robert Musil, *Precision and Soul: Essays and Addresses,* trans. Burton Pike and David S. Luft (Chicago and London: University of Chicago Press, 1990), 158.

it has stable frames.⁶ In the view of Musil's father, accepting the traditional moral code is as necessary as solid doorframes and, without it, the world would slide into random chaos and excess. Morality, in this sense, equates to the limitation of possibilities and freedoms. Mockingly, Ulrich's general retort to his father's position is to say that according to him a person's desires, sentiments and plans in life could only be achieved if first framed by "prejudices, traditions, obstacles, and barriers of all sorts, like a lunatic in his straightjacket."⁷ In Musil's view, accepting the prevailing moral guidelines and social roles was a way for people to reduce complexity and uncertainty in a world that was becoming increasingly complex: "Life is made easier when it is socially bound."⁸ This dependency on the moral guidelines of one's society and social situation can make one so accustomed to the moral order that it feels to them as though it is the natural state of existence; they can no longer fathom that other, and maybe better, ways of living, of organizing one's life, are possible.

In Musil's view, the realities of life changed fundamentally at the end of the nineteenth century; the rapid transformations of modern life made the prevailing moral guidelines, along with the symbols of the moral order, as outdated as a powdered wig. People could no longer believe in the symbols of the moral order, such as the old Emperor Franz Joseph, whose fading power Musil compared with the light of a star that died many years ago.⁹ But at the same time, the people longed, more than ever, for firm guidelines and order as they saw their living conditions change beyond recognition. Consequently, people desperately tried to adhere to the moral guidelines that they could no longer take seriously.¹⁰ The rapid changes of modernity dislodged the

---

6   Musil, *The Man without Qualities*, 15–16.
7   Ibid.
8   Musil, *Precision and Soul*, 174–75.
9   It is no coincidence that the literature of this period is filled with protagonists who are unable to take up the social position they were supposed to, and who no longer know what to do, from Rilke's Malte Laurids Brigge to Broch's Pasenow to Mann's Hans Castorp.
10 Musil, *Precision and Soul*, 130.

established order, causing a crisis in both personal and collective identity. People no longer knew what to believe, which ideas to endorse, or what to admire. There was a growing list of culture-pessimistic narratives about the state of society, with the cult around Oswald Spengler's *Der Untergang des Abendlandes* (*The Decline of the West,* 1918) and the influence of Max Nordau's *Entartung* (*Degeneration,* 1892) as two prominent examples. People needed to believe in the order in which they have a place, yet, in Kakania, Musil's satirical Austro-Hungarian Empire, a process had begun whereby people gradually lost this belief: "They no longer knew what their smiles, their sighs, their ideas, were for."[11]

In *The German as Symptom,* Musil describes the changes that occurred in the 1880s as a "lack of faith," which was both spiritual and secular.[12] People could no longer identify with the symbols, institutions, and the life roles they were supposed to employ. As Musil writes in his diaries: "Morality was not undermined but proved to be hollow."[13] The problems concerning morality were like an escalating vortex: the need for clear guidelines was greater than ever, but people could only turn to guidelines they no longer considered, increasing their frustration and need for firm guidelines like a vicious cycle spiraling out of control. This quagmire created an explosive and destructive psychological condition, which, according to Musil, paved the way for the catastrophes of the early twentieth century. The frustration about the complex present led to the desire for widespread destruction. In *The German as Symptom,* Musil wrote about the craving for a "metaphysical bang" coming out of discontent with the times: an "apparently human need to rip existence to shreds from time to time, and toss them to the winds, seeing where they fall."[14] It was this feeling which made people welcome the

---

11 Musil, *The Man without Qualities,* 575–76. Kakania is derived from the description *kaiserlich-königlich,* used by the administration of the empire.
12 Ibid., 159.
13 Robert Musil, *Diaries 1899–1941,* trans. Philip Payne (New York: Basic Books, 1998), 287.
14 Musil, *Precision and Soul,* 129.

outbreak of the First World War with a festive mood, as if spring had arrived.

Musil regarded, specifically, the popular rhetoric about the state, nation and race as an inadequate framework through which to approach society, and referred to these ideologically loaded notions as the mystical fetishes of his time. They were fetishized as an absolute good and credited with a form of moral agency. Musil said that these mystical fetishes were used as piecemeal recipes for all evils of modern life. Not only were they dangerous because they provided the people with an arousing narrative that could be politically abused, but also because they relayed all moral responsibility to some idealized abstraction outside of the individual:

> If, in good and evil, the "race" rather than the individual is made responsible for everything, the effect is exactly the same as if one were always making excuses for oneself: the result is not only that truthfulness and intellectual refinement become dulled, but also that all the germ cells of morality degenerate. When virtue is declared to be national property by predestination, the Lord's vineyard is expropriated and no one needs to work in it anymore. The individual is flattered into believing that he possesses everything desirable by merely contemplating the virtues of his "race": evidently a fool's paradise, our happy Germany, where roasted virtues fly into our mouths.[15]

Unable to come to terms with the complexity of the present, many were seeking their reference points in abstracted ideals to which the facts of the present were supposed to conform. This deprived them of the capacity to invent novel and better ethical guidelines more suited for modern life and so prolonged the feeling of frustration. We can now understand why Musil, shortly after the end of the First World War, wrote the following

---

15 Ibid., 106–7.

controversial assessment: "Germany's collapse was not brought about by her immoral, but by her moral, citizens."[16]

This explosive condition was by no means over after the end of the First World War. In 1921, Musil warned, in his essay "'Nation' as Ideal and Reality," that it would be a grave mistake to forget recent events and move forward. To ignore the circumstances and tensions that had caused the war would, he argued, inevitably cause the same destructive tensions to return: "By repressing it we would be sinking the foundations of a monstrous hysteria into the soul of the nation."[17]

The connection between a critique of morality and the play between inside and outside was already at the heart of the novel that made Musil a successful writer at the age of 26: *The Confusions of Young Törless* (1906). As a child, Musil was sent to the military boarding schools of Eisenstadt and Mährisch-Weisskirchen; his experiences there formed the material for this early work. Rainer Maria Rilke, who was briefly at the same school at Mährisch-Weisskirchen, had to be removed by his parents after less than a year, remaining traumatized by his stay there for the rest of his life. When Rilke read Dostoevsky's prison memoir *The House of the Dead,* he said it reminded him of the atmosphere at the school. Musil, who was much less shaken by his experience in the military academies than Rilke, nevertheless referred at the end of his life to the boarding school of Mährisch-Weisskirchen as "the arsehole of the devil."[18]

It was the purpose of these prestigious schools, where the wealthy Viennese families with positions in the administration and education systems of the Empire sent their children, to install, in the pupils, an unshakable sense of moral duty and an unquestionable loyalty to the Habsburg monarchy. The readers of *The Confusions of Young Törless* must have been shocked when Musil described the sadistic, homoerotic power games that went on at night in the remote corners of the school, includ-

---

16 Musil, *Diaries*, 287.
17 Musil, *Precision and Soul*, 103.
18 Musil, *Diaries*, 469.

ing punishment rituals amongst the pupils, while during the day a strict moral rule and military code reigned. The novel is now regarded as an exploration of the preconditions of what would become the violence and cruelty of the Nazi regime. While some regarded the book to be "prophetic," or a microcosmic tale depicting compactly the grotesque violence that would become official policy in Germany, this view is redundant when we know that Musil's point was to show that later outbursts of large-scale violence were the consequence of conditions that had been brewing for decades.

The boarding school that Törless is sent to is in a remote area of the empire, to keep the pupils away from all potentially "corrupting" influences of the big city. It comes across like a fortress, with high, solid walls, keeping the pupils "safe" from the threatening outside, such as the nearby village with its bars and prostitutes. When young Törless enters the institution that is supposed to instill in him the solid moral guidelines that should guide him throughout his life, he soon discovers that simply being a pupil in the school regime is not enough to still his moral confusions, especially when he is drawn into the erotic and sadistic games that go on at night and the possibility of visiting a prostitute who lives nearby. Törless also discovers that he does not have the proper notions to formulate his concerns or to think them through. He is not equipped with the skills to grasp and reflect upon his moral troubles, being used to adopting preexisting moral rules. He only had to follow the guidelines that the school, representing the values of society, was going to provide him, and not to reflect on them himself, something that proved to be utterly inadequate. Not finding the language to express his confusions, he shapes them into a generally acceptable manner for the school, namely into a mathematical question.

Törless cannot accept how an exact science, such as mathematics, can make use of imaginary numbers. When he asks this question to his mathematics teacher, he tells him that he is too young to comprehend such complex things and that he just has to believe. The impressive leather volume of Kant the teacher has in his room, inspired the hope in Törless to find the answers in Kant, but he soon realizes that he cannot relate to the abstractions he is trying to read alone in his room. At the end of the book, when all the nightly games have been discovered and Törless has to justify himself to the school authorities, he can only mumble unclear phrases. These sound like confused nonsense to his judges, who conclude that Törless has an unhealthy inclination towards speculative matters that could be directed towards the acceptable philosophical and theological channels. As Törless's moral and sexual crisis inevitably escalates, Musil provides the reader a glimpse of Törless's future as an adult, who has fully repressed the confusions of his adolescence, becoming a man "upon whom respect for the law and, to some extent, for public morals, has a calming effect [...]."[19] In this early work, the fortress-like school embodies the rigid moral codes which breed violence and rob the pupils of the capacity to make their own ethical reflections.

Similarly, in the opening pages of *The Man without Qualities,* the connection is made between the interiority of a home and an outdated form of morality. For Ulrich, living the lifestyle of his father would be unimaginable, which is presented in the beginning of the novel by the inability of Ulrich to live in the house of his father. The house of his father is described as an old-fashioned house, as "a sort of little château with short wings, a hunting lodge or rococo love nest of past times."[20] It unambiguously comes across as belonging to a bygone era: "it was basically seventeenth century, while the park and the upper story showed an eighteenth-century influence and the façade had been restored and somewhat spoiled in the nineteenth century, so that the whole had something blurred about it, like a double-exposed photograph."[21] The entire beginning of the novel stages the drastic contrast of modern urban life with past forms of living. Ulrich believes that the present requires a new

---

[19] Robert Musil, *The Confusions of Young Törless,* trans. Shaun Whiteside (London: Penguin Books, 2001), 126.

[20] Musil, *The Man without Qualities,* 6.

[21] Ibid.

style that breaks with the past and that follows completely different principles.[22] When he arrives at his father's home in 1913, after having been away for a long time, the idea that such a home would be his seems unimaginable. As Musil ironically writes: it is the house of a man with qualities. After trying to settle into the house, Ulrich feels out of place, wondering: "Is this life going to be mine?"[23]

Ulrich feels as if he walked into a home from an older century, in which everything has its place, but it would be a ludicrous idea that Ulrich would take his place in such an outmoded setting. As we have already seen, Ulrich looks at the hustle and bustle of the street from behind the window in the house of his father, who is of the opinion that "solid door frames" are required to walk through a door. From the fixed frame of the window, the world looks like chaos. The contrast between modern life "outside" and the prevalent framework to grasp society is made total. Ulrich cannot live according to the life roles, moral beliefs, symbols and style of the generation of his father; nor are these ideals adequate to make the best out of life in the modern city. What should he do instead? Ulrich chooses to take a year-long vacation to decide. Nevertheless, his father helps him to become a part of the elite group of aristocrats, businessmen and establishment figures who want to organize a grand jubilee for the Emperor Franz Joseph (which would never take place because of the First World War), the so-called "Parallel Campaign." Throughout *The Man without Qualities,* the reader follows the chaotic meetings in which this group fruitlessly tries to synthesize the best ideas of their time to find the one crowning idea which is supposed to represent Austria.

In Musil's analysis, modern society consisted of a plethora of fragmented domains. Those domains often existed with complete indifference for each other, or even worse, with mutual antagonisms. Now, the increasing fragmentation and segregation of different domains or systems in modern society has become

---

22 Ibid., 14–15.
23 Ibid., 16.

a well-known phenomenon. But how to deal with this fragmentation was, for Musil, a crucial concern. His present consisted, he believed, of a large amount of possibilities, but these did not come to fruition because different domains ignored each other or were at odds with one another. What was required, in Musil's view, was finding a way to combine different domains to create new ways of understanding. A theme that runs throughout *The Man without Qualities* is the clash between the world of the sciences and a more spiritual, religious or poetic experience of the world. Already in the opening sentence this contrast is staged, in which a pleasant day in Vienna is described in inhuman, dry scientific jargon. The contrast between scientific measurements and our daily experience of a day with nice weather is pushed to the extreme. Musil, who was trained as both an engineer and a philosopher, but who also had a keen interest in the experience of mysticism, was strongly opposed to the popular tendency amongst intellectuals of his time to denounce what they regarded as the mechanization of society due to an increasingly scientific worldview and to compensate for this by pleading for the irrational.[24] It was precisely the presentation of the present in terms of such a dualism, a world which is "too rational" versus a healthy "irrationalism," that made the dangerous frustration about modern society worse. Musil remarked that we do not have too much intellect and too little soul, but too little intellect in the matters of the soul. He believed that the most innovative methods and insights from the sciences had to be combined with the more subjective and intense insights from what could be called spiritual experiences. In the popular and intellectual discourse of the day, attempts were often made to combine these two in problematic ways. How this should be achieved was for Musil a crucial question.[25]

In *The Man without Qualities,* the incapacity to comprehend modern life is exemplified by the chaotic meetings of the Par-

---

[24] For more detailed information about Musil's life see Karl Corino, *Robert Musil: eine Biographie* (Reinbek bei Hamburg: Rowohlt, 2003).

[25] Musil, *Precision and Soul*, 147.

allel Campaign. These meetings bring together characters such as the aristocratic and conservative Tuzzi and Count Leinsdorf, Diotima who regards the meetings as her own prestigious salon, the German businessman and essayist Arnheim (for whom Walther Rathenau served as a model), and General Stumm von Bordwehr, who observes the events from a military perspective. Besides these, many more characters are presented in the novel, such as Ulrich's sister and counterpart Agathe, Clarisse, who romanticizes the irrational and, as gradually losing her mind, eventually develops a dangerous obsession for the psychotic serial-killer Moosbrugger and Clarisse's husband Walter, a failed artist with Wagnerian aspirations, amongst many others. The collective viewpoints of the characters form an overview of some of the popular theories and opinions circulating in Musil's time. Throughout *The Man without Qualities,* Musil exposes the inadequacy of these differing approaches for comprehending reality. The clashing of these inadequate perspectives comes across like a maddening cacophony. Initially, it is the hope of the members of the Parallel Campaign to collect the most intelligent people and the best ideas and to somehow synthesize them. Thus, Diotima was hoping to find the "crowning idea" representing Austria. This endeavor was doomed from the start, and the meetings descend into a dizzying flow of occasionally absurd new ideas and inventions. What Musil tried to show is that, the frameworks they adopt for grasping the complex present allow them to see only fragmented chaos, leading to a world in which perspectives clash or exist in parallel without the possibility of developing frameworks that transcend the prevailing categories. This problem is repeatedly figured in spatial terms.

In a striking segment, general Stumm heads to the national library to ask the librarians for a volume that presents an overview or synthesis of the best ideas of his time. In so doing, he hopes to solve the Parallel Campaign's problem of finding a "crowning idea" that transcends the huge diversity of circulating new ideas. The national library is a symbolic place in which all knowledge is not only stored, but also nicely ordered and categorized. Stumm discovers that the modern archive can assign each book neatly its proper place in the archive, but that there is no such thing as a book that can provide an overview of the content of the books, let alone provide a synthesis. One librarian even tells him that ordering the books into neat categories is only possible if one does not actually read the books. The rigid order goes at the cost of insight. The ordering system is a horizontal system of discrete categories, in which each book has its place. But such a system does not allow for the creative usage and combination of insights from different categories. It does not lead to a fruitful reproduction and formation of knowledge, but only continues the overwhelming feeling of being faced with a vast amount of knowledge. In this section, Musil prefigured the critique of the modern arc hive which writers such as W.G. Sebald developed decades later: that an archive can also bury the information it is storing, rather than preserving its existence.[26] An overly rigid order can hamper comprehension and perpetuate a form of disorder and conceptual stagnation. Instead, a more flexible way of ordering all this information is required.[27]

Towards the end of Part 2 of the novel *Pseudoreality Prevails* (1930), the rumors of the activities of the Parallel Campaign have caused an escalating suspicion amongst the people, to the extent that a demonstration is organized outside of the house of Tuzzi. That people mobilize to vent their anger at the activities of the Parallel Campaign is absurd because the members of the Parallel Campaign get absolutely nothing done. The incomprehension and incapacity of the Parallel Campaign is met with blind mass anger directed at a vague, unknown target. Musil is show-

---

26   For more about Sebald's critique of the modern archive, see J.J. Long, *W.G. Sebald: Image, Archive, Modernity* (New York: Columbia University Press, 2010).

27   Musil tried to develop such a flexible way of archiving himself in his extensive series of notebooks. These notebooks contained diary entries, thoughts, drafts for his writings, comments on books he read, and intellectual analyses. A short selection of the content, which does not do justice to the vast amount of notebooks Musil wrote, can be found in Robert Musil, Diaries. For more about this see Stijn De Cauwer, *A Diagnosis of Modern Life: Robert Musil's Der Mann ohne Eigenschaften as a Critical-Utopian Project* (Brussels: Peter Lang, 2014), 108–10.

ing how these two aspects — incomprehension because of too rigid frameworks and large-scale destructive frustration — are two sides of the same coin. Once again, Ulrich and the other members watch the approaching mob, shouting diverse slogans, from behind the window of the salon where their meeting takes place. The conceptual rigidity of the members of the Parallel Campaign is presented as a window frame through which one only sees random chaos resembling pure madness: "Ulrich had just walked over to the window when the marchers arrived. [...] A little further back, vehicles could be seen wedged into the crowd, while its relentless current flowed around them in endless black waves on which the foam of upturned faces seemed to be dancing."[28] The mob is presented like an ugly and frightening force, turned into a hideous spectacle from behind the window.

In *The Man without Qualities,* Ulrich is a character who gradually wants to break away from the rigid and deeply entrenched perspectives of his peers. He wants to develop alternative views on the world, which are compared with provisional experimental hypotheses. A way of escaping one's ordinary disposition towards the world and of obtaining a radically new vision is by experiencing something akin to a sudden mystical experience. In front of the window, Ulrich experiences such an alteration of his state of mind, which inverses the spatial setting of inside and outside, each described as a stage:

> With his eyes still moving from the threatening open-mouthed faces to the high-spirited ones farther back, and his mind refusing to absorb any more of this spectacle, he was undergoing a strange transformation. [...] The two stages had their way of fusing into one without regard for the fact that he was standing in between them. Then his sense of the room behind him contracted and turned inside out, passing through him or flowing past him as if turned to water, making for a strange spatial inversion, Ulrich thought, so that the people were passing behind him. Perhaps he had passed

---

28 Musil, *The Man without Qualities,* 685–86.

> through them and arrived beyond them at some zero point, or else they were moving both before him and behind him, lapping against him as the same ever-changing ripples of a stream lap against a stone in their midst.[29]

This sudden change in experience breaks open the habitual categories of experiencing the world and allows for the formation of new ways of looking, though, in this passage, Ulrich does not know yet what to make of this experience.

A last example of Musil's use of spaces is his employment of the psychiatric hospital in *The Man without Qualities*. Towards the end of the published part of the novel, Clarisse is increasingly losing herself in her desire for a redemptive irrational outburst. The strange case of the psychotic killer of prostitutes, Moosbrugger has been on everybody's lips and in a warped twist Clarisse starts to romanticize this inhuman killer as a redemptive savior. To quench her unhealthy obsession with Moosbrugger, Clarisse, her brother, Ulrich, and Stumm pay a visit to the psychiatric hospital where Moosbrugger has been placed, but in the published parts of the novel they never get to see him. In one of the striking unpublished drafts for the continuation of the novel, which Musil left behind after his death, the visitors do get to see Moosbrugger, engaged in a game of cards with a priest and two doctors: a young unnamed hospital intern and an older visiting doctor, called Dr. Pfeifer, who works as a legal expert.[30] The card game that Clarisse, guided by Dr. Friedenthal, witnesses is organized by the doctors in order to observe Moos-

---

29 Ibid., 689.
30 When Musil died, he left behind a large amount of chapter drafts or drafts for possible continuations of *The Man without Qualities*. For a long time, Musil scholars erroneously tried to "reconstruct" the continuation of the novel for Musil. This is now regarded as a mistake. The fragments consist of different possible and parallel continuations, and these fragments are today considered to be part of the complex text which is the *The Man without Qualities*. For more on the complications with the editions of *The Man without Qualities*, see Walter Fanta's "The Genesis of *Der Mann ohne Eigenschaften*," in A Companion to the Works of Robert Musil, ed. Philip Payne, et al. (Rochester: Camden House, 2007), 251–84.

brugger in a more casual setting. The two doctors at the table strongly disagree on the case of Moosbrugger. What is at stake is the question of whether Moosbrugger is sane and can be sentenced to death, or is sick and hence not accountable for his actions and should be committed to a psychiatric hospital. Both doctors are hoping to provoke Moosbrugger into a statement that can prove one of their respective cases, but Moosbrugger remains a silent enigma. Soon, it becomes clear that the reasoning adopted by the doctors is flawed and twisted. They have to warp the premises of their theoretical positions to make their respective points. Especially when the doctors use their medical knowledge to draw a legal judgment about Moosbrugger, Musil exposes the strong conflation of medical knowledge and moral judgments. Significantly, while the two doctors are arguing and quarrelling, it is the rather silent priest who wins the card game. The decision on Moosbrugger is ultimately a moral decision, not a scientific or clinical one.

In an article in which she analyzes this chapter draft, Patrizia McBride emphasizes that the card game is not only about Moosbrugger, but first and foremost a competition between conflicting domains, using incommensurable validity claims, all striving for final authority on this matter.[31] For the young intern, defending the domain of psychiatry, issues of guilt or personal accountability have no place in his scientific approach. He is concerned with medical observation and explanation, but not with moral or metaphysical questions. The legal expert on the other hand will insist on the moral, but non-scientific, categories of guilt and non-guilt. The rather silent priest will defend the incapacity of human reason and understanding in issues of guilt and culpability. This short chapter draft is, in a sense, a compact summary of Musil's analysis of the modern impasse: incompatible domains struggle over the case of Moosbrugger, with completely incommensurable claims and terminology, and, because of this, no understanding is achieved of the enigmatic

---

31 Patrizia C. McBride, "On the Utility of Art for Politics: Musil's 'Armed Truce of Ideas,'" *The German Quarterly* 73, no. 4 (2000): 366–86.

and incomprehensible Moosbrugger. The ultimate basis for the judgment is the prevailing morality of society. Musil shows here that the psychiatric and the legal worlds are essentially pervaded by this prevailing morality.

For Musil, what makes the world seem mad are these fragmented domains and viewpoints working against each other, increasing the confusion, without being able to transcend this fragmentation and form new and more fruitful approaches. Geoffrey C. Howes reveals the insanity in Musil's writings as derivative of a struggle between systems that are logical only as self-contained arguments.[32] The scene in the psychiatric hospital forms a microcosm of the world "outside," and, as one doctor confesses, the uncertainty of knowledge, a general condition of society.[33]

In *The Man without Qualities,* Musil stages the inadequacy of different prevailing opinions, theories and conceptual approaches, along with the ensuing incomprehension and frustration. In so doing, he hoped to move beyond theoretical limitations and unproductive fragmentation to find new hypotheses and creative possibilities. He regarded his novel as a vast experimental station in which one could uncover new ideas and relationships and could construct alternative ontological models "to invent the inner person."[34] These new connections, combinations and possibilities could only be found amid the complexity of daily life, not in a secluded refuge from it.

---

32 Gemma Blackshaw and Sabine Wieber, eds., *Journeys into Madness; Mapping Mental Illness in the Austro-Hungarian Empire* (New York, Oxford: Berghahn Books, 2012), 142.
33 Ibid,. and Musil, *The Man without Qualities,* 1638.
34 Musil, *Precision and Soul,* 64.

Bibliography

Blackshaw, Gemma, and Sabine Wieber, eds. *Journeys into Madness: Mapping Mental Illness in the Austro-Hungarian Empire*. New York, Oxford: Berghahn Books, 2012.

Corino, Karl. *Robert Musil: eine Biographie*. Reinbek bei Hamburg: Rowohlt, 2003.

De Cauwer, Stijn. *A Diagnosis of Modern Life: Robert Musil's Der Mann ohne Eigenschaften as a Critical-Utopian Project*. Brussels: Peter Lang, 2014.

Fanta, Walter. "The Genesis of *Der Mann ohne Eigenschaften*." In *A Companion to the Works of Robert Musil*, edited by Philip Payne, Graham Bartram, and Galin Tihanov, 251–84. Rochester: Camden House, 2007.

Huyssen, Andreas. *Miniature Metropolis: Literature in an Age of Photography and Film*. Cambridge: Harvard University Press, 2015.

Long, J.J. *W.G. Sebald: Image, Archive, Modernity*. New York: Columbia University Press, 2010.

McBride, Patrizia C. "On the Utility of Art for Politics: Musil's 'Armed Truce of Ideas.'" *The German Quarterly* 73, no. 4 (2000): 366–86. DOI: 10.2307/3072757.

Musil, Robert. *Posthumous Papers of a Living Author*. Translated by Peter Wortsman. Brooklyn: Archipelago Books, 2006.

———. *Diaries 1899–1941*. Translated by Philip Payne. New York: Basic Books, 1998.

———. *Precision and Soul. Essays and Addresses*. Translated by Burton Pike and David S. Luft. Chicago and London: University of Chicago Press, 1990.

———. *The Man without Qualities*, 2 volumes. Translated by Sophie Wilkins and Burton Pike. London, New York: Vintage International, 1995.

Schwartz, Agatha. *Gender and Modernity in Central Europe: The Austro-Hungarian Monarchy and Its Legacy*. Ottawa: University of Ottawa Press, 2010.

5

Artful Arrangements: Interior Space in Edmond de Goncourt's *La maison d'un artiste*

Erin E. Edgington

Edmond de Goncourt's *La maison d'un artiste* (1881) is a difficult work to classify within the large body of Goncourt non-fiction, primarily because it seems to sit astride generic boundaries, incorporating elements of some of the brothers' better-known projects, notably art historical works like *L'art du XVIIIe siècle* and their voluminous journals.[1] It is a catalogue, characterized by long lists of objects and possessions, but it is nonetheless stylized, not only because long narrative passages recounting key episodes related to the collections under discussion accompany the lists, but also because the lists themselves only rarely read as such. What the reader finds in the pages of its two volumes is not only documentary text, but also paragraphs of prose that serve as a record while maintaining a readability that is lacking in most other contemporary catalogues, including those prepared to accompany the eventual sales of the Goncourt collections.

---

1 On the relationship between the literature and the collecting practices of the Goncourt brothers, see Dominique Pety, *Les Goncourt et la collection: De l'objet d'art à l'art d'écrire* (Geneva: Droz, 2003).

At its most superficial level, the text is defined by multiple boundaries. Indeed, the work's several chapters represent not only textual divisions, but physical divisions as well, since they divide the home in the same way that its walls do, so that the text becomes a kind of hyper-detailed schematic. That the chapter divisions function as delimiters of physical as well as textual space is likewise made apparent by the fact that the two volumes that make up the work progress logically through the space as if the reader were actually touring the home, with volume one beginning in the vestibule and volume two taking the reader through the home's private spaces, concluding in the garden. The very purpose of this text, it would seem, is to grant a larger audience access to the home, allowing them to cross its threshold and disappear into a fabricated environment as far removed as possible from the banality and the unpleasantness of typical, everyday life.

Speaking purely in terms of its basic organization into chapters, the text is both taxonomical and hierarchical; while certain spaces, notably the salons and the library (which doubles as a workspace), are described in lengthy chapters, and others, like the vestibule, receive shorter descriptions, every space is addressed in order. If on the surface the text seems to follow a very straightforward order, though, upon closer inspection its internal boundaries reveal themselves to be as permeable as the spaces it facsimiles, and equally as subject to disruption. This is true on several levels: first, some of the Goncourt collections are large enough to require space in more than one room and, therefore, in more than one chapter; this is the case, for instance, of the collection of French works on paper, which occupies both salons and the stairwell. Second, episodes related to collections displayed in one space sometimes take place in another part of the house, subtly challenging the authority of the chapter headings; one such episode, to which I will return in what follows, is a key narrative passage that functions as a perfect microcosm of this already claustrophobic work. Third, multiple collections sometimes intermingle within individual spaces, as in the dining room where an heirloom serving-board is foiled by an imported folding screen decorated with a floral motif. This kind of juxtaposition is a key feature of this and other Goncourt works, and one that Pamela Warner has explored in more detail; significantly, she notes that Edmond's practice of pairing French and Far Eastern objects is linked with his overall tendency to "[see] Japanese art through eyes deeply familiar with eighteenth-century France," a tendency that "caused [him] to find connections in surprising places."[2] According to noted collector Samuel Bing, writing in the introduction to the catalogue for the sale of the Goncourt collections in 1897, "the honor of having affirmed the solidarity of all the arts, and the fact that they ought to be grouped, not according to their local origins, but rather according to the affinities between them, belongs to the Goncourts."[3]

The Literary within the Documentary

Given the grand scale and exceptional quality of the brothers' collections, and the work's title, where the term *artiste* clearly references their *écriture artiste* while simultaneously emphasizing its links with the plastic arts tradition precisely via its erasure of the term *écriture*, it is not particularly difficult to think of the home as a museum space. Indeed, Edmond himself makes the comparison fairly explicit with his continual insistence upon the quality of his objects and upon his own skill in arranging them. We might just as easily imagine the artist's home as a gallery of his work, or else as a work in its own right. Juliet Simpson has called attention to the way in which the title designates *La maison d'un artiste* "as a work of singular artistry" as well as noting "a growing interest in the art-work potential of the domestic

---

2 Pamela Warner, "Compare and Contrast: Rhetorical Strategies in Edmond de Goncourt's Japonisme," *Nineteenth-Century Art Worldwide: A Journal of Nineteenth-Century Visual Culture* 8, no. 1 (2009): n.p.

3 "c'est l'honneur des Goncourt d'avoir affirmé que tous les arts sont solidaires, qu'il faut les grouper, non suivant des origines locales, mais selon des parentés de sentiment" (Samuel Bing, "Les arts de l'Extrême-Orient dans les collections des Goncourt," in *Collection des Goncourt: Arts de l'Extrême-Orient* [Paris: Motteroz, 1897], iii).

home."⁴ Considering the space from this perspective suggests a fourth boundary that is disrupted by the work, namely, that between institutionalized display spaces and private domestic space.

All of these disruptions owe in some sense to the work's identity as a catalogue, that is to say, as a realistic representation of the home's contents. If we take the text at face value, we might say that artistic intentionality is lacking in it, since a catalogue may be categorized as a purely documentary text. Immediately, though, we are confronted again with the title and its incontrovertible designation of its author's profession. To begin to appreciate the work as something more than a detailed, prosaic exegesis of fin-de-siècle aesthetics, then, it becomes necessary to consider the breakdown of boundaries not only within the home's rooms and within the text's chapters, but also between genres. *La maison d'un artiste* is a hybrid: like most of the many hundreds of catalogues published in the second half of the nineteenth century to accompany high-profile art auctions, it is comprehensive, offering all the detail another enthusiast could desire; unlike these texts, it includes narrative passages.

These passages and the anecdotes they recount are easily justified from a literary perspective. As would such passages in an extended work of fiction, they punctuate the text, adding variety and interest beyond that provided by the objects themselves. This uneven weighting of description and action in *La maison d'un artiste* is complementary to the novelistic aesthetic that developed over the course of the nineteenth century in which descriptions of objects balance narrative. Edmond's stories, like the collections that run the gamut from centuries-old Chinese and Japanese porcelain to custom-bound editions of contemporary literature, vary widely and include tales reproduced from books in the library, as well as intimate stories about the life he shared with his brother (for whom Malin Zimm has called the work "a kind of epitaph") and his own solitary life following

---

4   Juliet Simpson, "Edmond de Goncourt's *Décors*—Towards the Symbolist *Maison d'art*," *Romance Studies* 29, no. 1 (2011): 2.

Jules's death. Importantly, they are equally characterized by an instability between past and present, and memory and reality.⁵

Indeed, although its narrative is sparser, *La maison d'un artiste* is easily grouped with paradigmatic novels of collecting. The collection of works on paper, which includes works by Old Masters like Fragonard and Boucher, recalls the art collection in Balzac's *Le cousin Pons,* for example, and the links between Edmond's catalogue and Huysmans's *À rebours* are undeniable.⁶ The misfit collection amassed by Flaubert's *Bouvard et Pécuchet,* too, is worth mentioning, since *La maison d'un artiste* is essentially a record of the same kind of project, but undertaken by two discerning collectors rather than two clueless, bourgeois retirees. This darkly funny novel has more to do with Edmond's catalogue than might at first be evident, for if we can agree that Edmond and Jules had a good eye for works of art and other objects that would appreciate in value, we cannot say that they benefitted from extraordinary means in the purchasing of their collections. However, the key aspect of Flaubert's unfinished novel that finds an echo in Goncourt's exactly contemporary narrative catalogue is the notion of collecting as a social rather than a solitary endeavor.

Turning first to the work's identity as a reminiscence on the good times he shared with Jules, then, I cite a remark Goncourt makes early in the text as he enumerates the dining room's contents, recalling fond memories of the dinner parties they used to give. He writes: "At that time, we were two: practically a married couple entertaining. Today the dining room is nothing more than the dining room of a lonely old man."⁷ This remark not

---

5 Malin Zimm, "Writers-in-residence: Goncourt and Huysmans at home without a plot," *The Journal of Architecture* 9, no. 3 (2004): 307.
6 See Bertrand Bourgeois, "*La maison d'un artiste* et *À rebours*: Du livre comme objet de collection à la maison-œuvre d'art," *Voix Plurielles* 5, no. 1 (2008), for a detailed comparative analysis of the two works.
7 "Dans ce temps [...] nous étions deux: c'était presque un ménage qui recevait [...] Aujourd'hui la salle à manger [...] n'est plus que la salle à manger d'un vieil homme seul" (Edmond de Goncourt, *La maison d'un artiste* [Paris: Charpentier, 1881], 1:21. *Hereafter cited as *MA*). All translations are my own.

only suggests the closeness the two brothers shared in life, but also casts Edmond in the role of the widower who preserves, or conserves, the domestic space following the death of his spouse. Indeed, Claire O'Mahony has noted that Goncourt's constant engagement with the house following Jules's death seems to have functioned as a coping mechanism for that loss.[8] If his sentimentality is hard to overlook, this is hardly a case where a death is the only catalyst for conservation. While this is made clear enough by the fact that Goncourt mentions any number of cherished objects purchased after Jules's death, it is also significant that he considers, at some length, his own passion for collecting, in the chapter devoted to the *Cabinet de travail* where he traces the development of his identity as an *amateur* back to his childhood.

Goncourt begins with a pathologizing reflection on his collecting practice, musing, "I have often wondered about my passion for trinkets, which has made me miserable and happy all my life. Finding in my memory those manic days of unreasonable purchases, I have wondered if this disease was an accident or whether it was hereditary."[9] His introduction of the notion of heredity here lacks the connotations of decline it so often carried in the nineteenth century. Rather than acknowledge himself and Jules as the termini of their family tree, Goncourt instead positions himself at the pinnacle of his family's line of collectors; he passes over his father, who took a greater interest in practical objects, naming his mother and aunt, who were themselves collectors and with whom he experienced "the first and expansive happiness of acquisition," as his key role models.[10] Recalling

---

8   Claire O'Mahony, "*La maison d'un artiste*: The Goncourts, Bibelots and Fin de Siècle Interiority," in *Writers' Houses and the Making of Memory*, ed. Harald Hendrix (London: Routledge, 2008), 189.

9   "souvent je me suis interrogé sur cette passion de bibelot qui m'a fait misérable et heureux toute ma vie […] retrouvant dans ma mémoire ces journées maladives d'achats déraisonnables […] je me demandais si cette maladie était un accident […] ou si ce n'était plutôt une maladie héréditaire" (*MA*, 2:354).

10 "le premier et expansif bonheur de l'acquisition" (*MA*, 1:357).

their shopping trips, he deduces that it was these women "who made me the collector that I was, that I am, and that I will be all my life."[11] These reflections suggest that Goncourt's transcription of the home makes it both a monument to himself and to his legacy in the same way that certain objects in the home, like the serving board mentioned above, function as surrogates for the late Jules while others recall relatives more distant in time. The urge to monumentalize, common to artists of all stripes, is straightforwardly set out in his journal entry for July 7, 1883 — which Brigitte Koyama-Richard has already connected with *La maison d'un artiste* — where he writes: "It is an ongoing preoccupation of mine to survive myself, to leave behind me images of my person and of my house."[12]

Certainly, the home Goncourt created and catalogued excels the stereotypically overdone literary nineteenth-century interior, but it does so in a counterintuitively (though perhaps insincerely) unpretentious way. For example, he asserts that the collection of works on paper demonstrates "what a poor devil can amass by spending a little money on one thing."[13] Obviously anyone who is consistently spending money on art and collectibles cannot properly be said to be lacking means, yet Goncourt points to certain works that he was genuinely unable to purchase that still haunt him; one striking example is a Boucher drawing of Madame de Pompadour that he likens to "a woman that something stupid [money] kept you from possessing."[14] He equally mentions works he did purchase at a discount that he wishes he could have paid full price for, like a Jean-Michel

---

11 "qui ont fait de moi le bibeloteur que j'ai été, que je suis, et que je serai toute ma vie" (*MA*, 1:357).

12 "C'est chez moi une occupation perpétuelle [...] à me survivre, à laisser des images de ma personne, de ma maison" (Edmond de Goncourt, *Journal des Goncourt: Mémoires de la vie littéraire*, 9 vols. [Paris: Charpentier, 1887–96], 6:269). For Koyama-Richard's comments see Brigitte Koyama-Richard, "*La maison d'un artiste*: Edmond de Goncourt et l'art japonais," *Hikaku Bungaku: Journal of Comparative Literature* 40 (1997): iii.

13 "ce qu'un pauvre diable [...] en massant un rien d'argent sur une seule chose, peut faire" (*MA*, 1:28).

14 "une femme qu'un rien stupide vous a empêché de posséder" (*MA*, 1:51–3).

Moreau that he purchased for 400 francs after its owner was unable to get her asking price of 1,000, and notes his regret over not having had the money to spend.[15]

If the collections were assembled according to bourgeois financial considerations (indeed, the house itself, purchased for 100,000 francs, is characterized as an "unreasonable purchase for the bourgeois reason [again, money]" in their journal), they nonetheless evince the aristocratic attitudes of their owners.[16] It is clear, for instance, that the brothers had no particular intention of selling what they purchased at a profit, despite selling off part of their collection in 1856 to refine it, even if Edmond sometimes lists auction prices for comparable items. To be sure, the collection included many objectively valuable objects and works of art whose value only appreciated, particularly as the years passed and *ancien régime* collectibles again became desirable and, importantly, as the vogue for all things "Oriental" gained momentum. However, to continue with the comparison between this private home and the public museum, a space whose primary aim is to broaden a given collection's audience, it is worth noting the slippage between Goncourt's eagerness in the role of interior decorator and his comparable passion in the role of curator; he genuinely loves these objects, but he also understands them as belonging to an important collection, and he is by no means blind to their significant market value.

In this sense, aesthetic and affective attachment seem to be on almost equal footing in the text. As I noted above, Goncourt's sentimentality is in evidence in many spaces throughout the home; in his bedroom, there is another family heirloom, a small chest that belonged to his grandmother and housed her *cachemires,* where he stores sentimental objects that evoke her and other departed family members, such as a bank register dating from the Directory, his mother's wedding ring, his

---

15 *MA*, 1:118–19.
16 Koyama-Richard emphasizes how the house itself is instrumental in the acquisition of the collections (Koyama-Richard, "*La maison d'un artiste*," ii). See also Edmond de Goncourt, *Journal des Goncourt,* 3:234: "achat [...] déraisonnable pour la raison bourgeois."

father's military cross, and a lock of his sister Lili's hair.[17] Yet, interestingly given the very personal nature of this object, the most significant element of this particular décor, and the focus of the narrative text describing it, are the tapestries that line its walls and to which Goncourt seems equally attached. It is these works that truly succeed in transporting him away from the nineteenth-century present and into the past, and that make "this bedroom a bedroom of the last century."[18] He describes at length the ways in which these embroidered works interact with the light in the room at various times of the day noting that they are particularly suggestive (and lifelike) in the semi-lucid moment between dreaming and waking.[19] He wonders why tapestry, which he likens to painting throughout this passage, does not seem to inspire children's curiosity when "an exchange of curiosity, of faith, and of affection with the tapestry's characters" might be possible.[20] In addition to his personal longing for a time before his brother's death, then, Goncourt experiences a kind of aesthetic longing to step from his already rarified reality into the even more beautiful worlds represented in the various works of art that fill his home.

This need to exchange reality for beauty, in the absence of any real human companionship, can only be satisfied via interaction with the collections as is made evident in descriptions offered in several chapters over the course of the work. Indeed, as the bedroom is enjoyable because of its pleasingly diverting tapestries, the *Cabinet de l'Extrême Orient* and the boudoir are equally prized for their capacity to inspire; as Goncourt puts it, "even now when I prepare to write a bit of text that does not contain the slightest knickknack, I need to spend an hour in this Oriental [sic] cabinet and boudoir."[21] In spite of Goncourt's se-

---

17 *MA*, 2:199.
18 "cette chambre une chambre du siècle passé" (*MA*, 2:200).
19 *MA*, 2:203.
20 "un commerce de curiositié, de foi, d'affection avec les personnages de tapisserie" (*MA*, 2:202).
21 "À l'heure présente [...] quand je me prépare à écrire [...] un morceau où il n'entre pas le moindre bric-à-brac [...] j'ai besoin de passer une heure dans

clusion within the interlocking universes of his collections and his writing, in *La maison d'un artiste* he nevertheless recounts the odd encounter with the outside world.

A *Bibelot* Unlike Any Other

However, when external reality forces its way into the house, as it did during the siege of Paris in the winter of 1870–1871, Goncourt is still compelled to aestheticize the experience. Although decidedly less cheerful than the animate tapestries of his bedchamber, Goncourt's reminiscence on the lack of food that accompanied the siege is one of the most memorable narrative passages in the entire text, and one of the most overtly literary. The episode opens the chapter devoted to the *Petit Salon*, although it partially occurs in the garden. In addition to blurring the literal spatial boundary between the two spaces, as well as those separating documentary from literary prose and reality from art, it also destabilizes what is perhaps the key dichotomy of the work by rendering a precious *bibelot*, by definition a useless object, utilitarian.

A significant narrative passage both in terms of length and content, the account of the siege is dominated by a rare description of Goncourt's interactions with another living being, his pet hen Blanche. Focusing on the two-month period from December 1870 to January 1871 (mere months after Jules's death on June 30, 1870), Goncourt evokes the severity of the situation by describing how he took refuge in the *Petit Salon*, the room that, after the siege, would house his most prized collection of seventeenth- and eighteenth-century works on paper and of which a detailed catalogue follows. He remembers the time he spent in this room where "the shock of cannons made the picture frames fall," recalling, in particular, the dire lack of food that plagued the city and hinting at the lengths to which Parisians and their suburban counterparts had to go to eat at all.[22] He mentions his

---

ce cabinet et ce boudoir de l'Orient" (*MA*, 2:349).

22 "l'ébranlement du canon faisait tomber les cadres" (*MA*, 1:22).

meager provisions, six fowl, which, in the end, were insufficient to his needs, but with which he nevertheless had to make do for primarily *aesthetic* reasons.²³

Blanche is the last of these six birds. Unsurprisingly enough, she has managed to survive up to this point because she is beautiful, and it seems that her looks even make up for some of her many less desirable personality traits. I use the term consciously following Goncourt, who highlights her "girlish charms" and notes how "she gave such a human expression to her clucks and cackles."²⁴ It is worth quoting at length from the text in order to emphasize the ways in which her pleasing appearance foils her disagreeable demeanor:

> This hen or, to be more precise, this pullet, all white, prettily spotted, and coquettishly crested, was the most impudent little beast that I ever met. Jumping on the table as my lunch was served, she cleared half of the meager plate with two pecks as quick as lightning. And what an amusing spectacle she made when we got to the bread, which looked for all the world like a poultice larded with toothpicks. First, she began to juggle the little pieces we threw to her, at once disdainful and angry, pouting all day until she finally decided to eat the bread that night.²⁵

This combination of aesthetic beauty, which of course is heavily feminized in Goncourt's account by way of such adverbs as "pret-

---

23 *MA*, 1:22.
24 "allures si gamines" & "elle donnait à ses gloussements, à son caquetage un langage si humain" (*MA*, 1:23).
25 "Cette poule ou, pour mieux dire, cette poulette, toute blanche, et joliment cailloutée, et coquettement huppée, était bien la plus impudente petite bête que j'aie jamais rencontrée, sautant sur la table, au moment où on me servait à déjeuner [...] et de deux coups de bec rapides comme des éclairs, nettoyant la moitié du maigre plat. [...] Et l'amusant spectacle qu'elle me donna, quand nous arrivâmes à ce pain qui ressemblait à un cataplasme lardé de cure-dents. Elle commençait à jongler avec les petits morceaux qu'on lui jetait, à la fois dédaigneuse et colère [...] demeurait rognonnante toute la journée, et ne se décidait à manger le pain du siège que le soir" (*MA*, 1:22–3).

tily" and "coquettishly," with the "amusing spectacle" of Blanche's behavior is a rare one within this carefully curated environment.

The majority of the objects that make up the collections, even if they are sometimes anthropomorphized within Goncourt's narratives, are appealing to him precisely because they are inanimate; their lifelessness complements his own solitude. The peculiar relationship he forms with Blanche, then, is a reflection not only of his real and unsatisfied need for companionship, but also of his inability to relate to anyone, or anything, unless it equally stimulates his capacity for aesthetic appreciation. Indeed, immediately following this long enumeration of Blanche's peculiar attributes and faults, he summarizes his attitude toward his pet in an unexpected way, writing: "in short, I became attached to her."[26] In the midst of this life-or-death situation, which saw many Parisians eating street animals and other things far less savory than the salt cod and substandard bread on which Goncourt and his one remaining domestic were expected to subsist, Blanche's counterintuitive survival depends equally on her attractiveness and on the uniqueness of her manners.[27]

Her curious attachment to Goncourt elicits the same attachment from him; he even combs her "with a fine comb every morning."[28] Apart from the kindness Blanche seems to show him, it is clear that Goncourt's reaction is motivated in no small part by what he perceives as her vanity. While Blanche's behavior is quite typical of any domesticated bird, it is easily interpreted as contrasting with the behavior of the non-domesticated ones that have already left Paris and as being a confirmation of the affection he has attributed to her.[29] If Goncourt is certainly aware that a hen is rather less capable of escape than wild birds with the capacity to fly, he is nevertheless swayed by her antics and continues to enjoy the company of Blanche the pet (a creature

---

26 "somme toute, je m'y étais attaché" (*MA*, 1:23).
27 *MA*, 1:23.
28 "tous les matins […] au peigne fin" (*MA*, 1:23).
29 *MA*, 1:23.

who fits in nicely with the other beautiful objects that populate the home) instead of making the most of Blanche the provision.

His executioner's hand, however, is only stayed temporarily. As the situation grows increasingly desperate, Goncourt realizes that he has no choice and, having eaten everything in the house down to his goldfish, he asks his domestic to kill Blanche but, unfortunately, she does not know how.[30] Goncourt himself is no better equipped for the task but, knowing that it will have to be accomplished somehow, he begins to seek a method to "effectuate the creature's passing without making her suffer."[31] While this would seem to be an exceedingly simple task (after all, the domestic must know where a sharp knife is kept), Goncourt instead gives careful thought to the matter. Luckily, he remembers that he possesses "a Japanese sabre whose blade rivals the scimitar with which Saladin used to cut feather pillows in half."[32]

Once again, the object selected, clearly a precious *bibelot*, highlights the tension between the literal conflict (and its attendant hunger), and the sentimental/aesthetic one surrounding Blanche. Although the exact nature of his feelings about his pet become muddled as the passage draws to a close, Goncourt explicitly establishes the parallel between the two conflicts immediately after deciding on the sabre by alluding to the "tempest of Prussian shells" that occupied the sky at that moment.[33] Certainly what follows constitutes a kind of microcosmic reproduction of the ongoing battle as Goncourt confronts his curious adversary but, unlike the war itself, he casts his personal conflict in unmistakably aestheticizing terms.

The next few lines of the passage, which set up the execution that follows, are much more literary than documentary in tone. Goncourt first equates Blanche with more exotic animals, noting how she "questioned the sky with the mistrustful look of

---

30 *MA*, 1:23.
31 "faire passer de vie à trépas la bestiole sans la faire souffrir" (*MA*, 1:23).
32 "un sabre japonais, dont la trempe, m'avait-on dit, valait la trempe des cimeterres avec lesquels le sultan Saladin coupait en deux un coussin de plumes" (*MA*, 1:24).
33 "ouragan d'obus prussiens" (*MA*, 1:24).

the animals in the Jardin des Plantes at that time, who seemed to ask from the depths of their cages if the storm that had been raging overhead for two months would ever end."[34] This remark, another instance in which Goncourt projects his own fear of and disillusionment with the war onto his pet, humanizing her, leads into a second description of Blanche's unique personality. As Goncourt summons her into the garden, she hesitates, not only because of the frightening sounds of the shells flying overhead, but also because she has become used to the lifestyle of a cherished pet; "sensitive to the cold, she hesitated to step outside."[35] However, it is a characteristic exacerbated by her domesticity that is ultimately her undoing as "gluttony triumphs" and Blanche follows the trail of crumbs Goncourt has left to lure her out of the house.[36]

What has been, up to this point, an account of Goncourt's atypical domestic life subtended by the action of the war quickly shifts focus, foregrounding the physical conflict that his coddling of his last real provision had concealed. Indeed, the fatal moment is related in quasi-epic terms: "I moved carefully and, at the exact moment she raised her neck to swallow a morsel a little larger than the others, I cut off her head with my Japanese sabre every bit as skillfully as an executioner of that land."[37] In spite of his admission, only paragraphs earlier, that he had never before slaughtered an animal, Goncourt seems to relish the act that he had thus far avoided. Importantly, though, it is not bloodlust, nor even his increasing hunger, that drives him but, seemingly, his delight at using and successfully manipulating the beautiful

---

34 "interrogeait le ciel avec le regard défiant des bêtes du Jardin des Plantes d'alors, — et qui avaient l'air, du fond de leurs cabanes, de demander si l'orage qui tonnait là-haut depuis deux mois n'allait pas finir" (MA, 1:24).

35 "la frileuse hésitait à se risquer dehors" (MA, 1:24).

36 "la gourmandise [triomphe]" (MA, 1:24).

37 "Je prenais bien mes mesures, et au moment où elle relevait le cou pour la déglutition d'un morceau un peu plus gros que les autres, avec mon sabre japonais, je lui détachait la tête aussi bien qu'aurait pu le faire un bourreau du pays du sabre" (MA, 1:24).

weapon. Of course, the presumed authenticity of his stroke is only one more literary cliché aggrandizing the scene.

Of these, Goncourt includes many more in the final lines of the passage, which ultimately aestheticize the grim event so fully that its farcical tone re-emerges. The aftermath of the execution is, of course, predictable, the chicken runs around with her head cut off, but the description of this macabre commonplace softens the line between the ridiculous and the sublime as its register rapidly shifts. Upon delivering the fatal blow, Goncourt is unsurprised when "the decapitated hen begins to run."[38] In fact, he seems to be extending his portrait of the willful hen from whom he would expect nothing less.

However, what begins as an expression of subtle annoyance continues into a vivid image of the scene as the bird's erratic movements "leave a red trail behind her on the snow in the alley and across the garden to the crystalized shrubs."[39] The blood spilling out onto the white snow is an image that aligns itself at once with the conflict in progress within the much larger, bleak landscape of the city, and references the poetic fascination with the pairing of white and red that is evident, for example, in Hugo's overtly epic "Le parricide." If red blood spilling on pristine white snow explicitly evokes battle, though, it is nonetheless linked with the classical trope of feminine beauty in which vermillion lips contrast with porcelain skin that is easily applied to Blanche in this instance.

The description goes on to reference the appropriately inhospitable weather that backgrounds Blanche's continued animation and to offer more details related to the manner of her movements; "she kept stumbling around, frenetically flapping her wings, a plume of blood spurting out of her neck in place of her head."[40] Already verging on a return to the wry humor that

---

[38] "la poulette décapitée se met à courir" (*MA*, 1:24).

[39] "[laissent] derrière elle un sillon rouge sur la neige de l'allée, et à travers le jardin aux arbustes cristallisés" (*MA*, 1:24).

[40] "elle allait toujours sur ses pattes titubantes, battant frénétiquement des ailes, — une aigrette de gouttelettes de sang, au-dessus de son col coupé, à la place de tête" (*MA*, 1:24).

had characterized the passage up until the execution, the wordiness of the description, which covers, at most, a few moments, renders it strangely hyperbolic. Even so, Goncourt's last word on Blanche underlines his original, sardonic attitude toward her. Although he first expresses regret at having killed the only sympathetic being in his life, he glibly dismisses the episode in the next clause, writing "all the more so because, I must admit, she was horribly tough," and then abruptly transitioning to the period following the conflict and into an introduction to the catalogue proper.[41]

In addition to getting a laugh out of the *mot* that concludes the passage, though, we also ought to note how Goncourt's actions subtly, and counterintuitively, undermine the whole project of collecting. I mentioned above that the sabre he selects is a valuable *bibelot,* but it bears repeating that the essential quality of such an object, indeed, the source of its value, is its very uselessness and impracticality. A collected object's worth is more directly proportional to its formal beauty than to its possible functional beauty, even in cases like this one where its form clearly evokes a specific function. To employ a collectible for its intended purpose, as any collector knows, can only decrease its value over the long term and, as such, it is not only Goncourt's instrumentalization of his sabre that is provocative, but also the fact that he keeps a record of the unorthodox use he makes of it. It is even fair to say that Goncourt glorifies his use, or misuse, of the sabre by boasting of his prowess with the blade. At the very least, the passage does not conform to the expectations of the catalogue genre narrowly defined. This is one episode where narrative asserts itself over description and an object becomes important because of what it allows Goncourt to do rather than because of how it looks in his home.

Equally significant is the way in which this episode re-emphasizes Goncourt's isolation from the rest of the world and presents the home as a kind of self-sufficient microcosm. Certainly,

---

[41] "d'autant plus que, je dois l'avouer, elle était horriblement dure, Blanche" (*MA,* 1:25).

under the circumstances, a literal siege, such isolation is to be expected, but what is unexpected here is the fact that Goncourt is not forced to eat, as many Parisians were, cats and rats, but rather subsists on food that is, if not much more appetizing, a great deal more elegant. Indeed, not only does he eat a hen that he formerly combed each morning as she interacted with her reflection in the mirror, but he is also able to do so only by killing one lovely thing with another. It is worth noting again that, in his long search for the perfect instrument for this task, it never enters his mind to simply retrieve a cleaver from the kitchen, a room that, like other practical spaces, is not described in the otherwise exhaustive text.

A final justification for understanding this particular narrative passage as the work's most literary is to be found in its literal and metaphorical proximity to the jewel in the Goncourt crown, the collection of French works on paper. This story is, tellingly, the textual stepping stone that links Goncourt's survival to the survival of the works on paper that are the home's central collection. A minimal visual break in the text separates this story from the passage leading up to the more formally organized catalogue of works on paper, which begins with his assertion that it was the war that gave him incentive to "create a sort of museum of the drawings from the French School collected by he and his brother over many years."[42] Goncourt is alone and, at times, obviously lonely, but the house and its collections offer him much needed comfort.

Conclusion

Although he does it in his *préambule,* and therefore outside the textual version of the house proper, Goncourt is forced to admit, in spite of his melancholy, that the nineteenth century has brought about one positive change with regard to décor: "Existence is no longer external as it was in the eighteenth century; the

---

42 "faire une espèce de musée des dessins de l'école française recueillis par [son frère et lui] depuis longues années" (*MA,* 1:25).

human organism has come to want the four walls of his home to be agreeable, pleasing, amusing to the eye."[43] Goncourt's artistry in the creation of his own charming interiors finally remains subordinated to his primary artistic endeavor, recording them textually. As he puts it in a journal entry roughly contemporary with the text's publication, "Literature is my sacred mistress; trinkets are my whores. Never will the sacred mistress suffer for the upkeep of the whores" (February 25, 1880).[44]

Ultimately, if the collections served the affective function of preserving the past and transporting Goncourt back to happier, less lonely days, or else to other times and places altogether, the text is equally forward-looking and fulfills as well the aesthetic function of monumentalizing the house and its curator/cataloguer. Not only does it pay tribute to Jules's legacy and the brothers' past exploits, but it also fulfills Edmond's goal of projecting his identity as an individual and as an *amateur* into the future. Because the property was designated to become the headquarters of the *Académie Goncourt,* the Goncourt collections were eventually sold off as part of its funding scheme, and the text is now the only place where it can still be accessed in its integrity.[45] Indeed, while the several series of photographs that were made of the home offer an alternative representation of it in its heyday, they do not present as complete an account as Goncourt's narrative catalogue. Although his desire to offer access to this private space might seem unusual given that the home very

---

43 "l'existence n'est plus extérieure comme au XVIIIe siècle [...] la créature humaine [...] a été poussée à vouloir les quatre murs de son *home* agréables, plaisants, amusants aux yeux" (*MA,* 1:2).

44 Koyama-Richard, "*La maison d'un artiste*," iii. See also Edmond de Goncourt, *Journal des Goncourt,* 6:107–8: "La littérature, c'est ma sainte maîtresse, les bibelots, c'est ma putain; pour entretenir cette dernière, jamais la sainte maîtresse n'en souffrira."

45 As per Goncourt's will, each of the elected members of the academy is entitled to "an annual pension of 6000 francs" (une rente annuelle de 6000 francs) (Hugh Chisholm, ed., *Encyclopedia Brittanica,* 11th edn., vol. 12 [Cambridge: Cambridge University Press, 1911], 231, s.v. "Goncourt, De, Edmond"). The funds for these pensions, and indeed for the Prix Goncourt itself, initially derived from the sale of the collections.

clearly served as a sanctuary from the increasing grittiness of modern life, it is fitting that, in hindsight, the textual facsimile of his home, which because of its textuality takes on the role of the "sacred mistress," is the most faithful representation of Edmond's personal *chef-d'oeuvre,* while the *bibelots,* his whores, have all been sold off. In a sense, then, Edmond's narrative catalogue, or "catalogue novel," amounts to a reasonably successful attempt to resolve the paradox of material possessions.[46] You cannot take them with you, but you can write them into your own history in such a way that they come to sustain both your individual memory and, quite literally, your artistic legacy.

---

46 Zimm, "Writers-in-Residence," 306.

Bibliography

Balzac, Honoré de. *Le cousin Pons.* Paris: Calmann-Lévy, 1847.

Bing, Samuel. "Les arts de l'Extrême-Orient dans les collections des Goncourt." In *Collection des Goncourt: Arts de l'Extrême-Orient,* i–v. Paris: Motteroz, 1897.

Bourgeois, Bertrand. "*La maison d'un artiste* et *À rebours*: du livre comme objet de collection à la maison-œuvre d'art." *Voix Plurielles* 5, no. 1 (2008): n.p.

Chisholm, Hugh, ed. *Encyclopedia Brittanica,* 11th Edition, Volume 12. Cambridge: Cambridge University Press, 1911.

Flaubert, Gustave. *Bouvard et Pécuchet.* Paris: Lemerre, 1881.

Goncourt, Edmond. *La maison d'un artiste.* 2 vols. Paris: Charpentier, 1881.

Goncourt, Edmond and Jules de Goncourt. *Journal des Goncourt: Mémoires de la vie littéraire.* 9 vols. Paris: Charpentier, 1887–96.

———. *L'art du XVIIIe siècle (1859–1875).* 3 vols. Paris: Charpentier, 1881–82.

Hugo, Victor. "Le parricide." In *La légende des siècles.* Paris: Lévy-Hertzel, 1859.

Huysmans, Joris-Karl. *À rebours.* Paris: Charpentier, 1884.

Koyama-Richard, Brigitte. "*La maison d'un artiste*: Edmond de Goncourt et l'art japonais." *Hikaku Bungaku: Journal of Comparative Literature* 40 (1997): 172–88. DOI: 10.20613/hikaku.40.0_188.

O'Mahony, Claire. "*La maison d'un artiste*: The Goncourts, Bibelots and Fin de Siècle Interiority." In *Writers' Houses and the Making of Memory,* edited by Harald Hendrix, 187–202. London: Routledge, 2008.

Pety, Dominique. *Les Goncourt et la collection: De l'objet d'art a l'art d'ecrire.* Geneva: Droz, 2003.

Simpson, Juliet. "Edmond de Goncourt's *Décors* — Towards the Symbolist *Maison d'art.*" *Romance Studies* 29, no. 1 (2011): 1–18. DOI: 10.1179/174581511X12899934053202.

Warner, Pamela. "Compare and Contrast: Rhetorical Strategies in Edmond de Goncourt's *Japonisme.*" *Nineteenth-*

Century Art Worldwide: A Journal of Nineteenth-Century Visual Culture 8, no. 1 (2009): n.p. https://www.19thc-artworldwide.org/component/content/article/55-spring09/spring09article/61-compare-and-contrast-rhetorical-strategies-in-edmond-de-goncourts-japonisme.

Zimm, Malin. "Writers-in-Residence: Goncourt and Huysmans at Home without a Plot." *The Journal of Architecture* 9, no. 3 (2004): 305–14. DOI: 10.1080/13602360412331296125.

6

In Her Chambers: Spaces of Fiction in Elsa Morante

Gabrielle E. Orsi

Elsa Morante (1912–1985)[1] is recognized today as one of the major figures of modern Italian literature. The Morantian imagination is captivated by enclosed spaces: gardens, islands, prisons, palaces, tombs, and labyrinthine streets. This essay will go beyond cataloguing such spaces, to trace how Morante uses space to theorize the novel (*romanzo*) and its creation, particularly through the private room or chamber, which Morante calls *la camera*, *la stanza*, and diminutive forms thereof. The chamber and the associated domestic spaces reveal their function as a space of fiction in four key works: the short story "Il gioco segreto" ("The Secret Game," 1937) and the novels *Menzogna e sortilegio* (*House of Liars*, 1948), *L'isola di Arturo* (*Arturo's Island*, 1957), and *Aracoeli* (1982).

Yet these Morantian spaces are, ultimately, I will argue, ambiguous: both welcoming and haunting, splendid and unwholesome. The chamber hosts the eruption of fantasies that, though

---

[1] Elsa Morante won Italy's prestigious Viareggio prize in 1948 for her first novel, *Menzogna e sortilegio* (translated as *House of Liars*), the Strega prize in 1957 for her second novel, *L'isola di Arturo* (*Arturo's Island*), and the Prix Medici for her final novel, *Aracoeli*.

dazzling, also cause deep unease. The classically Morantian plot is the evasion of an often grim or disappointing reality via a secret dream world of fantasy, memory, and texts. And hence Morantian spaces, though at times wildly lush, fall into decay, and reflect the problems of their texts. Additionally, exterior and domestic spaces entwine or overlap each other in Morante's writing: *L'isola di Arturo* features a garden in a house upon an island, for example. Thus, nature offers no space or escape from domestic discontents.

An iconoclastic, deeply private novelist, Morante left a rather sparse body of essays. As Enrico Palandri has remarked, rather than illuminating her writing, Morante's essays "serve her purpose of concealment of the space necessary to create."[2] Indeed, Morante's characters — like Morante herself — cherish their privacy, seeking secrecy and enclosure. Exposure, often in the form of bright light, is associated with painful realizations, the end of illusions.[3] In the following, I read texts by Morante against themselves as keys to better understanding her writing.

Entering the "Secret Game" of Stories

Morante's early prose, from the 1930s, offers an important introduction to her writing; in this body of work, she rehearses the spatiality, themes, and the use of memory as wellspring of narration that characterize her subsequent novels.[4] The short

---

[2] Enrico Palandri, "Narrative and Essays: The Ethical Commitment of Elsa Morante," in *Under Arturo's Star: The Cultural Legacies of Elsa Morante*, eds. Stefania Lucamante and Sharon Wood (West Lafayette: Purdue University Press, 2006), 267.

[3] I have argued elsewhere that with her novella "Lo scialle andaluso," Morante conducts an experiment in exposing the private space of fantasy that she does not subsequently repeat. See Gabrielle Orsi, "'Lo Scialle Andaluso': Performance, Performativity, and the Creativity of Elsa Morante," in *Elsa Morante's Politics of Writing: Rethinking Subjectivity, History, and the Power of Art*, ed. Stefania Lucamante (Madison: Fairleigh Dickinson University Press, 2015), 119–28.

[4] Elsa Morante and Giuseppe Pontremoli, *Le bellissime avventure di Caterí dalla trecciolina e altre storie*, 2nd edn. (Trieste: Einaudi Ragazzi, 1998), 266.

story "Il gioco segreto" stands out as a guide to reading Morante.[5] Uniformly regarded as among Morante's most important stories, Morante herself indicated its stature by titling one of the two short-story collections published in her lifetime as *Il gioco segreto* (1941).[6] Michael Caesar comments that with this story, "Morante appears to be testing the forces of the imagination, marking out the limits in which she as a writer will perform."[7] This story previews the illusions and shattering disenchantments of Morante's novels; it introduces the power of fantasy to transform and even usurp reality, and the pitfalls of acquiring a taste for beautiful illusions. Moreover, the story's chivalric romances herald Morante's later plumbing of the *romanzo*, which in Italian means "romance" as well as "novel."

"Il gioco segreto" — like much of Morante's prose from the 1930s — is marked by outbursts of dramatic fantasy, which often coincide with traumatic, liminal events such as death, illness, or puberty in the characters' lives. "Il gioco segreto" links storytelling, decorated domestic interior space, passionate reading, childhood, and illness — a nexus that repeats in subsequent Morante works. The secret game of the story's title shows how Morante portrays the construction of fiction, offering a template for her works in which imaginative creation must unfold in seclusion, in confined spaces, away from scrutiny (indeed, the secret

---

  Giuseppe Pontremoli employs this term of preistoria in his afterword to *Le bellissime avventure di Caterì dalla trecciolina e altre storie*.
5 Carlo Sgorlon, *Invito alla lettura di Elsa Morante* (Milan: Mursia, 1972), 40. Carlo Sgorlon, for instance, describes "Il gioco segreto" as revealing not only Morante's talent, but also the keys of her narrative: "il gusto del fittizio, gli incanti e l'evasione dal reale attraverso la fantasia e la recitazione." All subsequent translations are mine unless otherwise indicated; to the best of my knowledge, this story has not been translated. See also Umberto Pirotti, "Sulle opere giovanili d'Elsa Morante," *Studi e problemi di critica testuale* 53 (1996): 180. Raffaele Donnarumma notes the relationship between *Menzogna e sortilegio*, Morante's first novel, and "Il gioco segreto." Raffaele Donnarumma, "*Menzogna e sortilegio* oltre il bovarismo," *Allegoria* 11, no. 31 (1999): 121–35.
6 Elsa Morante, *Il gioco segreto; racconti* (Milan: Garzanti, 1941), 260.
7 Michael Caesar and Peter Hainsworth, *Writers & Society in Contemporary Italy: A Collection of Essays* (Leamington Spa: Berg Publishers, 1984), 214.

game ends when the children's parents interrupt them at play). Such space is a Morantian *sine qua non*. In an autographical touch, the secret game is modeled upon one played by Morante herself as a child.[8]

What is this secret game? It is mimetic: a staging by three aristocratic children, Giovanni, Pietro, and Antonietta, of the strange romances they discover in their palace. Each child impersonates characters from the texts. Moreover, the children are all in poor health — Giovanni suffers from seizures, for example — and so their play takes on a feverish, hallucinatory quality. For instance, the children believe they see the characters from the books depicted in the palace's frescoes. As this connection between the children's game and space in which they play indicates, the secret game has a very specific spatial dimension.

The story's initial scene introduces the dreariness which envelopes the children, inspiring them to create the dramatic secret game. Their palace stands in a dusty piazza, across from a trickling fountain adorned with a strange marble face — "a patrician house in ruins, once pompous, now dilapidated and squalid."[9] Their family, the Marchesi, occupy only a small section of the mansion; its other, uninhabited rooms are full of dust, and from the walls hang fragments of tapestries. The walls and ceilings are frescoed with radiant clouds, nude cherubs, splendid ladies, and bounteous garlands; or regal figures on camels or in gardens among monkeys and falcons.[10] The fountain, tapestries and frescoes herald Morante's tendency to employ ekphrasis in her writing. Statues, in particular, appear prominently in other stories in the same collection, such as "Via dell'Angelo" and "La nonna," both also from 1937, and recur in *L'isola di Arturo* and *Aracoeli*. Such artwork, incorporated into the space for the game, indicates its status as a space of and for art.

---

8   Ilaria Splendorini, *Menzogna e sortilegio di Elsa Morante: Una scrittura delle origini* (Florence: Le Lettere, 2010), 6.

9   "una casa patrizia in rovina, una volta pomposa, ora disfatta e squallida" (Elsa Morante, *Lo scialle andaluso* [Turin: Einaudi, 1963], 77).

10 Ibid., 78.

Furthermore, this palazzo encloses a garden, surrounded by a high wall, in which a few imprisoned plants languish.[11] This pattern of a domicile with an inner sanctum returns in both *Menzogna e sortilegio* and *L'isola di Arturo*; gardens especially reappear in *L'isola di Arturo* and *Aracoeli*. The children's rapture with their secret game and their ill health are paralleled by the garden's sudden yet sickly flourishing as this "garden-prison acquired a fictitious life."[12] The garden's feebleness and later decline suggests that there can be no flight into a "green world," a freer, more authentic realm of nature, beyond the palace walls.[13] Though Morante implicitly parallels nature — the living vegetation of the garden — and the mimetic artifice of the texts, her interest clearly lies in the latter.

Indeed, inner rather than outer flight is what preoccupies Morante: as the garden's withering presages, the children's fantastical escape into the characters of their romances is fleeting. And like the garden, the "fictitious life" that the romantic texts offer fades, heralding the discontents with fiction that Morante will develop in greater detail in her first novel, *Menzogna e sortilegio*.

Though the atmosphere of "Il gioco segreto," with its *hortus conclusus* and mansion, is generally oppressively claustrophobic, it is also simultaneously claustrophilic as the enchanting secret game is staged privately indoors, within those frescoed walls. Even when Giovanni attempts to flee the *palazzo* after the game ends, he succumbs to a sort of epileptic fit and is carried back inside unconscious: the story closes with the tableau of Antonietta keeping vigil at his bedside. The importance of "Il gioco segreto" as a fundamental text for Morante is evident when regarding *Menzogna e sortilegio* which repeats and expands upon this crucial interplay among interior space, the arts, illness, childhood, and secret stories.[14]

---

11 Ibid.
12 "giardino-carcere acquistava una vita fittizia" (ibid., 83–84).
13 Northrop Frye, *Anatomy of Criticism: Four Essays* (New York: Athenaeum, 1966), x, 383.
14 Elsa Morante, *House of Liars*, trans. Adrienne Foulke and Andrew Chiappe, 1st edn. (New York: Harcourt, 1951), 565.

Menzogna e sortilegio: Into the chamber

Morante's first novel, *Menzogna e sortilegio*, like "Il gioco segreto," weaves together the time of childhood, interior space, and text. The prologue is key, as it shows Morante theorizing the *romanzo*, with a shift towards the creation of text in such a space, not simply the enjoyment of texts there, as was the case in "Il gioco segreto." In the prologue, the protagonist Elisa de Salvi (whose name echoes Elsa Morante's own) defines her writing, which is inextricable from the chamber in which she dwells. She declares that she will unravel the enigma of the past and replace the entrancing legends she has imagined with her family's actual history. By displacing falsehoods with the truth, she will finally liberate herself from her room and from her family's habitual deceptions.[15]

Thus, the novel's immediately announced central endeavor is a therapeutic reworking of the secret game in the new space of the chamber, the *camera* or *cameretta*. As in "Il gioco segreto," reading and writing, the very construction of the novel itself, remain troubled: though Elisa has a room of her own in which to read and write, she aims to escape from it.[16]

Furthermore, if in *Menzogna e sortilegio*, the palace halls of "Il gioco segreto" have contracted to a single room, the garden has been entirely displaced from within the house. Instead, the Sicilian countryside serves as the novel's natural space. Indeed,

---

15 Elsa Morante, *Menzogna e sortilegio* (Turin: Einaudi, 1994), 18.
16 Gaston Bachelard writes that the house is "our first universe, a real cosmos in every sense of the word," and that the house shelters an "ultimate poetic depth," which being a closed and maternal space, retains and integrates memories, images, and dreams. Certainly, his insight into "the power of attraction of all the domains of intimacy" says much about Morante's choice of setting for *Menzogna e sortilegio*; however, his assertion that such intimate spaces join being with well-being, in a self-evident "topophilia," is not borne out by Elisa's morbid enclosure in her room. More cogent for Elisa's case is his observation that "there exists for each one of us an oneiric house, a house of dream-memory, that is lost in the shadow of a beyond of the real past" (Gaston Bachelard, *The Poetics of Space,* trans. Maria Jolas [New York: Orion Press, 1964], 6–9, 12).

the divide between city and countryside is crucial in *Menzogna e sortilegio*: country latifundia provide the wealth enjoyed by the upper class, such as the Cerentano family, relatives of Elisa's mother Anna who play important roles in the novel. Meanwhile, other characters, such as Cesira, Elisa's paternal grandmother, and Francesco, Elisa's father, crave such wealth and status and seek it in town. Though physically peripheral the countryside is integral to the plot: amorous encounters there between Alessandra, Elisa's peasant maternal grandmother, and Nicola Monaco, the Cerentano estate administrator who often moves between these two realms, result in Francesco's birth, and thus lead to Elisa.[17] *Menzogna e sortilegio* often feels urban and claustrophobic with its Roman and Sicilian cityscapes, confined domestic interiors, and labyrinthine streets — yet the countryside, a space of constrictions and poverty, is far from idyllic. Morante does not romanticize the countryside or make it picturesque; instead, it is there that Francesco falls ill with the smallpox that will disfigure him and alter his life.

Throughout the novel, Elisa remains in her Roman home, an inheritance from her adoptive mother Rosaria. The house, once opulent, is now moldering like the palace of the Marchesi. More precisely, Elisa remains alone in her hushed, dim room, curtained off from the rest of the apartment and lined with mirrors and fantastic books. Elisa does not cross her room's threshold except via fantasy and memory. "In this little room," explains Elisa, "I have spent, nearly buried, the majority of the time that I have lived in this house. In the company of my books and of myself, like a contemplative monk [...]."[18]

Elisa traces manifold links among enclosure, fantasy, and illness or insanity; she reveals that she suffers from the disease of *menzogna*, "deceit," which she describes as a form of delusional

---

17 Intriguingly, *Vita di mia nonna* (*My Grandmother's Life*) was the title of the first 1943 draft of what would eventually become *Menzogna e sortilegio*.
18 "In questa cameretta io ho consumato, quasi sepolta, la maggior parte del tempo che ho vissuto in questa casa. In compagnia dei miei libri e di me stessa, come un monaco meditativo [...]" (Morante, *Menzogna e sortilegio*, 17).

fantasy that plagues both branches of her family. Those afflicted eschew reality for the surrogate reality of their fantasies, "not recognizing any happiness possible apart from non-truth!" Elisa claims to surpass her grandmother Cesira and her mother Anna in becoming her family's greatest victim of *menzogna,* inaugurating the metaphors of storytelling as deception and disease that permeate the novel.[19]

In the prologue's second section, titled "Santi, Sultani e Gran Capitani in camera mia" ("Saints, Sultans, and Great Leaders in My Room"), Elisa explains how she came to be cloistered for the past fifteen years in her room, after the deaths of her parents. "Really, my life [...] stops at the day that saw me, a girl of 10, enter here for the first time [...] Even today, in a certain sense, I have remained arrested at that childhood summer: around which my soul has continued to revolve and flutter without rest, like an insect around a blinding lamp."[20]

Elisa, described as both young and old, male and female, is an ambiguous figure.[21] And with its contradictory images of stillness and movement, time and timelessness, the prologue blurs the boundaries of Elisa's room, establishing her ability to engender the subsequent novel.[22] Elisa's room thus frames and contains all other places in the novel: it is the novel's originating space.[23]

The image of a closed room that is paradoxically both enticing and repellent has deep roots for Morante, as this dream, recorded in her 1938 diary, shows: "I wish to enter that unoc-

---

[19] "non riconoscendo nessuna felicità possibile fuori del non-vero!" (ibid., 21).

[20] "In realtà, la mia vita [...] s'arresta al giorno che mi vide, bambina di dieci anni, entrar qui per la prima volta [...] Ancora oggi, in certo modo, io sono rimasta ferma a quella fanciullesca estate: intorno a cui la mia anima ha continuato a girare e a battere senza tregua, come un insetto intorno a una lampada accecante" (ibid., 17).

[21] Ibid. 12.

[22] Stefania Lucamante, *Elsa Morante e l'eredità proustiana* (Fiesole: Edizioni Cadmo, 1998), 5. Stefania Lucamante observes that, for Elisa, as for Proust's Marcel, her room's isolated space is a prerequisite for gazing upon the past.

[23] Felix Siddell, *Death or Deception: Sense of Place in Buzzati and Morante* (Leicester: Troubador, 2006), 23–24. As Felix Siddell observes, Elisa's room is the original space of the novel.

cupied and closed room. Finally, I have the key, I enter. It's an enchanting room, with rather old furniture, a bit provincial, antique damasks, a very small bed [...] The window that opens on the garden is narrow, but almost as tall as a door, supported by slender columns. But the room reeks of death."[24]

Annis Pratt, in describing archetypal patterns in women's fiction, writes that "Young woman heroes begin outside the enclosure into which they must be drawn [...] it is for this reason that at its roots the *bildungsroman* [for women] is essentially a novel of selfhood rather than of social conformity."[25] Pratt's insight is particularly apt for the Miss Havisham-esque Elisa, who begins her narration by asking who she is. In her house's mirrors, Elisa's "treacherous reflection" startles her, and upon recognizing herself, she asks, "'Who is this woman? Who is this Elisa?'" Elisa swims like a jellyfish, which in the original Italian is the evocative word *medusa*, in "these funereal lonely waters."[26] Her inability to tranquilly recognize her own reflection anticipates her unreliability as a narrator and the uncertainties of her enterprise. These treacherous reflections also herald the text's ambiguous, even deceitful representations, such as the letters her mother Anna forges.[27]

---

24 "Io voglio entrare in quella stanza disabitata e chiusa. Infine, ho la chiave, entro. È una stanza incantevole, con mobili piuttosto vecchi, un po' provinciali, antichi damaschi, un picolissimo letto [...] La finestra che dà sul giardino è stretta, ma alta quasi come una porta, sorrettta da colonnine sottili. Però la stanza odora di morte" (Elsa Morante, Cesare Garboli, and Carlo Cecchi, eds., *Opere*, Vol. 2 [Milan: Mondadori, 1988], xxxi).

25 Annis Pratt, *Archetypal Patterns in Women's Fiction* (Bloomington: Indiana University Press, 1981), 37. For Paola Azzolini, Elisa's room is a kind of sealed labyrinth, countering the external voyage of the masculine Bildungsroman with an internal, domestic, feminine voyage. See Paola Azzolini, *Il cielo vuoto dell'eroina: Scrittura e identità femminile nel Novecento italiano* (Rome: Bulzoni, 2001), 184–85.

26 "'Chi è questa donna? Chi è questa Elisa?'" and "queste funebri acque solitarie" (Morante, *Menzogna e sortilegio*, 11–12).

27 Sharon Wood concludes that this and other instances of mirroring reveal Morante's "perception of the instability of the subject is reflected in a narrative in which ambiguity and uncertainty provides the dynamic both of text and subjectivity. If narrative becomes the mirror to reflect not so much

Interestingly, in her counterfeit letters, purportedly from her cousin Edoardo Cerentano, Anna as author also retreats to a closed space. She imagines Edoardo dwelling in a subterranean mansion with her. This palace, as sepulchral as Elisa's dim room, has torches, candelabras, lamps, glistening jewels, but no light from the sun or stars. Elisa, reading the letters, makes an observation that also fits her room: "Perhaps the palace which, according to these triumphant messages, you would be the lord of is in reality your prison. And we almost seem to discern, in the depths of those walled rooms, your tearful countenance."[28]

Notably, Elisa describes Anna's death as the vanishing of her mother's room, in a flash of the daylight Anna had shunned: "And the beloved maternal chamber, ablaze with the August noon, fled forever from my gaze, like a foreign ship."[29] Ultimately Elisa fails, hundreds of pages later, to leave her room — "Here I am, then, returned to the same point where my story began."[30]

---

the world as the mind-in-the-world, then that mirror is indeed bewitched." Sharon Wood, "The Bewitched Mirror: Imagination and Narration in Elsa Morante," *The Modern Language Review* 86, no. 2 (1991): 317–21.

28 "Forse, il palazzo di cui, secondo questi trionfanti messaggi, tu saresti il padrone, è in realtà il tuo carcere. E ci par quasi di scorgere, in fondo a quelle stanze murate, il tuo sembiante lagrimoso" (Morante, *Menzogna e sortilegio*, 595).

29 "E l'amata camera materna, accesa dal mezzogiorno d'agosto, fuggí per sempre dai miei sguardi, come una nave straniera" (ibid.). Alba della Fazia Amoia writes of daylight in *Menzogna e sortilegio*, "Full daylight [...] brings a perception of crushing realities: dashed hopes for honor, title, and wealth, unrequited love, and unslaked thirst for friendship" (Alba della Fazia Amoia, *20th-Century Italian Women Writers: The Feminine Experience* [Carbondale: Southern Illinois University Press, 1996], 82).

30 "Eccomi, dunque, tornata al punto stesso donde la mia storia ebbe principio (Morante, *Menzogna e sortilegio*, 704)." According to Sharon Wood, "the ambiguity which characterizes Morante's characters is mirrored in the fiction itself. The end of the novel brings us back to the originating moment of the text, and there is no guarantee that through her narrative Elisa will achieve her own liberation" (Sharon Wood, *Italian Women's Writing, 1860–1994* [London: Athlone, 1995], 158). Giuseppe Nava describes *Menzogna e sortilegio* as the sending of self-referential messages in a closed circuit. See Giuseppe Nava, "Il gioco segreto di Elsa Morante: I modi del racconto," *Studi novecenteschi: revista semestrale di storia della letteratura italiana contemporanea* 21, no. 47–48 (1994): 66.

Elisa's authorship is circular, riddling, debilitating. And her chamber, where reflections and reality, true and false, the dead and the living all mingle, where time and space bend, is not only the point where her narration originates: it is the text itself.

Another Elisa appears briefly in Morante's next novel, *L'isola di Arturo*: the witchy midwife Fortunata Emanuella, who lives alone with her Methuselah of a cat, a counterpart to Elisa's cat Alvaro. After the birth of Carmine Arturo, Arturo's half-brother, she prophesies the baby's fate, perhaps the final vision from within Elisa's chamber.[31]

L'isola di Arturo: Romance of the Rose

Elsa Morante's second novel, 1957's *L'isola di Arturo*, reveals the evolution of her notions of the *romanzo* and representation since *Menzogna e sortilegio*. In *L'isola di Arturo*, the space of the chamber — now called *stanza* or *stanzetta* — is linked to a new imagining of the process of literary creation, which Morante would expound upon in her 1959 essay, "Sul romanzo." I examine here a key moment in which metanarrative discourse appears in the novel: the dream of a major character, Romeo the Amalfitano.

L'isola di Arturo is narrated from an unspecified future time and without prelude by the adult Arturo, who recalls his childhood on Procida, an actual island in the Bay of Naples which Morante visited.[32] By limiting the novel to Arturo's Procidan childhood, Morante plays with the literary trope of the island as a (e)utopia and as a place of self-discovery and formation *à la* Robinson Crusoe. Alone, unschooled after his mother's death in

---

[31] Elsa Morante and Cesare Garboli, *L'isola di Arturo* (Turin: Einaudi, 1995), 194–95.

[32] It is interesting that Morante chooses an actual island for her second novel. Often, islands in Italian literature are off the map, such as Dante's Purgatory and Anna Maria Ortese's Ocaña. Morante also vacationed on the nearby island of Ischia in the 1950s. "L'isola d'Ischia, come un luogo letterario," *La Repubblica Letteraria Italiana,* April 1, 2002, http://www.repubblicaletteraria.it/Ischia_letteratura.html..

childbirth, Arturo grows up idolizing his absent father Wilhelm Gerace, whose name is perhaps an homage to the prototypical *Bildungsroman* by Johann Wolfgang von Goethe, *Wilhelm Meisters Lehrjahre* (*Wilhelm Meister's Apprenticeship*).

Wilhelm's marriage to a poor Neapolitan girl, Nunziatella, followed by the revelation of his homosexual love affair with Tonino Stella, a petty criminal housed in Procida's jail, reveals him to be vain, arrogant, and deceitful, rather than the hero of Arturo's dreams. Clinging to his code of honor, the adolescent Arturo decides to leave Procida to prove his valor in combat as World War II erupts. However, the adult narrator observes tersely, as the novel ends, that in the army, his unit was composed of boys his own age, a rather bleak picture since he was only sixteen, and hints that the war was merely the inglorious slaughter his friend Silvestro had predicted.[33]

L'isola di Arturo resembles its precursor in some respects; it is also set in southern Italy, reiterating Morante's preference for the *Mezzogiorno* as a setting. The same kinds of confined, ekphrastic spaces present in "Il gioco segreto" and *Menzogna e sortilegio* appear, chiefly Arturo's house, dubbed by Procidan fisherfolk the "Casa dei Guaglioni," a dilapidated baroque former monastery and barracks with an inner garden; and Procida's well-known Bourbon prison in the zone called Terra Murata, or "Walled Land."

The furnishings and walls in Casa dei Guaglioni are scarred with a web of graffiti and drawings, occasionally scratched out, reminiscent of Angelica and Medoro's impassioned carving of their initials on trees in *Orlando Furioso*.[34] The beds in

---

33 Morante and Garboli, *L'isola di Arturo*, 370.
34 Ibid., 24–25. Ludovico Ariosto and Marcello Turchi, *Orlando Furioso*, 17th edn., 2 vols. (Milan: Garzanti, 2000), 1305 (Canto LXXII). See Canto XXIII of *Orlando Furioso*, in the second volume of the Garzanti edition, for Angelica and Medoro's carving. One of the names carved on the wall, "Taniello," seems drawn from the work of the marchese di Caccavone, marquis of Caccavone, Raffaele Petra, 1798–1873, Neapolitan aristocrat and author, often of satirical works, who participated in the flourishing of the Neapolitan epigrammatic genre. Petra's Taniello confesses his amorous sins to a priest in "'A confessione 'e Taniello." Thus, perhaps Morante is offering an inside

the house are adorned with inlaid mother-of-pearl and intricate painted landscapes.[35] The house's untended luxuriant inner garden contains a variety of decaying objects, exotic plants, and two mysterious faded terracotta statues.[36] Evoking Elisa's house in *Menzogna e sortilegio*, Casa dei Guaglioni, despite being superstitiously shunned by Procidan women, projects "the illusion of a past of great-grandmothers and grandmothers, of ancient feminine secrets."[37]

Arturo's narration, like Elisa's, draws upon memories of childhood. But Arturo has already crossed the threshold and departed from Procida, and now, as he looks back, yearns to return to his island. Intriguingly, when Morante was interviewed in 1952, she shared her initial plan that *L'isola di Arturo* would be the memoir of a young man in an African prison; but eventually, due to her dissatisfaction with the first chapter, she would decide to simply start the novel *in medias res*. Thus, in the published version of the novel Arturo narrates the story of his childhood on Procida from an unknown time and place: there is no longer a single evident imprisoning chamber like Elisa's that is the source of narration.[38]

Romeo the Amalfitano, owner of Casa dei Guaglioni, which he bequeathes to Wilhelm, evokes *Menzogna e sortilegio*'s Elisa. Romeo, who has become blind, insists that he now enjoys more vivid, fantastic dreams.[39] In one of his dreams, *Romeo l'Amalfitano*

---

joke, since the Casa dei Guaglioni was formerly a monastery. Raffaele Petra Marchese di Caccavone and Antonio Palatucci, *Tutto Caccavone: Edizione critica*, 2nd edn. (Naples: La Nuova Cultura Editrice, 1980), 85.

35 Morante and Garboli, *L'isola di Arturo*, 22.
36 Ibid., 16.
37 "l'illusione di un passato di bisavole e di nonne, e di antichi segreti femminili" (ibid., 17).
38 Giuliana Zagra, *Santi, sultani e gran capitani in camera mia: Inediti e ritrovati dall'archivio di Elsa Morante* (Rome: Biblioteca Nazionale Centrale di Roma, 2012). See also Graziella Bernabò, *La fiaba estrema: Elsa Morante tra vita e scrittura* (Rome: Carocci, 2012), 122. I discuss the adulthood of Arturo and the time from which he narrates. Gabrielle (Popoff) Orsi, "Elsa Morante's *L'isola di Arturo* and *Aracoeli*: Remembering and Reconciling with the Fascist Past," *Quaderni del '900* 11 (2011): 19–26.
39 Morante and Garboli, *L'isola di Arturo*, 59.

wanders through vast meadows of roses and realizes that all souls are either roses or the bees who seek the roses' nectar.

This is not the first time Morante uses apian imagery: *Menzogna e sortilegio* opens with a poem "Ai personaggi" ("To the Characters"), in which that novel's characters are flowers with Elisa as their servant and *pronuba ape,* "pollinating bee," and the novel's final poem, "Canto per il Gatto Alvaro" also features bees.[40] Thus, reading Romeo's dream in metanarrative terms seems appropriate. His dream supersedes the bees of those poems by introducing the roses. These roses do not understand "their own mysteries," and the first rose of all is God.[41]

Rome describes the activity of the swarm of bees in his dream: "It goes and robs a little honey from all the roses, to carry it to the hive, into its cells."[42] Other *stanzette* appear at key junctures in the novel: Nunziatella gives birth to Carmine Arturo in a *stanzetta*;[43] Stella languishes in a *stanzetta* in the prison; and, Arturo finds refuge in a fisherman's *stanzetta* on the shore of the beach during the last night he spends in Procida before departing to take up arms.[44]

Incidentally, Morante's diary entries from 1952 show her attention to her own dreams while at work on *L'isola di Arturo*—she writes of a beach on Procida where she wandered with a small boy, feeling sad and lonely, and of roses and a mysterious letter arriving on her birthday.[45]

The comparison of melliferous bees to writing is longstanding, as Morante was surely aware. Seneca's example of the bees

---

[40] Morante, *Menzogna e sortilegio,* 705–06.

[41] "i propri misteri" (Morante and Garboli, *L'isola di Arturo,* 66–67). Cristina Della Coletta examines the roses in terms of the desire they enact. See Cristina Della Coletta, "The Morphology of Desire in Elsa Morante's L'isola di Arturo," in *Under Arturo's Star: The Cultural Legacies of Elsa Morante,* 149–51.

[42] "Va, e ruba a tutte le rose un poco di miele, per portarselo nell'arnia, nelle sue stanzette" (Morante and Garboli, *L'isola di Arturo,* 66–67).

[43] Ibid., 199.

[44] For Stella in a *stanzetta,* see ibid., 314. For Arturo's grotto as a *stanzetta,* see ibid., 360.

[45] Morante, Garboli, and Cecchi, *Opere,* lxv–lxvi.

in his letter to Lucilius was frequently cited in the Italian debates over literary imitation during the Renaissance.⁴⁶ Apiculture is the subject of Book IV of Virgil's *Georgics*. Morante taught Latin in her younger days of financial struggle, and her knowledge of the classics, particularly Virgil, is demonstrated by her reference to Euryalus in the poem that prefaces *L'isola di Arturo*, as well as such later works as her play "La serata a Colono," inspired by Sophocles' "Oedipus at Colonus," derived from her 1968 genre-bending work *Il mondo salvato dai ragazzini*.

Perhaps, as Teresa de Lauretis writes in regards to Umberto Eco's *Il nome della rosa,* the rose has become "so dense with literary allusions, references, and connotations that it no longer has any, and thus appears to refer to what Baudrillard has called the implosion of meaning: a rose is a rose is a rose is a black hole, as it were."⁴⁷ However, Morante's essay "Sul romanzo," provides a key for these roses and bees. In the essay, which appeared

---

46 Seneca writes, as translated by Richard M. Gummere, "We should follow, men say, the example of the bees, who flit about and cull the flowers that are suitable for producing honey, and then arrange and assort in their cells all that they have brought in; these bees, as our Vergil says, 'swell their cells with nectar sweet.' It is not certain whether the juice which they obtain from the flowers forms at once into honey, or whether they change that which they have gathered into this delicious object by blending something therewith and by a certain property of their breath. [...] We also, I say, ought to copy these bees, and sift whatever we have gathered from a varied course of reading, for such things are better preserved if they are kept separate; then, by applying the supervising care with which our nature has endowed us, - in other words, our natural gifts—we should so blend those several flavors into one delicious compound that, even though it betrays its origin, yet it nevertheless is clearly a different thing from that whence it came" (Lucius Annaeus Seneca, *Ad Lucilium Epistulae Morales,* trans. Richard M. Gummere, Vol. 2 [New York: G.P. Putnam's Sons, 1917], 75–77). For more on literary imitation in the Renaissance, see Martin L. McLaughlin, *Literary Imitation in the Italian Renaissance: The Theory and Practice of Literary Imitation in Italy from Dante to Bembo* (Oxford: Clarendon Press, 1995), viii, 314. G.W. Pigman III discusses Renaissance imitation and bees in detail. See G.W. Pigman III, "Versions of Imitation in the Renaissance," *Renaissance Quarterly* 33, no. 1 (1980): 1–32.

47 Teresa de Lauretis, "Gaudy Rose: Eco and Narcissism," *SubStance* 14, no. 2 (1985): 19.

just two years after the publication of *L'isola di Arturo* and which constitutes her most explicit statement on the novel and the author's role, she insists that the author must rework her own experience of reality into what she terms poetic truth. In the essay, Romeo's roses become the writer's very medium, language itself.

> The word is always renewed in the very act of living, and (unless civilization crumbles) it cannot decline into a practical object, spent and worn out. Every other instrument can wither or decay, but the word is reborn naturally along with life, each day, fresh as a rose [...] words, being the names of things, are the things themselves. A rose is a rose is a rose is a rose.[48]

For Morante, language renews eternally and great art is a rejuvenating force; as Arturo concludes, "eternally each pearl of the sea copies the first pearl, and each rose copies the first rose."[49] If roses are language, then the text is constructed of *stanzette* for the roses' honey. Among the wonders of Naples that Nunziatella recounts to Arturo is this miracle, encapsulating Morante's vision: "A nun, delicate and tiny, who had been dead for more than seven hundred years; but she was always as beautiful and fresh as a rose, so that, inside her crystal urn, she resembled a doll on display [...]."[50]

---

48 "La parola si rinnova sempre nell'atto stesso della vita, e (a meno di una enorme frana della civiltà) non può scadere a oggetto pratico, spento e logoro. Ogni altro strumento può deperire, o decadere, ma la parola rinasce naturalmente insieme alla vita, ogni giorno, fresca come una rosa [...] le parole, essendo i nomi delle cose, sono le cose stesse. Una rosa è una rosa è una rosa è una rosa" (Morante, Garboli, and Cecchi, *Opere,* 1516–1517).

49 "in eterno ogni perla del mare ricopia la prima perla, e ogni rosa ricopia la prima rosa (Morante and Garboli, *L'isola di Arturo,* 301)." Myriam Swennen Ruthenberg glosses Morante's roses, writing, "Language too obeys this very law of eternal mutation by which everything is born out of a previous experience, yet maintains essentially the same internal characteristics [...]" (Myriam Swennen Ruthenberg, "Romancing the Novel: Elsa Morante's L'isola di Arturo," *Romance Languages Annual* 9 [1997]: 339).

50 "Una suora, delicata e minuscola di persona, la quale era morta da piú di settecento anni; ma era sempre bella e fresca come una rosa, cosí che, den-

Furthermore, in "Sul romanzo," Morante depicts the writer's search for language as being conducted with the "adventurous and almost heroic feeling of he who searches for an underground treasure, [...] that word, and none other, that represents the precise object of his perception, in his reality."[51] She thus grounds words in hidden spaces of treasure, like the cells of the honeycomb of her bees.

Wilhelm dismisses the importance of names — he quotes Shakespeare's Juliet on roses and their aroma with a self-consciously ironic wink to Romeo's own name.[52] But in *L'isola di Arturo* names and words do matter: the novel begins in fact with Arturo's pride in his own name as echoing both the legendary King Arthur and Arcturus, the brightest star in the northern celestial hemisphere. Arthur dreams of glorious exploits, particularly travel and combat, the deeds of a knight errant, to make a lasting name for himself: "*Arturo Gerace* should be known in all countries!"[53] Such braggadocio constitutes a masculine rhetoric of conquest, travel, and adventure, the subjects of Arturo's favorite books; it is no coincidence that the young Arturo enjoys plotting future journeys on his maps, writing himself into their open spaces.

Moreover, the books Arturo likes best tell stories of those who have renowned names, in contrast to the "obscure race of women" who are confined to "rooms and little rooms," in clear contrast to Elisa of *Menzogna e sortilegio*, his stepmother Nunziatella, and the other secluded women of Procida.[54] Ironically, the child Arturo, in his endless wait for Wilhelm's return to

---

tro la sua urna di cristallo, somigliava a una bambola in vetrina [...]" (Morante and Garboli, *L'isola di Arturo*, 101).

51 "sentimento avventuroso e quasi eroico di chi cerca un tesoro sotterraneo," "quell'unica parola, e nessun'altra, che rappresenta l'oggetto preciso della sua percezione, nella sua realtà" (Morante, Garboli, and Cecchi, *Opere*, 1506).

52 Morante and Garboli, *L'isola di Arturo*, 57–58.

53 "Arturo Gerace si deve conoscere per tutti i paesi!" (ibid., 116).

54 "oscuro popolo delle donne" and "camere e stanzette" (ibid., 49). For a comparison of Arturo's and Elisa's libraries, see Marco Bardini, "Arturo tra libri e certezze assolute," *Narrativa* 17 (2000): 89–99.

Procida, assumes a classically feminine role: from Ariadne on Naxos, to Calypso on Ogygia, to Circe, the Mediterranean has long been populated in myth with women lingering on islands like Procida.

Arturo's desire to make a name for himself in the space of the wider world is thwarted; and his present disenchanted adulthood far from Procida is elided in the text.[55] Instead of describing adventures, he nostalgically returns to his childhood on the small island, whose own name is often equated with its famous prison — to most people, he notes, Procida "means the name of a jail."[56] His tale ultimately springs from the confined, ambiguous space of his island, his "stanzetta." Arturo cries, in a metaphor evocative of the settings of *Menzogna e sortilegio*: "And the island, what had it been so far for me? A land of adventure, a blissful garden! Now, instead, it appeared to me to be a bewitched sensual mansion [...]."[57]

At the novel's end, Arturo journeys off the page into silence, crossing the sea to leave Procida. He previously called the open sea, "an indifferent splendor" and "a field without direction, worse than a labyrinth."[58] Its blankness is indecipherable, illegible; its expanse contrasts with the confined yet creative stanzette of the text. In her final novel, *Aracoeli*, Morante will map her protagonist's journey beyond Italy to Spain, and will replace the

---

55 For a more extensive discussion of Arturo's adulthood, see Orsi, "Elsa Morante's *L'isola di Arturo* and *Aracoeli*."
56 "significa il nome d'un carcere" (Morante and Garboli, *L'isola di Arturo*, 14–15). Luisa Guj writes that the island is "the ambiguous symbol of Arturo's bondage to his own fantasies from which he has to break free in the final crossing of the sea. That the island is not the place of freedom which it seems to be to the unaware child is suggested by the ominous shadow cast by the penitentiary [...]" (Luisa Guj, "Illusion and Literature in Morante's L'isola di Arturo," *Italica* 65, no. 2 [1988]: 144–45).
57 "Il gioco segreto": "E l'isola, per me, che cos'era stata, finora? un paese d'avventure, un giardino beato! ora, invece, essa mi appariva una magione stregata e voluttuosa [...]" (Morante and Garboli, *L'isola di Arturo*, 267).
58 "uno splendore indifferente" and "un campo senza direzione, peggio d'un labirinto" (ibid., 40).

chamber as a locus of creativity with the most original generative space of all: the womb.

Inner Space: *Aracoeli*

In her final novel, *Aracoeli*, published in 1982, Morante revises her use of space once more. Otherworldly dimensions such as eternity, Eden, the womb, death, and heaven appear; and Spain, rather than southern Italy, looms large.[59] Now substituting the womb for the chamber, Morante attempts to stretch the limits of language and mimesis in the novel, to utilize the "fabulous code [*codice favoloso*]" of the body and the mysteries of interior space.[60] Morante had used the outpouring of her characters' memories to construct her novels since her first writings in the 1930s, yet, *Aracoeli* differs from its predecessors by defining memory as corporeal.

With this turn towards corporality, the chamber falls from its prior privileged status as the wellspring of language, of the text. Indeed, the novel often shows the acts of translation, speech, and reading as frustrated or impossible in its rooms. Yet, in *Aracoeli* the body and the womb are also ambiguous; sources of suffering and death as well as life. Though she breaks with her usual textual/spatial paradigm, Morante continues to include the iconic garden space of her earlier works.

Aracoeli is the story of Manuele's quest for his dead Spanish mother Aracoeli. Morante breaks with her usual sequestration of her protagonists, sending Manuele in November 1975 to the Spain of a moribund General Franco. With childhood memories interrupting the narration of this journey, Manuele moves,

---

59 With Aracoeli, Morante anticipates, to some extent, the trajectory that Danielle Hipkins describes in her study of space in three women writers from hermetic, fantastic confined spaces to national, even international spaces. Hipkins explains that Morante is credited as an influence by at least one of the authors she examines, Paola Capriolo. See Danielle E. Hipkins, *Contemporary Italian Women Writers and Traces of the Fantastic: The Creation of Literary Space* (London: Legenda, 2007), 59.
60 Morante, Garboli, and Cecchi, *Opere*, 1041.

in his words, "in the double direction of the past and of space."[61] However, Manuele's real wish is not to find Aracoeli's home village of El Almendral in Spain, but to return to her womb, to "reenter her. Nest myself inside her, in my only den, by now lost who knows where, in what sheer drop."[62] This impossible union of bodies, inner space, and time would create a being he calls the *niñomadrero,* a fusion of himself and his mother Aracoeli. Aracoeli's own name is richly evocative: "altar of heaven."[63] By sending Manuele to Spain in *Aracoeli,* Morante moves through space that is mythic in her works, not simply across the Mediterranean. As Elisa Garrido observes, "Spain, more specifically Andalusia, always represented for Elsa Morante the epitome of the mythic, uncontaminated land, the essential south."[64] Morante's novella "Lo scialle andaluso," one of her most important non-novelistic works which anchors a 1963 collection of her shorter fiction, links Andalusia specifically to artistic production: the Andalusian shawl of the title is part of a dancer's theatrical wardrobe worn one memorable night by her son, a duo who anticipate Aracoeli and Manuele.[65] Throughout the novel, Spanish mingles with the original Italian, often in the forms of Aracoeli's lullabies, folklore, and in amalgamations of Italian and Spanish by both Aracoeli and Manuele. Spanish words and neologisms, like *niñomadrero,* point towards the mythic spaces of Aracoeli's body and Spain, and the time of Manuele's childhood.[66]

---

61 "nella doppia direzione del passato e dello spazio" (ibid., 1046).

62 "rientrare in lei. Rannicchiarmi dentro di lei, nell'unica mia tana, persa oramai chi sa dove, in quale strapiombo" (ibid., 1058).

63 For more on Aracoeli's name, see Manuele Gragnolati and Sara Fortuna, *Power of Disturbance: Elsa Morante's* Aracoeli (London: Legenda: 2009), xii, 189. See also Concetta D'Angeli, *Leggere Elsa Morante: Aracoeli, La Storia e Il mondo salvato dai ragazzini* (Rome: Carocci, 2003), 142.

64 Elisa Martinez Garrido, "Between Italy and Spain: The Tragedy of History and the Salvific Power of Love in Elsa Morante and María Zambrano," in *The Power of Disturbance: Elsa Morante's* Aracoeli, 119.

65 See Orsi, "'Lo scialle andaluso,'" See also Gabrielle Orsi, ""TATR GLORIA": Theater and Theatricality in Elsa Morante," *L'anello che non tiene: Journal of Modern Italian Literature* 24 (2012): 161–75.

66 Francisco Javier García Melenchón, "The Spanish Language in Elsa Morante's Narrative Works," presentation at The Davy Carozza International

Importantly, the gardens of *Aracoeli* such as "Totetaco" (Rome's Monte Sacro quarter) or El Almendral in Spain combine space and time into a lost unity, akin to Arturo's island childhood, as the novel's original garden referent, the Garden of Eden, clarifies. "We were whole before Genesis; and it is possible that the expulsion from Eden could be understood, in its hidden sense, as an ambiguous and provocative game," muses Manuele, recasting the *gioco segreto* of the children of Morante's early story. Moreover, as part of this game, God has concealed a "secret fruit [*frutto segreto*]," in the world which would make humans equal to the gods, who, unlike the schizoid Manuele, are still whole, because they are outside of time and do not require memory to retrieve the past.[67] Manuele's disintegration, his regressive quest, are thus explained as the result of his lapsarian time-bound mortality, his exile from the garden.

Strikingly, unlike Morante's previous protagonists, the voracious readers Elisa, Arturo, and the three children of "Il gioco segreto," Manuele rejects reading. After being equipped with new eyeglasses as a child he is overwhelmed, experiencing a nightmarish visual overload: "reflecting swiftly, as if bewitched, in the white blaze of too many electric bulbs, among the multiple mirrors [...] the crowded street, glowing with neon and streetlights, attacked me with its never before seen spectacle of horror."[68] The sudden clarity of vision strikes him violently as

---

Conference: Elsa Morante and The Italian Arts, Washington, D.C., October 25–27, 2012. Francisco Javier García Melenchón of the University of Barcelona describes the semantic fields Morante uses. He argues that Elsa Morante discovers in the Spanish language what he dubs a "lexicon of origins." This special use of Spanish by Morante is possible since her Italian readers can understand or nearly understand Spanish words, yet Spanish remains an alien language, estranging them. He also observed that Morante's Spanish is not correct, which he finds significant.

67 "Eravamo integri prima della Genesi; e può darsi che la cacciata dall'Eden vada intesa, nel suo senso occulto, per un gioco ambiguo e provocatorio" (Francisco Javier García Melenchón, "The Spanish Language", 1289).

68 "rimbalzando fulmineamente, come stregato, nell'incendio bianco dei troppi bulbi elettrici, fra gli specchi multipli [...] la strada affollata, rutilante di neon e di fanali, m'investí col suo mai veduto spettacolo di orrore" (Francisco Javier García Melenchón, "The Spanish Language", 1258–59).

he perceives an "atrocious world [*mondo atroce*]," where human faces are chiseled with cruel wrinkles he had never before perceived. A similar blinding light—"a well of midday light, terrible and blinding"—envelopes him when Aracoeli rejects his desperate, furtive attempt to reconnect with her by breast-feeding while she sleeps after his sister Encarnación's death.[69] Like the wash of bright light at Anna's death in *Menzogna e sortilegio*, such light marks the end of illusions harbored in darkness, in secret inner space.

Furthermore, Manuele eschews representation—he insists that his memory, the basis for his narration, is physical. For instance, he insists that he hears, not a memory of his mother's voice, but rather her actual physical voice. He also describes obscure organs of memory, still unknown to science, that exist in another dimension yet register all sensory perceptions of our dimension, and perhaps of others as well which operate "in a zone outside of space, but of limitless movement."[70] And he suggests that each newborn's eyes bear the imprint of previous lives, which act as a lens, shrouding vision with its "fabulous forms and colors," that fade over time like a fresco's colors, to be finally erased by adult memories.[71]

Morante returns in *Aracoeli* to the lexicon she previously utilized in *Menzogna e sortilegio* and *L'isola di Arturo*, specifically, diminutives of *camera* and *stanza,* such as *cameretta* and *stanzetta*.[72] Yet, these rooms are degraded versions of the chambers of fiction of Morante's previous novels, as the diminutive *cameraccia* makes clear, for instance, when Manuele questions the very existence of his journey, speculating that it is a fantastic, absurd dream he is having while on drugs "in some lousy rented room

---

[69] "un pozzo di luce meridiana, terribile e accecante" (ibid. 1302).

[70] "in una zona esclusa dallo spazio, però di movimento illimitato" (Morante, Garboli, and Cecchi, *Opere*, 1047–48).

[71] "forme e colori favolosi" (ibid., 1177).

[72] Morante could have utilized other Italian words, such as *bugigattolo, stambugio," "stanzino, stambugetto, stambugino, stambugiolo* to describe rooms in *Aracoeli* but instead uses *camera* and *stanza* again.

in Milan."[73] Moreover, Manuele is strangely unable to speak his mother's native Spanish, the language she cooed to him in the "little room on the city's edge," "our nocturnal little room," where they lived in his early childhood, in the Roman neighborhood of Monte Sacro, which he childishly dubbed "Totetaco."[74] Manuele works in the cramped offices of Editore Ypsilon, in its *stanzette*. As the novel closes, he is reunited with his father Eugenio in another wretched *stanzetta*, strewn with litter.[75]

Moreover, the decorations and art characteristic of Morante's previous works only briefly appear in *Aracoeli*: chiefly in Manuele's visit to a brothel, which unlike the house of Rosaria, the prostitute who is Elisa's benefactor in *Menzogna e sortilegio*, is not defunct though it is equally sumptuous and decrepit. And evoking Arturo's Casa dei Guaglioni, this brothel is inscribed with graffiti. "In certain niches, perhaps once occupied by ornamental statues, one could now see pencil scribbles and dirty handprints." This brothel is only "a deformed, wretched labyrinth."[76] The dwindling of the ekphrastic traces of previous works in *Aracoeli* corresponds to Morante's shift away from the chamber as the key creative space to corporality, specifically the womb.

Evincing the substitution of the womb for the chamber is Aracoeli's explanation to the child Manuele that during her pregnancy the baby, Encarnación, exists in "a warm little room [*una stanzetta calda*]," illuminated with a small diamond hung from her earlobe. Manuele imagines the fetus as a miniature, perfect copy of Aracoeli; meanwhile Aracoeli busies herself frantically sewing and embroidering an ever-increasing number of baby clothes and linens.[77] More copies appear as Aracoeli's womb is

---

73 "in una qualche mia cameraccia d'affitto a Milano" (Morante, Garboli, and Cecchi, *Opere*, 1115).
74 "cameretta di periferia," and "la nostra cameretta notturna" (ibid., 1275). Elisa's cameretta is, of course, also in Rome. Concetta D'Angeli discusses Aracoeli's language. See D'Angeli, *Leggere Elsa Morante*, 45.
75 Morante, Garboli, and Cecchi, *Opere*, 1447.
76 "Dentro certe nicchie, forse occupate un tempo da statue ornamentali, si vedevano scritte sbilenche a carboncino e impronte di mani sporche" and "un deforme, misero labirinto" (ibid., 1138).
77 Ibid., 1274–75.

also described as an *alveare* and a *nido*, a "beehive" and a "nest," which yearns to generate a living *muñeca*, "doll," a replacement for the dolls and puppets of her childhood, cast aside in her adolescence as "dead things [*cose morte*]."[78]

Yet, in *Aracoeli* the womb is also equivocal, not simply a source of life. Like the chambers of previous novels, the womb is linked to death: from the grotesquely mutated orphans that Manuele's grandmother tends, to Encarnación's death soon after birth.[79] Encarnación's name of "incarnation" and her premature death suggest that embodiment in the world is as fraught as the retreat from the world represented by Elisa. Ultimately, Manuele sees each birth as a "birth sentence [*condanna alla nascita*]."[80] Manuele in fact describes the body as a deep mystery, "a tomb, that we carry close," whose darkness is blacker than that of the tomb.[81]

One important mirror in *Aracoeli* harks back to the many mirrors of Elisa's room in *Menzogna e sortilegio*, yet also shows how in *Aracoeli* Morante is moving from a space of textual production, the private chamber, towards corporeality, towards the inner space of the body and its reproductivity. Manuele associates Aracoeli's name with a certain ornate mirror in his parents' bedroom, now lost. Its glass is new and shiny, but the frame is "old and faded in its gilting, was of a majestic seventeenth-century style."[82] Observing that "certain wizards [*certi negromanti*]" insist that mirrors are bottomless abysses, swallowing the past and perhaps also the future, he wonders if this mirror's "underwater worlds [*mondi subacquei*]" still contain his memory, and will recompose it out of nothingness.[83] Importantly, Manuele's first uncertain memory is the reflection in this mirror of himself as an infant nursing at Aracoeli's breast, and this tableau of

---

78 Ibid., 1167.
79 Ibid., 1424.
80 Ibid., 1172–73.
81 "un sepolcro, che ci portiamo appresso" (ibid., 1333).
82 "vecchia e impallidita nelle dorature, era di uno stile secentesco maestoso" (ibid., 1048–49).
83 Ibid.

their lost harmony reminds him (in one last moment of ekphrasis) of a painting of the Madonna and child.[84] In Spain, Manuele travels through the province of Almería — he claims its name means "mirror" in Arabic.[85] As Manuele approaches his final destination of Aracoeli's village in Almería, he reveals that he has tried to travel "from reflection to reflection, towards the unspeakable treasure of my extreme body."[86] His body and its locations thus figure and map his quest: inner space rather than Spain is the destination.

Finally, as Manuele voyages through Spain, he realizes that El Almendral does not appear on any map, reiterating the ambiguity, the unintelligibility, in short, the epistemological issues surrounding his quest.[87] Manuele admits that he has relied upon imagination for his quest to Spain. "And I know already that my present analysis and its supposed results are imaginary, imaginary as is my entire story (and all other stories, or Stories, mortal or immortal)."[88] This declaration reveals the text's fabrication, while insisting on the fabricated nature of all (hi)stories and questioning how stories can be told.

As *Aracoeli* concludes, wasps dolefully replace the bees of previous texts. As flying messengers, they are the last of the novel's many angelic, winged, and feathered beings, bearing an

---

84 Ibid., 1178. Although this memory evokes Jacques Lacan's mirror-stage, it does not conform exactly to the mirror-stage's tableau, since the infant Manuele gazes into Aracoeli's eyes rather than the mirror and enjoys their union rather than a sense of individual autonomy. Accordingly, he does not scrutinize his own body and its borders. However, his later dissatisfaction with his aged and sexed body, heightened by a gaze at his nude self in a mirror, does seem to follow Lacan's argument that the wholeness of the mirror-stage is ultimately illusory. See Jacques Lacan, *Écrits: A Selection*, trans. Alan Sheridan (New York: Norton, 1977), xiv, 338.
85 Morante, Garboli, and Cecchi, *Opere*, 1087.
86 "di riflesso in riflesso, verso il tesoro indicibile del mio corpo estremo" (ibid., 1248).
87 Ibid., 1047.
88 "E so già che la mia presente analisi e i suoi pretesi risultati sono immaginari, come immaginaria, del resto, è l'intera mia storia (e tutte le altre storie, o Storie, mortali o immortali)" (ibid., 1452).

Annunciation.[89] Learning of his father's death Manuele feels pierced "as if by the sting of a huge wasp, penetrating me from the neck through my throat." He concludes, in the novel's final line "certain individuals are more inclined to weep out of love than over death."[90]

Manuele's *piangere d'amore* is a wordless, bodily response that replaces the textual endeavors of previous narrators. Yet, this painful weeping can also be read in poetic terms: as Manuele's beloved caretaker, Daniele explains to him in a dream while plucking spines from a flying fish, "there is no thorn without a rose."[91] From the pricking of such thorns the novel is born, fresh as a rose.

By reinterpreting the important spaces of her earlier works in *Aracoeli*, Morante redefines the *romanzo* one last time: questioning, through Manuele's condition of existential and epistemological crisis, what language itself can accomplish, what can be known. The ultimate secret, creative space in Morante's writing, that of the womb in *Aracoeli*, figures the gap between creation and representation, between the artifice of literature and as Romeo puts it in *L'isola di Arturo*: "that little artistic and fatal hand that has shaped all things in the universe."[92]

The closed space of the chamber, accompanied by the cluster of other iconic Morantian spaces such as the garden, the house, and the island, are important throughout Morante's oeuvre as a space of and for fiction, as this chapter has traced. However, these spaces never lose their ambiguity: they remain attractive but elusive, voluptuous but crumbling. Even the womb is simultaneously life-giving and death-dealing. If wondrous, beautiful

---

89 Hanna Serkowska discusses the angelology of *Aracoeli*. Hanna Serkowska, "The Maternal Boy: Manuele, or the Last Portrait of Morante's Androgyny," in *Under Arturo's Star*, 157–87.

90 "come di un pungiglione di vespa grossissima, che dal collo mi penetrasse fino in fondo alla gola" and "certi individui sono piú inclini a piangere d'amore, che di morte" (Morante, Garboli, and Cecchi, *Opere*, 1454).

91 "non c'è spina senza rosa (ibid., 1409).

92 "quella manina artistica e fatata che ha formato tutte le cose dell'universo (Morante and Garboli, *L'isola di Arturo*, 124)."

and fresh as a rose, these spaces are also imbued with death and disease, like the Neapolitan nun lying rosy in her glass coffin. That such confined spaces falling into decay seem necessary for Morante's art demonstrates that these spaces figure the discontents she perceived in representation throughout her long career. Like the mirrors that her characters gaze into, the private ludic, creative spaces archetypal in Morante's writing reflect enchantments and deceptions.

Bibliography

Amoia, Alba della Fazia. *20th-Century Italian Women Writers: The Feminine Experience*. Carbondale: Southern Illinois University Press, 1996.

Ariosto, Lodovico, and Marcello Turchi. *Orlando Furioso*. 17th edn. Milan: Garzanti, 2000.

Azzolini, Paola. *Il cielo vuoto dell'eroina: Scrittura e identità femminile nel Novecento italiano*. Rome: Bulzoni, 2001.

Bachelard, Gaston. *The Poetics of Space*. Translated by Maria Jolas. New York: Orion Press, 1964.

Bardini, Marco. "Arturo tra libri e certezze assolute." *Narrativa* 17 (2000): 89–99.

Bernabò, Graziella. *La fiaba estrema: Elsa Morante tra vita e scrittura*. Rome: Carocci, 2012.

Caesar, Michael, and Peter Hainsworth. *Writers & Society in Contemporary Italy: A Collection of Essays*. Leamington Spa: Berg Publishers, 1984.

D'Angeli, Concetta. *Leggere Elsa Morante: Aracoeli, La Storia e Il mondo salvato dai ragazzini*. Rome: Carocci, 2003.

De Lauretis, Teresa. "Gaudy Rose: Eco and Narcissism." *SubStance* 14, no. 2 (1985): 13–29. DOI: 10.2307/3685048.

Della Coletta, Cristina. "The Morphology of Desire in Elsa Morante's *L'isola di Arturo*." In *Under Arturo's Star: The Cultural Legacies of Elsa Morante*, edited by Sharon Wood and Stefania Lucamante. West Lafayette: Purdue University Press, 2006.

Donnarumma, Raffaele. "*Menzogna e sortilegio* oltre il bovarismo." *Allegoria* 11, no. 31 (1999): 121–35.

Frye, Northrop. *Anatomy of Criticism: Four Essays*. New York: Athenaeum, 1966.

García Melenchón, Francisco Javier. "The Spanish Language in Elsa Morante's Narrative Works." Presentation at the Davy Carozza Elsa Morante and The Italian Arts Conference, Washington, D.C., October 25–27, 2012.

Garrido, Elisa Martinez. "Between Italy and Spain: The Tragedy of History and the Salvific Power of Love in Elsa Morante and María Zambrano." In *The Power of Disturbance: Elsa Morante's Aracoeli*, edited by Manuele Gragnolati and Sara Fortuna, 118–128. London: Legenda, 2009.

Guj, Luisa. "Illusion and Literature in Morante's *L'isola di Arturo*." *Italica* 65, no. 2 (1988): 144–53. DOI: 10.2307/479190.

Hipkins, Danielle E. *Contemporary Italian Women Writers and Traces of the Fantastic: The Creation of Literary Space*. London: Legenda, 2007.

Lacan, Jacques. *Écrits: A Selection*. Translated by Alan Sheridan. New York: Norton, 1977.

Lucamante, Stefania. *Elsa Morante e l'eredità proustiana*. Fiesole: Edizioni Cadmo, 1998.

McLaughlin, Martin L. *Literary Imitation in the Italian Renaissance: The Theory and Practice of Literary Imitation in Italy from Dante to Bembo*. Oxford: Oxford University Press, 1995.

Morante, Elsa. *Il gioco segreto; racconti*. Milan: Garzanti, 1941.

———. *House of Liars*. Translated by Adrienne Foulke and Andrew Chiappe. 1st edn. New York: Harcourt, 1951.

———. *Lo scialle andaluso*. Turin: Einaudi, 1963.

———. *Menzogna e sortilegio*. Turin: Einaudi, 1994.

———. *Opere. I Meridiani*. Vol. 2. Milan: Mondadori, 1988.

Morante, Elsa, and Cesare Garboli. *L'isola di Arturo*. Turin: Einaudi, 1995.

Morante, Elsa, Cesare Garboli, and Carlo Cecchi, eds. *Opere. I Meridiani*. Vol. 1. Milan: Mondadori, 1988.

Morante, Elsa, and Giuseppe Pontremoli. *Le bellissime avventure di Caterí dalla trecciolina e altre storie*. 2nd edn. Trieste: Einaudi Ragazzi, 1998.

Nava, Giuseppe. "Il gioco segreto di Elsa Morante: I modi del racconto." *Studi Novecenteschi: Revista semestrale di storia della letteratura italiana contemporanea* 21, no. 47–48 (1994): 53–78.

Orsi, Gabrielle E. "'Lo scialle andaluso': Performance, Performativity, and the Creativity of Elsa Morante." In *Elsa Morante's Politics of Writing: Rethinking Subjectivity, History, and the*

Power of Art, edited by Stefania Lucamante, 119–28. Madison: Fairleigh Dickinson University Press, 2015.

———. "Elsa Morante's *L'isola di Arturo* and *Aracoeli*: Remembering and Reconciling with the Fascist Past." *Quaderni del '900* 11 (2011): 19–26.

———. "'TATR GLORIA': Theater and Theatricality in Elsa Morante." *L'anello che non tiene: Journal of Modern Italian Literature* 24 (2012): 161–75.

Palandri, Enrico. "Narrative and Essays: The Ethical Commitment of Elsa Morante." In *Under Arturo's Star: The Cultural Legacies of Elsa Morante,* edited by Stefania Lucamante and Sharon Wood, 257–67. West Lafayette: Purdue University Press, 2006.

Petra, Raffaele, *Marchese di Caccavone and Antonio Palatucci.* Tutto Caccavone: Edizione critica. 2nd edn. Naples: La Nuova Cultura Editrice, 1980.

Pigman III, G.W. "Versions of Imitation in the Renaissance." *Renaissance Quarterly* 33, no. 1 (1980): 1–32. DOI: 10.2307/2861533.

Pirotti, Umberto. "Sulle opere giovanili d'Elsa Morante." *Studi e problemi di critica testuale* 53 (1996): 159–84.

Pratt, Annis. *Archetypal Patterns in Women's Fiction.* Bloomington: Indiana University Press, 1981.

Ruthenberg, Myriam Swennen. "Romancing the Novel: Elsa Morante's *L'isola di Arturo*." *Romance Languages Annual* 9 (1997): 336–41.

Samaritani, Fausta. "L'isola d'Ischia, come un luogo letterario." *La Repubblica Letteraria Italiana,* April 1, 2002. http://www.repubblicaletteraria.it/Ischia_letteratura.html.

Seneca, Lucius Annaeus. *Ad Lucilium Epistulae Morales.* Translated by Richard M. Gummere, Vol. 2. New York: G.P. Putnam's Sons, 1917.

Serkowska, Hanna. "The Maternal Boy: Manuele, or the Last Portrait of Morante's Androgyny." In *Under Arturo's Star: The Cultural Legacies of Elsa Morante,* edited by Stefania Lucamante and Sharon Wood, 157–87. West Lafayette, Indiana: Purdue University Press, 2006.

Sgorlon, Carlo. *Invito alla lettura di Elsa Morante*. Milan: Mursia, 1972.
Siddell, Felix. *Death or Deception: Sense of Place in Buzzati and Morante*. Leicester: Troubador, 2006.
Splendorini, Ilaria. *Menzogna e sortilegio di Elsa Morante: Una scrittura delle origini*. Florence: Le Lettere, 2010.
Wood, Sharon. "The Bewitched Mirror: Imagination and Narration in Elsa Morante." *The Modern Language Review* 86, no. 2 (1991): 310–21. DOI: 10.2307/3730532.
———. *Italian Women's Writing, 1860–1994*. London: Athlone, 1995.
Zagra, Giuliana. *Santi, sultani e gran capitani in camera mia. Inediti e ritrovati dall'archivio di Elsa Morante*. Rome: Biblioteca Nazionale Centrale di Roma, 2012.

7

The Inscapability of Dwelling in Yoknapatawpha County

Stefanie E. Sobelle[1]

At the opening of William Faulkner's *As I Lay Dying* (1930), Jewel Bundren walks into a window of a cotton house, through the building, and out the opposite window without breaking stride — as if the house were not there at all. Described as having a "wooden face," Jewel is materially one with the log house. It does not impact his sense of self; it *is* his self. There is no distinction between interior and exterior for Jewel; he has no periphery. Rooms exist differently for his introspective brother, Darl, who narrates this remarkable scene. For Darl, rooms are the spaces in which he explores his selfhood. Whereas Jewel is one with an uninhabited house, Darl is alienated by uninhabited rooms — he avoids entering the cotton house entirely, and a bedroom creates for him an uncomfortable existential crisis.[2] This contrast between Jewel and Darl demonstrates two ways

---

1   An expanded version of this essay comprises a chapter in my forthcoming book with Oxford University Press on "the architectural novel."
2   In a scene later in the novel, Darl meditates on the strangeness of rooms and their ontological implications — the ways in which you "are" or "are not". Because Jewel does not have such existential thoughts, Darl suggests that he must know he "is" (William Faulkner, *As I Lay Dying* [New York: Vintage Books, 1987], 72).

that architecture — in particular, interior space — functions in Faulkner's fiction — 1) as metonymic of the characters themselves and 2) as symbolic of the complex psychological, social, and political events unfolding in and around them. Faulkner brings these two functions together through narrative perspective. Architecture for Faulkner is thus not only a metaphor but also an organizing principle for the novel's construction. His treatment of interiority functions differently than the ways interiority is experienced by his characters; whereas Darl's and Jewel's interiorities are constrained by their respective personal limitations, the reader moves easily between the textual rooms that comprise their inner lives. In other words, the architectural structures — assemblages of closed rooms — within Faulkner's more experimental novels are often at odds with or challenged by the open architecture of the novels. This essay argues that Faulkner's inquiry into domestic relations in American culture unfolds in the formal experimentation of his multi-perspectival narratives, a literary technique comparable to the open planning of modernist architecture contemporary to their publication.

Faulkner's literary architecture resembles the work of Frank Lloyd Wright, whose open plans — a break from traditional closed rooms in an attempt to accomplish a fluidity of interior space by eliminating confining walls between rooms — were a significant contribution to architecture. Wright designed rooms so that the corner of one would no longer be an endpoint but a space itself, thus expanding the perception of space within the house and the viewpoints from which it could be experienced.[3] The viewer, then, much like Faulkner's reader, ultimately defines the space, not the limits indicated by the container of the house itself. By reading Faulkner's formal experimentation through the open planning of Wright's architecture, I will show how novels like *As I Lay Dying* and, even more pertinently, *Absalom, Absalom!* (1936), become an architecture — not only analogues of it.

---

3   See Sandy Isenstadt, *The Modern American House: Spaciousness and Middle-Class Identity* (Cambridge: Cambridge University Press, 2014), 67.

Faulkner's interest in space — both interior and geographical — is inextricable from his writing. Faulkner privileged domestic settings for his works, just as he was informed by the region of Mississippi in which he crafted them. Famously, he charted *A Fable* (1954) by the days of the single week that passes in the novel on the walls of his study at his 1840s Greek Revival house, Rowan Oak — a kind of merging of built and literary environments.[4] This practice of writing on walls is then a way of understanding how "home" functions in some of his novels — as a screen onto which one projects an imaginative alternative to the architecture of the house.

As I have argued elsewhere, in architecture, the term "inscape," though rarely used, describes the realm of the interior in opposition to a surrounding exterior landscape.[5] Inscape, like landscape, is experiential, dependent on perspective. An author's efforts to depict inscape aim to capture interiority as experienced on two registers: first, by the characters in the novel, and second, by the reader of the book. Like the novel, the home is an imaginative space with limitless possibilities, as opposed to the more rigid structure of the book or house that contains it. To speak of any sort of "scape" is necessarily to be speaking of experience, and so architectural inscapes are not merely metaphors for literary explorations of mindscapes more generally.[6]

---

4 His work is an example of what David Spurr means when he argues that "literature's encounter with the built environment is essential to its definition of what is sometimes called modernity" (David Spurr, *Architecture & Modern Life* [Ann Arbor: University of Michigan Press, 2012], ix).

5 See Stefanie Sobelle, "Inscapes: Interiority in Architectural Fiction," *Interstices* 12 (2011): 59–67. In this article, I explain that inscape is a term that has been used in several ways, such as the poetic sense of inscape of Gerard Manley Hopkins, which meant the inherent quality of a thing, or Roberto Matta's Surrealist, aesthetic term, which refers to the representation of the mental landscape of an artist. For my purposes here, the term describes the realm of the interior in opposition to a surrounding exterior — inscape as opposed to landscape. My definition, while evocative of its predecessors, extends the treatment of domestic interiority beyond prevailing readings of the house as a metaphor for the psychological.

6 Ted Atkinson even titled a review essay "Faulknerscapes," as a nod to the prevalence of 'scapes in Faulkner's work (*Studies in the Novel* 42, no. 4

Faulkner's literary experimentation reorganizes how a reader moves through text, just as modernist architecture contemporary to his writing of the novel reorganized how an inhabitant moved through domestic space. Nonetheless, the houses in *Absalom, Absalom!* are consistently nineteenth-century structures, and Yoknapatawpha County, littered with neo-classical structures, is deeply indebted to material architectural history. In *William Faulkner and the Tangible Past,* architecture historian Thomas Hines demonstrates a parallel between the architecture of Faulkner's fictional county and the genres/aesthetics of the novels themselves. *Absalom,* he argues, falls under the categories of both tragedy, in the Greek sense, and Gothic, in the medieval and then Romantic sense. As these two genres come together in Faulkner's fiction, they also coalesce in styles of building in the period. As Hines suggests, "American romantics, particularly in the South, found comfort not only in 'yesterday,' but in the 'days before yesterday.'"[7] Faulkner is writing in a period for which architecture takes a turn away from the historical and ornamental toward modernist houses that attempted to harmonize nature and home through an emphasis on transparency — a merging of inscape and landscape.

Hines suggests that the Gothic Romanticism of the nineteenth century plants seeds for what in the early twentieth century grows into something like Wright's "organic" architecture. Wright, a student of Louis Sullivan, argued for new structures to reflect and accommodate contemporary society. Organic architecture was meant to be an architecture that evolves naturally out of context. In "Organic Architecture" (1910), he asserts that a building must be treated holistically with its furnishings and its surroundings and argues that a "human dwelling place" should be a complete work of art, each element inextricable from the next, rather than a "composite of cells."[8] The dwellings within

---

[2010]: 471–78).

7 Thomas S. Hines, *William Faulkner and the Tangible Past: The Architecture of Yoknapatawpha* (Berkeley: University of California Press, 1996), 75.

8 Frank Lloyd Wright, "Organic Architecture," in *Programs and Manifestoes on 20th-century Architecture,* ed. Ulrich Conrads (Cambridge: MIT Press,

Absalom are indeed "cells," often imprisoning (think of Rosa's father in his attic), arranged as separate rooms. Wright's open plans were a response to this imprisonment and to the transformation of domestic life that occurred at the turn of the twentieth century, when servants had a less prominent or completely absent role in most American households.

To reiterate, *Absalom*'s narrative structure likewise allows the reader entries into and through them over time and space — a kind of open planning for the reader, if not for the characters. The reader is then the ultimate inhabitant of the space of the novel. Faulkner had expressed particular concern for some of the federally funded modernist projects of the New Deal, and Hines suggests that he was equivocal about modernism, as new buildings so often replaced old buildings that had become a part of the vernacular of his region.[9] Faulkner might have known of Wright. Several Wright houses were constructed in Mississippi, two when Wright was working under Louis Sullivan and two much later: The Charnley Summer Residence and Guest House (1890, Ocean Springs, severely damaged by Hurricane Katrina); the Sullivan Residence (1890, a house for Louis Sullivan in Ocean Springs, destroyed by Hurricane Katrina); the Welbie Fuller House (1951, a Usonian house in Pass Christian); and Fountainhead (1954, the J. Willis Hughes Usonian house in Jackson). The houses in Faulkner's fiction may not be of the modernist variety, but this "open planning" of Wright's is nonetheless in parallel with Faulkner's narrative construction.

The writing of *Absalom* follows a move in domestic architectural design in the early twentieth century that focused on spaciousness as an ideal, a goal, and a concept. Sandy Isenstaadt has outlined this shift extensively in *The Modern American House: Spaciousness and Middle-Class Identity*, tracing the increased importance of "spaciousness" as a value in Middle Class America throughout the twentieth century.[10] Isenstaadt dedicates a

---

1971), 25.
9 Hines, *William Faulkner and the Tangible Past*, 121.
10 Isenstaadt, *The Modern American House*, 7–8.

bulk of his study to the rise of glass, both as a material and a design principle, which coincided in the late nineteenth century with a prioritizing of "light and clean air" as "necessary for good health" and a correspondence between windows and imaginative, progressive thinking.[11] Glass allowed the outside to come in, creating an effect of both interior volume and a connection with the wider world.[12] Furthermore, the arrival of European architects into the US in the 1920s and onward — architects who prioritized the use of glass in design, such as Mies van der Rohe and Richard Neutra — changed the possibilities for domestic architecture in the US.[13] The impact of glass architecture from the late nineteenth century through the early twentieth affected the ways in which writers understood narration and novelistic interiority, experimenting with methods of perspective, as exemplified by Faulkner's *Absalom, Absalom!*, in which Faulkner wrote inscapes into his novels thematically and formally. Faulkner's inscapes, in other words, are expanded by his multi-perspectival narratives, which both offer unusual views into characters' lives and out to the exterior worlds beyond them.

Faulkner's literary inscapes find a predecessor in Henry James, who was well aware of the rise of architecture and architectural materials in the late nineteenth century, which, as Curtis Dahl has argued of his work, are signifiers: "they become part of the 'language' through which James expresses American as opposed to British values, [...] he shows himself a magnificent literary architect."[14] Most of James's novels and stories feature houses of some sort: for example, the haunted country house in *Turn of the Screw* (1898); the existential city house in "The Jolly Corner" (1908); the museum-like house in *The Spoils of Poynton* (1897); or Ralph Touchett's ancestral estate, Isabel Archer's arrival at Gilbert Osmond's villa, and Isabel's attic in her own birth

---

11 Ibid, 147, 151.
12 Ibid., 158.
13 Ibid., 161–64.
14 Curtis Dahl, "Lord Lambeth's America: Architecture in James's 'An International Episode,'" *Henry James Review* 5, no. 2 (1984): 89–92.

home in *The Portrait of a Lady* (1881).[15] Architecture in these novels indexes the structures that constitute human experience and in this way was, for James, significant not only for its representational setting and for the symbolism embedded in various styles, but also as a way of understanding how narrative itself should be structured. James's allegorical use of architecture to describe narrative is well known, best exemplified by his theory of "the house of fiction" in his 1908 "Preface" to the 3rd volume of the New York edition of *The Portrait of a Lady*:

> The house of fiction has [...] not one window, but a million [...] they have this mark of their own that at each of them stands a figure with a pair of eyes, or at least with a field-glass, insuring to the person making use of it an impression distinct from every other [...] The spreading field, the human scene is the "choice of subject"; the pierced aperture, either broad or balconied or slit-like and low-browed, is the "literary form"; but they are, singly or together, as nothing without the posted presence of the watcher — without, in other words, the consciousness of the artist.[16]

James's use of free indirect discourse, described here as a literary form open enough to allow the reader to watch "the spreading field" within, looks forward to the kind of multiperspectivism of Faulkner by focusing both on the reader's act of watching, or of looking through, and of the architect's, or writer's, construction of a work that exposes the interior worlds of multiple subjects at

---

15 Elizabeth Boyle Machlan writes that the houses Isabel inhabits correlate to genres of the novel — genres that would be identifiable both to Isabel and to the reader. Thus, each house represents a narrative for Isabel, and, according to Boyle Machlan, illuminates the ways in which architecture is central to the ways in which humans understand themselves and their experiences. See Elizabeth Boyle Machlan, "'There are Plenty of Houses': Architecture and Genre in The Portrait of a Lady," *Studies in the Novel* 37, no 4 (2005): 395.

16 Henry James, *The Portrait of a Lady* (New York: Houghton-Mifflin Riverside Edition, 1956), Preface.

once.[17] James imagines an impossible house with a million apertures; Faulkner's walls are likewise so pierced that they often disintegrate entirely, allowing for both an acute sense of interiority and an opening up of narrative space.

Whereas the divide between inscape and landscape is dissolved for Jewel, in Faulkner's *Absalom, Absalom!*, the narration of architectural inscapes plays at the border between characters' experiences of domestic space and the storytellers' perceptions of those characters and of themselves. Rosa, Compson, Quentin, and Shreve narrate decades of local history, and the central house in the novel, Sutpen's Hundred, exists primarily through their gossip and stories. *Absalom*'s houses are not capable of sheltering their inhabitants; they instead become characters themselves, signifying not the subjects who inhabit them as much as the post-Civil War nation — and in Faulkner's present, the late depression-era world — in which they dwell, "as though," Rosa Coldfield says, inadvertently alluding to Jewel, "houses actually possess a sentience, a personality and character [...] inherent in the wood and brick."[18] These houses tend toward the stuffy, the ominous, the inescapable, and the uninhabitable, whether it be the massive Sutpen's Hundred or the confined Coldfield house. They then counteract the transparent ideal of the modernist architecture contemporaneous with the writing of the novel. Yet, modernism's architectural idealism still manages to express itself in Faulkner's literary experimentation, even within the regional South's historicized structures and novel forms. The novel's dense, repetitive structure becomes, analogically, a literary house in which the reader is kept outside certain rooms of knowledge, allowed only into the zones of inherited information that the narrators have to offer. This chapter's title thus refers both to the interior 'scapes of Faulkner's spaces as well as to this imprisoning, in*escapable,* nature of them.

---

17 Ellen Eve Frank further discusses James's use of architecture in *Literary Architecture: Essays Toward a Tradition* (Berkeley: University of California Press, 1983), 182–83.

18 William Faulkner, *Absalom, Absalom!* (New York, Vintage Books, 1990), 67.

With his overlapping blocks of story, Faulkner employs the spatial, temporal, and narrative tools of modernism to depict a vernacular landscape still mired in the pre-modern, similarly to how European Modernist architecture arriving in the United States around the time he was writing did not at first change the ordinary landscape so much as change the way in which it could be understood. While modernist architecture was initially criticized for disrupting expected entries into a structure — a front door might be located in the back of a building — causing confusion for its occupants at the exterior, the result is a more profound experience of the interior. Architect David Leatherbarrow has argued, for example, that the long entry of Wright's Robie House delays the full experience of the interior, making its inevitability all the more striking for the entrant.[19] Similarly, modernist novels that disrupt expected entries into the text — such as the dense and recursive narrative organization of *Absalom* — offer expansive interiors, new possibilities compared to more traditional literary habitats. One might argue that the work demanded of the reader by the text produces a work that is likewise all the more rewarding. Readers cannot settle complacently into compartmentalized narrative rooms, finding comfort in predictable characters, linear narratives, and unambiguous narration. Instead, *Absalom*'s innovative structure suggests another mode of habitation, a resistance to the implicate limitations of the domestic settings it appropriates. As such, it offers the modern reader an escape from the sorry fate of its characters by allowing the movement across and through rooms more unique, say, to the respective reader.

That is, Faulkner treats an interior that is not the self, the psychological, or not only so, but rather one of experience and knowledge more broadly. In a Q&A in 1958, Faulkner explains this readerly habitation in a response to a student who asks him if there is any one "right" view in the novel, or if it is all just thirteen ways of looking at a blackbird, alluding to Wal-

---

19 See, for example, David Leatherbarrow, "Disorientation and Disclosure," *Interstices* 12 (2011): 95.

lace Stevens. Faulkner replies, "I would like to think [that the truth], comes out, that when the reader has read all these thirteen different ways of looking at the blackbird, the reader has his own fourteenth image of that blackbird which I would like to think is the truth."[20] Thus, the overlapping, interpenetrating stories of the novel attempt a kind of Wrightian interiority and transparency — insofar as transparency is a kind of truth, in Faulkner's sense.

Faulkner understands, however, that that truth shifts depending on who is looking through the window. He is therefore not only exploring a metaphor but also is designing a direct connection between space and experience. The space of the house and the space of the novel are social spaces, in Henri Lefebvre's notion of social space, but they are social spaces that can be inhibited or concealed by two co-dependent illusions — illusions of transparency and illusions of opacity, or what Lefebvre calls realism — idealism and materialism. He contradicts the nineteenth-century notion of transparency as an opening up, arguing that transparency is an "illusion," a "trap." The trap is the following: outdated or devolving "historical and political forces" enact this so-called transparency, as if their images are based in nature. As such, they "naturalize" the "rational," and nature itself is rendered nostalgic, a nostalgia that then supersedes the rational.[21] Faulkner traces this form of nostalgia through the recurrence of events, ideologies, and structures over time. The spatial, in other words, can either reify or challenge the temporal; it can engender nostalgia or undermine it.

Sutpen's Hundred, the primary house in the novel, houses this nostalgia and is importantly at odds with the design of the novel's architecture, preventing its inhabitants from dwelling with intention in the ways made possible for Faulkner's readers. Furthermore, it is metonymic of the characters: Sutpen's house

---

20 Session: May 8, 1958, Audio File, The William Faulkner Collection. Department of Special Collections. University of Virginia Library.

21 Henri Lefebvre, *The Production of Space*, trans. Donald Nicholson-Smith (Oxford: Blackwell, 1991), 27–30.

is more of an extension of Sutpen than symbolic of his psychology, in a way similar to the relationship between Jewel and the cotton house in the earlier *As I Lay Dying*. In a sense, Faulkner here responds to James — instead of a house with a million windows through which to peer, the house *is* Sutpen himself. As a plantation, it maintains the power structures in which Sutpen participates, whether or not he is present to orchestrate them. This relationship of Sutpen to his rooms is explained when he returns from the war to find Charles Bon dead, his son Henry a refugee, and his estate in disrepair:

> He wasn't there [...] [he was a] waiting grim decaying presence [...] of the house itself, talking that which sounded like the bombast of a madman who creates within his very coffin walls his fabulous immeasurable Camelots and Carcassonnes. Not absent from the place, the arbitrary square of earth which he had named Sutpen's Hundred [...] He was absent only from the room [...] a part of him encompassing each ruined field and fallen fence and crumbling wall of cabin or cotton house or crib [...].[22]

Upon return, Sutpen is as empty as his house is of sons, as decayed as his house is because of the war — he encompasses the "crumbling walls," and as such, he, like Darl, cannot be, ontologically, in his room, for he is not. His only choice is to restore his house if he is to hope for a return to his self.

However, while Jewel does have the opportunity to narrate his own section of his novel, readers have no access to Sutpen's interiority — no window. Furthermore, the reader is given very little description of the interiors of the house on the estate of Sutpen's Hundred. Yet, its profound and imprisoning interiority is central, both for the major events that take place and the ways those events are narrated. Rather than explain characters' identities — their full mindscapes, the total ways they experience their lives — by how they are aware of architecture as produc-

---

22 Faulkner, *Absalom, Absalom!*, 129.

tive of a particular experience of home, *Absalom* excavates characters' mindscapes for clues as to what their concept of home entails. The storytellers' narrations are then a kind of negative characterization of the house itself.

The bold — and even gauche — "grand design" Sutpen has for his house, which he hires (or forces) a French architect to design, is strikingly parallel to the construction of the US capitol, designed in the 1790s in the classical tradition by Charles L'Enfant, a Frenchman who was raised at Versailles and who was committed to what he called a "grand plan" for the young nation's headquarters.[23] Sutpen sees his house not as the humble dwelling of a single man, but as a classical symbol for greatness and power. We are not totally without descriptions of the house. For example, Compson at one point compares Sutpen's Hundred (and all its inhabitation) to Bluebeard's castle, implying it to be a Gothic mansion (in contrast to the classical implications of the White House, though both styles were prevalent in Southern architecture), referring to the late seventeenth-century (1698) fairy tale in which the nosy third wife of an infamous, dangerous nobleman, having been forbidden to enter one of the rooms in her husband's castle, takes the opportunity of his absence to let herself in and discovers the hanging bodies of Bluebeard's former wives.[24] She survives her husband's wrath and prevails in the story, inheriting the estate and marrying a more pleasing spouse. The house, then, is the organizing principle for the story's plot and its unfolding, similarly so in Faulkner, for which Sutpen plays Bluebeard and his wife Ellen presumably Bluebeard's wife (albeit fated otherwise).

In *Absalom*, the narration operates linearly, but the blocks of story are overlapped and remittent, a structure that has been called "cubistic," "montage-like," and "vorticist." Critics such as Hugh Kenner and Andreas Huyssen have denied *Absalom*'s participation in any kind of avant-gardism, claiming its politics to

---

23 David P. Handlin, *American Architecture* (London: Thames & Hudson, 2004), 65.
24 Faulkner, *Absalom, Absalom!*, 47.

be too regionally Southern and its author too individualistic for group mentality. Still, *Absalom* was published in 1936 during the New Deal and the Spanish Civil War; as much as Faulkner is a Southern, American writer, he is also a self-identified international modernist, concerned with similar issues of war, class, and power — domestic and international — and attempting similar aesthetic experiments in simultaneity, dynamism, multiple perspectives, and stream of consciousness.[25] Teasing textual and literal boundaries, his novelistic innovations were in parallel both with the formal antics of the literary European avant-garde and the geographical innovations of American writer Sherwood Anderson. One critic has even referred to *Absalom* as antifascist, Sutpen and his grand design being a metaphor for the encroachment of totalitarianism.[26]

Faulkner was familiar with avant-gardism and Modernism more broadly: in 1925, he took a trip to Europe (his only trip until he accepted his Nobel Prize nearly thirty years later), where he visited private collections of Matisse and Picasso and Cezanne,

---

25 Hugh Kenner, in "Faulkner and the Avant-Garde," insisted that because Faulkner is operating out of an oral tradition he could not be employing the literary experiments of the militaristic, group-minded European avant-garde. Yet, both literary and architectural modernism emerged from similar concerns, regardless of Faulkner's appreciation or lack thereof (see Hugh Kenner, "Faulkner and the Avant-Garde," in *Faulkner, Modernism, and Film: Faulkner and Yoknapatawpha*, eds. Ann J. Abadie and Evans Harrington [Oxford: University Press of Mississippi, 1978], 182–96). Andreas Huyssen accused Faulkner of "insisting on the dignity and autonomy of literature, rather than to the iconoclastic and anti-aesthetic ethos of the avant-garde which attempted to break the political bondage of high culture through a fusion with popular culture and to integrate art into life." Yet, he located Faulkner as merely an American writer and misses that while Faulkner's concerns may not be the institutionalism of high art, and his needs were not necessarily to subvert such institutions, he nonetheless wrote from the margins (Andreas Huyssen, *After the Great Divide: Modernism, Mass Culture, Postmodernism* [Bloomington: University of Indiana Press, 1986], 31).

26 Ted Atkinson argues for Faulkner's political awareness in *Faulkner and the Great Depression: Aesthetics, Ideology, and Cultural Politics* (Athens: University of Georgia Press, 2005).

all of whom impressed him, particularly Cezanne.[27] During this trip, he attended what he called in a letter to his mother, a "very very modernist exhibition [...] futurist and vorticist."[28] Before this trip, while living in New Orleans and writing for the *Times-Picayune,* he had been experimenting with his interest in vortices, writing in "Mirrors on Chartres Street" (1925), "The moon had crawled up the sky like a fat spider and planes of light and shadow were despair for the Vorticist schools."[29] This passage at least alludes to Faulkner's working out of certain European avant-garde tendencies.

These tendencies are also evident in Faulkner's use and representation of interior space in the novel. While the narrators all consider Sutpen's Hundred to be a mausoleum too grand for its own good, characters live only in a very few of its rooms, and the novel's most significant events occur at its thresholds, or entries, rather than its interior (Henry's warning by Sutpen, Clytie's stopping Rosa on the stair, and a few deaths are the only significant events in the novel to take place inside the house). In one critical scene, Quentin, describing Sutpen's being turned away as a youth from the front door of Tidewater Plantation by a black manservant, tells Shreve that

> he seemed to kind of dissolve and a part of him turn and rush back through the two years they had lived there like when you pass through a room fast and look at all the objects in it and you turn and go back through the room again and look at all the objects from the other side and you find out you had never seen them before, rushing back through those

---

[27] Joseph Blotner, *William Faulkner: A Biography* (Jackson: University Press of Mississippi, 2005), 160.

[28] From a "Letter to Mrs. M.C. Falkner, 18 Aug. 1925," in William Faulkner, *Selected Letters of William Faulkner,* ed. Joseph Blotner (New York: Vintage Books, 1978), 13.

[29] William Faulkner, *New Orleans Sketches,* ed. Carvel Collins (Jackson: University of Mississippi Press, 2002), 16.

two years and seeing a dozen things [...] he hadn't even seen [...] before.³⁰

Here, Faulkner uses the metaphor of walking twice through a room to describe two years passing, as if each year were the same, though experienced differently, as if one walks through a room twice to understand that which was missed before. Space becomes a metaphor for time. The motion and the dynamism of this passage reflects, perhaps, an experience of vorticism, or at least of cubism, in motion — the attempt to experience all angles and aspects of a room simultaneously and while in motion — in order to represent the flashes of memory and thought, which can occur in a single instant. The novel's construction is confined within the limits of consciousness; the reader, like Rosa, is prevented from knowing certain things, and like Quentin and Shreve, is responsible for reconstructing the information, only possible by walking through the novel's rooms, examining its contents again from new perspectives.

Any examination of space and twentieth-century literature must contend with Joseph Frank's groundbreaking "The Idea of Spatial Form" (1945), in which, referring to Eliot's "The Wasteland," Frank defines spatial form as essentially a kind of literary cubism, for which conventional syntax is subordinated to a structure that prioritizes paratactic "word-groups" that are apprehended together and at once.³¹ He claims that modernist writers designed their works to be understood spatially, in a moment, rather than over time — a contradiction from the idea that modernists ranging from Proust to Joyce were in fact more engaged with the sequential qualities of memory and time.³²

---

30 Faulkner, *Absalom, Absalom!*, 186.
31 Joseph Frank, *The Idea of Spatial Form* (New Brunswick: Rutgers University Press, 1991), 14.
32 Ibid., 10. In an attempt to represent the fragmentation and violence of modernity (what Frank would call "a relation of disequilibrium with the cosmos"), Cubism, for example, strove to achieve a visual spontaneity and immediacy, representing all angles, all dimensions of an angle, all movement, simultaneously. Frank suggests, "In Braque, the Fauves or the Cubists, the

Frank admits that time and space are inextricably intertwined but suggests this emphasis on space as a kind of idealization on the part of artists.[33] However, Frank spends less time discussing that space also works as a persistent theme within the literature he discusses.

Faulkner brings time and space together in his spatial form. When Faulkner famously said in *Requiem for a Nun* (1951), "The past is never dead. It's not even past," he replaced the temporal, historical home, whether it be antebellum, reconstruction, depression-era, etc., with a spatial home that erases the discretion between these individual moments.[34] While most readers associate these words with Faulkner's penchant for writing the ways in which we inherit tragic events of history, they are also a kind of direction to understanding how time passes in *Absalom*, wherein over seventy years are recursively retold in the present tense, events collapsing through the act of storytelling into a synchronic zone, no longer functioning sequentially or temporally but spatially, re-experienced in two very particular confined spaces — the living room of Rosa Coldfield and the dormitory room of Quentin Compson. These are, for the most part, the rooms in which the novel takes place.

Rosa's "dim hot airless room," "somehow smaller than its actual size," operates as a counterpoint to Sutpen's mansion, Sutpen himself "not a being" but "a barracks filled with stubborn back-looking glass ghosts." His house was "a shell marooned and forgotten in a backwater of catastrophe," described in a parenthetical in *Requiem for a Nun* as "something like a wing of

---

naturalist principle has lost its dominance. We are asked only to accept the work of art as an autonomous structure giving us an individual vision of reality; and the question of the relation of this vision to an extra-artistic 'objective' world has ceased to have any fundamental importance" (30). No matter how disjunctive the elements of a Cubist painting may appear, they are, as he says of the chapters of Barnes's Nightwood, "like searchlights, probing the darkness each from a different direction yet ultimately illuminating the same entanglement of human spirit" (34).

33 Ibid., 61.
34 William Faulkner, *Requiem for a Nun* (New York: Random House, 1951), I.iii, 73.

Versailles glimpsed in a Lilliput's gothic nightmare."[35] It is after all designed by a French architect, modeled after another architect who hailed from Versailles.[36] These descriptions also reveal a way of thinking about being at home in the antebellum South; home in the novel may in part be about finding one's home or place in history, yet there are several histories overlapping here in one geographical space. The novel, like the Coldfield house, is smaller on the inside than the outside. It is small in time as well; despite purporting to cover nearly a century of history, *Absalom* takes place on two different days during one year. Faulkner seems to suggest that time does not really pass at all — that history is nothing more than a series of repeated (timeless) events. Rosa, who lives through Reconstruction, reconstructs her story for Quentin, hoping that in turn, he will reconstruct it again in the north by writing it for publication.[37] Here, Faulkner enacts Frank's spatial form; *Absalom*'s multi-perspectival spatial form, its overlapped storytelling, allows it to access multiple timeframes circumscribed within a confined present.

If home is partly found in history, then home is not an event per se but just one amongst the possible positions in the aftermath of its retellings; Rosa refers to Bon's murder as "an echo, but not the shot," having seen "a closed door" but one she never entered.[38] Rosa is the character who is closest to the events of the novel, and yet she witnesses nothing. While, as I have suggested, *Absalom*'s most significant events — Henry's murder and Sutpen's rejection at Tidewater — occur at the thresholds of houses, their retellings occur inside inflexible walls. Unlike Bluebeard's wife, Ellen and her younger sister Rosa never take full occupa-

---

35 Faulkner. *Absalom, Absalom!*, 3, 6, 7, 105. Faulkner, *Requiem for a Nun*, I.iii, p. 32. Description in *Requiem* quoted in William Ruzicka, *William T. Faulkner's Fictive Architecture: The Meaning of Place in the Yoknapatawpha Novels* (Ann Arbor: UMI Research Press, 1987), 46.

36 While it was not uncommon to borrow from European architecture in the South, baroque Versailles contrasts the architecture of Southern plantations. Perhaps for this reason, among others, Sutpen and his grand design are so maligned by their neighbors.

37 Faulkner, *Absalom, Absalom!*, 5.

38 Ibid., 121.

tion of their houses and are thus never freed of their ghosts.[39] The first pages of the novel present Rosa as a character who has lived the same way for decades, as if time has not passed. She was never a child, and she never ages, but she lives perpetually in the stories she has been told and the story she tells Quentin, hoping that he will, when he moves to Harvard, retell it in writing, forever mythologizing — and even reifying — the South. For forty-three years, she wades in this fetid swamp of the past, haunted by events she never witnessed, only inherited through stories. Time warps for Sutpen as well. Faulkner describes the duration of arriving at Tidewater only to be turned away as "a very condensation of time which was the gauge of its own violence."[40] On the one hand, the recursivity of the novel's structure implies an infinite repetition and inescapability of events. However, its retellings, the infinite perspectives into those events, might alter them and thus mutate them into something altogether different.

William Ruzicka, in *Faulkner's Fictive Architecture,* refers to Faulkner's houses as an "imaginative architecture" and claims that if one builds a house in order to inhabit a place, then Sutpen's house is nothing more than a possession, an attempt to gain what he is denied in his youth when turned away from the Tidewater Plantation.[41] As the novel describes it, "vanity conceived that house and, in a strange place and with little else but his bare hands and further handicapped by the chance and probability of meddling interference [....] built it."[42] If Ruzicka is correct, because Sutpen was never granted access he does not truly understand that which he tries to obtain. He does not have the proper shibboleth, to use one of the novel's favorite terms. Jefferson's townspeople understand this, and they keep him, the Other, at arm's length from day one. To put it another way, Faulkner's house fails to become a home because even within

---

39 Clytie, on the other hand, may be said to have full access, being a slave and a sister who inhabits multiple domestic zones, and thus takes full occupation of the house, thus able to be the one with final control over its fate.
40 Faulkner, *Absalom, Absalom!,* 201.
41 Ruzicka, *William T. Faulkner's Fictive Architecture,* 2–3; 57.
42 Faulkner, *Absalom, Absalom!,* 39.

the novel, Sutpen's Hundred is a fiction — an impossible and tragic ideal. Sutpen's house becomes otherworldly, a place of fiction for himself and those speculating as to the intentions that drove him to build a house out of nothing. Inscape and landscape, interiority and exteriority, become ontological zones between which the novel hovers. By the time the novel ends — with Quentin at Harvard in the North, explaining his strange world to Shreve — the entire South has become mythological, a fantastic place, much like Sutpen's Hundred.

In a 1956 interview for *The Paris Review* with Jean Stein, Faulkner suggests that the writer has the power to freeze history and to dispatch characters and readers into different temporal zones. He implies that writing is a way to immortalize, but that events of the past can be re-awakened and relived through the act of reading.[43] The Sutpen house pulls everything toward and into itself. It arrests motion, and the characters can only get so far from it. There is a way in which time stands still in *Absalom*, and Sutpen's "grand design" is "precisely the image of perpetuity — permanence, long-standing, enduring heritage, a local habitation and a name etched against contingency."[44] Wright's houses, if designed from the inside outward, work centrifugally, the inhabitation of the house being an interplay between space and subject. Faulkner's houses, and novel, operate centripetally, racing faster toward an internalized center, for which truth can only exist when processed by the reader. The architecture and the recursivity of *As I Lay Dying* and *Absalom, Absalom!* (as well as of *The Sound and the Fury* [1929], even if not discussed in this chapter) then exemplify Faulkner's theory of history as infinitely interiorized, or within.

The outmoded house is thus an implosive tomb. Rosa's father encloses himself in the attic of their house, presaging Henry's return home to die. The Sutpen house ultimately burns down

---

43 William Faulkner, "The Art of Fiction," interview by Jean Stein, *The Paris Review* 12 (1956): 28–52.
44 Ruzicka, *William T. Faulkner's Fictive Architecture*, 47.

and disappears.[45] What remains, however, is the book itself to be read by, inhabited by, many individuals over time and space. While the characters are entombed in its interiors, *Absalom* invites the reader to occupy the novel in new ways, to work with the text to build new narratives. Rather than a hermetic, self-referential container, *Absalom, Absalom!* is, in this sense, a design for living.

---

45 Faulkner, *Absalom, Absalom!*, 301.

Bibliography

Atkinson, Ted. "Faulknerscapes." *Studies in the Novel* 42, no. 3 (2010): 471–79. DOI: 10.1353/sdn.2011.0011.

———. *Faulkner and the Great Depression: Aesthetics, Ideology, and Cultural Politics.* Athens: University of Georgia Press, 2005.

Blotner, Joseph. *William Faulkner: A Biography.* Jackson: University Press of Mississippi, 2005.

Dahl, Curtis. "Lord Lambeth's America: Architecture in James's 'An International Episode.'" *Henry James Review* 5, no. 2 (1984): 80–95. DOI: 10.1353/hjr.2010.0145.

William Faulkner. *Absalom, Absalom!* New York, Vintage Books, 1990.

———. *As I Lay Dying.* New York: Vintage Books, 1987.

———. "Letter to Mrs. M.C. Falkner, 18 Aug. 1925." In *Selected Letters of William Faulkner,* edited by Joseph Blotner. New York: Vintage Books, 1978.

———. *New Orleans Sketches.* Edited by Carvel Collins. Jackson: University of Mississippi Press, 2002.

———. *Requiem for a Nun.* New York: Random House, 1951.

———. Session: 8 May 1958. Audio File. The William Faulkner Collection. Department of Special Collections. University of Virginia Library.

———. "The Art of Fiction." Interview by Jean Stein. *The Paris Review* 12 (1956): 28–52.

Frank, Ellen Eve. *Literary Architecture: Essays Toward a Tradition.* Berkeley: University of California Press, 1983.

Frank, Joseph. *The Idea of Spatial Form.* New Brunswick: Rutgers University Press, 1991.

Handlin, David P. *American Architecture.* London: Thames & Hudson, 2004.

Hines, Thomas S. *William Faulkner and the Tangible Past: The Architecture of Yoknapatawpha.* Berkeley: University of California Press, 1996.

Huyssen, Andreas. *After the Great Divide: Modernism, Mass Culture, Postmodernism.* Bloomington: University of Indiana Press, 1986.

Isenstaadt, Sandy. *The Modern American House: Spaciousness and Middle-Class Identity.* Cambridge: Cambridge University Press, 2014.

James, Henry. *The Portrait of a Lady.* New York: Houghton-Mifflin Riverside Edition, 1956.

Kenner, Hugh. "Faulkner and the Avant-Garde." In *Faulkner, Modernism, and Film: Faulkner and Yoknapatawpha,* edited by Ann J. Abadie and Evans Harrington, 182–96. Oxford: University Press of Mississippi, 1979.

Leatherbarrow, David. "Disorientation and Disclosure." *Interstices* 12 (2011): 93–104. http://interstices.aut.ac.nz/ijara/index.php/ijara/article/viewFile/132/192.

Lefebvre, Henri. *The Production of Space.* Translated by Donald Nicholson-Smith. Oxford: Blackwell, 1991.

Machlan, Elizabeth Boyle. "'There are Plenty of Houses': Architecture and Genre in *The Portrait of a Lady.*" *Studies in the Novel* 37, no. 4 (2005): 394–410. https://www.jstor.org/stable/29533717.

Ruzicka, William. *William T. Faulkner's Fictive Architecture: The Meaning of Place in the Yoknapatawpha Novels.* Ann Arbor: UMI Research Press, 1987.

Sobelle, Stefanie. "Inscapes: Interiority in Architectural Fiction." *Interstices* 12 (2011): 59–67. http://interstices.aut.ac.nz/ijara/index.php/ijara/article/viewFile/128/188.

Spurr, David. *Architecture & Modern Life.* Ann Arbor: University of Michigan Press, 2012.

Wright, Frank Lloyd. "Organic Architecture." In *Programs and Manifestoes on 20th-century Architecture,* edited by Ulrich Conrads, 25. Cambridge: MIT Press, 1971.

8

"The (Dis)Possessed": Djuna Barnes's *Nightwood* and the Modern Museum

Lindsay Starck

> *Sometimes in a phrase, the characters spring to life so suddenly that one is taken aback, as if one had touched a waxwork figure and discovered that it was a live policeman.*
> — T.S. Eliot on *Nightwood*[1]

In her introduction to Djuna Barnes's *Nightwood* (1937), Jeanette Winterson repeats T.S. Eliot's assertion that this is a book that must be read more than once. However, in the rush of modern life, she suggests, readers are not willing to set aside the necessary time. Books need to "be squeezed in," in contrast to the cinema, the theater, the gallery, or a concert, which require limited, fixed moments.[2] Winterson's invocation of the latter cultural venues are highly relevant to *Nightwood*, as the book's vivid and fragmented images recall the kinds of effects witnessed in

---

1   T.S. Eliot, introduction to Djuna Barnes, *Nightwood* (New York: New Directions, 1937), xx.
2   Jeannette Winterson, preface to Djuna Barnes, *Nightwood* (New York: New Directions, 2006), x.

early cinematography, its dramatic monologues and staging of characters in fixed scenes recall the theater, and the rhythm and musical pattern that T.S. Eliot observes in Barnes's prose link the novel to the world of music.[3] My focus in this essay is on the fourth space that Winterson brings to our attention: that of the museum gallery, in which "time" — quite literally — has been "set aside."

Nightwood is a text that readers have been struggling to define ever since its publication. In the *New York Times Book Review,* Alfred Kazin described it as "an experiment in the novel;" Dylan Thomas simply called it "a prose book."[4] Edwin Muir, one of the few critics of whom Barnes approved, insisted that the book was impossible to define according to any preexisting category and that its only contemporary influence was that of James Joyce.[5] As Monika Kaup reminds us, scholarly interpretations of Barnes's work since the 1920s and 1930s have seen two major phases: the first wave of Barnes scholars, following the example of T.S. Eliot and the New Critics, focused on her linguistic experimentation, her formalism, and her technique. Decades later, in the 1970s, feminist and new historicist critics highlighted the politics of her work, including subversive critiques of the patriarchal family, sexological theories, and depictions of lesbians in popular culture.[6] In the June 2014 issue of *Literature Compass,* Cathryn Setz (co-organizer of the first International Djuna Barnes Conference in 2012) suggests that the most recent phase of Barnes scholarship offers a series of alternative directions: the two most significant strands being "cultural histories of queer

---

[3] Eliot, introduction to *Nightwood,* xvii.

[4] Alfred Kazin, "An Experiment in the Novel," *The New York Times Book Review,* March 7, 1937, as quoted in Daniela Caselli, *Improper Modernism: Djuna Barnes's Bewildering Corpus* (Burlington: Ashgate Publishing Company, 2009), 51. Dylan Thomas, "Night Wood," *Light and Dark* (1937), as quoted in Caselli, *Improper Modernism,* 51.

[5] Edwin Muir, "New Novels," *The Listener* (28 October 1936), as quoted in Caselli, *Improper Modernism,* 52.

[6] Monika Kaup, "The Neobaroque in Djuna Barnes," *Modernism/modernity* 12, no. 1 (2005): 85–86.

sexuality" and "poetics, the archive, and intertextuality."[7] What contemporary critical texts such as Scott Herring's *Queering the Underworld: Slumming, Literature, and the Undoing of Gay and Lesbian History* (2007) and Daniela Caselli's *Improper Modernism: Djuna Barnes's Bewildering Corpus* (2009) share is a suspicion of scholarship that looks to "decode" Barnes's work; instead, Herring and Caselli — along with Julie Taylor in *Djuna Barnes and Affective Modernism* (2012) — analyze what Caselli terms "the politics of representation"[8] and Herring calls "a commitment to antirepresentation" in Barnes.[9] This chapter contributes to this fresh and productive branch of scholarship by reading *Nightwood* alongside a brief survey of the rise of the museum in the early twentieth century — a rise that took place (not coincidentally) during the same period in which Djuna Barnes and her compatriots were writing the most celebrated works of high modernism. I argue that reading the novel itself *as a museum* provides critical insight into these strategies of (anti)representation in Barnes and sheds new light on the distinctly modern juxtaposition of art with life, as well as the modernists' complicated relationship with the treasures and limitations of history.

This relationship is, I contend, inextricably bound up with the institution of the museum — a space that took on a new position of prominence at the turn of the twentieth century.[10] Modernist artists were forced to find ways to come to terms with this highly charged institution, existing as it did in a conceptual zone somewhere between the classical "house of the muses" from which it drew its name, and the "mausoleum" to which its critics made unfavorable comparisons. In "Valéry Proust Museum," Theodor Adorno famously called museums "family

---

7 Carolyn Setz, "'The Great Djuna:' Two Decades of Barnes Studies, 1993–2013," *Literature Compass* 11, no. 6 (2014): 367–87.
8 Caselli, *Improper Modernism*, 39.
9 Scott Herring, *Queering the Underworld: Slumming, Literature, and the Undoing of Lesbian and Gay History* (Chicago: University of Chicago Press, 2007), 165.
10 On the topic see Brian O'Doherty, *Inside the White Cube: The Ideology of Gallery Space* (Santa Monica: The Lapis Press, 1986), 14.

sepulchers of works of art."[11] Yet the museum was also the place where artists could play with the ideas of art and exhibition, as Duchamp demonstrated with his porcelain urinal in 1917 and his miniature museums from the 1940s through 1960s.[12] The museum represented an important juxtaposition, therefore, between artistic inspiration and the death of creativity, between the temple and the tomb. By structuring her novel as a museum, Barnes transforms the mausoleum into a productive space where figures on the margins of society can make a place for themselves.

I am not, of course, the first reader to have noted the significance of the museum in Barnes's text. On the contrary, her repeated use of the phrase "the museum of their encounter," which describes the home of Hedvig and Guido Volkbein, as well as the apartment of Nora and Robin, frequently crops up in analyses of the novel.[13] In "Exhibiting Domesticity: the Home, the Museum, and Queer Space in American Literature, 1914–1937," Kathryn Rose Taylor uses the motif of the home-as-museum to make an argument for Barnes's hybridization of public and private space. The home becomes "a space of public spectatorship" because the cohabitation of two homosexuals, Robin and Nora, transcends conventional notions of gender and domesticity that define the privacy of the home.[14] Mary Wilson expands the scope of the museum analogy beyond the public/private debate, invoking Henry James's famous metaphor of the "house of fiction" to show how Barnes "unhomes home" by creating "a modernist, experimental space of juxtaposition."[15] Other scholars, while not focusing on the particular effects of the museum, write on

---

11 Theodor Adorno, "Valéry Proust Museum" in *Prisms*, trans. Samuel and Shierry Weber (Cambridge: MIT Press, 1981), 175.
12 Kynaston McShine, *Museum as Muse: Artists Reflect* (New York: The Museum of Modern Art, 1999), 53.
13 For example, see Djuna Barnes, *Nightwood*, 7 and 61.
14 Kathryn Rose Taylor, "Exhibiting Domesticity: The Home, The Museum, and Queer Space in American Literature, 1914–1937," Ph.D. diss., UCLA, 2006, 96.
15 Mary Wilson, "No Place Like Home: Nightwood's Unhoused Fictions," *Studies in the Novel* 43, no. 4 (2011): 432.

closely related topics such as the novel's treatment of memory, history, and loss.[16] I pick up where Wilson left off, employing the hermeneutic of the museum to explain the experience of modern alienation — from self, from others, and from history — and dispossession.

Although in this chapter I draw upon the work of a variety of museum theorists, one of the texts most crucial to my analysis is Stephen Greenblatt's "Resonance and Wonder" (1990), a piece that continues to be regularly cited by contemporary museologists. Generally recognized as the founder of New Historicism — a mode of analysis he sometimes refers to as cultural poetics — Greenblatt focuses on the interrelationship between art and society, between aesthetic appreciation and the cultural context out of which that aesthetic originally emerged. In his essay on museums, he defines *resonance* as the ability of an object of display to breach its prescribed boundaries, extend to the world beyond and elicit for the viewer the culture from which it emerged. He defines *wonder* as capacity of the object of display to arrest the viewer's movement and demand attention.[17] *Nightwood*, like any good museum, displays elements of both resonance and wonder. However, the novel also exudes a sense of what Greenblatt considers the instability of objects, and the museum's performance as a monument "to the fragility of cultures."[18] Museums function, in other words, as a paradox: in their effort to immortalize artifacts of bygone moments and forgotten cultures, they underscore the ephemerality of culture and of all its elements: artistic, commercial, and human. Along these lines, I read *Nightwood* as a monument to the vulnerability

---

16 See especially Julie Taylor, *Djuna Barnes and Affective Modernism* (Edinburgh: Edinburgh University Press, 2012) and Julie Abraham, "Woman, Remember You: Djuna Barnes and History," in *Silence and Power: A Reevaluation of Djuna Barnes,* ed. Mary Lynn Broe (Carbondale: Southern Illinois University Press, 1991), 252–70.

17 Stephen Greenblatt, "Resonance and Wonder," in *Exhibiting Cultures: The Poetics and Politics of Museum Display,* eds. Ivan Karp and Steven D. Lavine (Washington DC: Smithsonian Institution Press, 1991), 42.

18 Ibid., 43–44.

of human beings and the fragility of their relationships. "The modern child has nothing left to hold to, or, to put it better, he has nothing left to hold with," says the Baron. "We are adhering to life now with our last muscle — the heart."[19] Flirting with sentimentality, anathema to modernism, the novel recounts a series of heartbreaks, both personal and broadly cultural.[20]

At its core, the pain of *Nightwood* is the pain of dispossession: Felix enters the world already stripped of his history just as he — and Nora after him — will be stripped of Robin. I use the term "stripped" here literally as well as figuratively to imply the characters' dispossession from society, to suggest their status as outsiders from the official record of history. The transformation of their houses and their lives into museums and museum pieces underscores their desire to "hold to" — in the words of the Baron — all that has left them and all they have left. Thus, Barnes's use of the museum becomes crucial because it signifies the impossibility of possession. The wonder of the museum, as Greenblatt argues, in entwined with consumption, yet the paradox at the heart of most art museums is that visitors are highly aware of their not being able to consume the objects.[21] An encounter with the museum, in this light, reflects the same frustration of expectations readers experience when they confront the famously impenetrable text of Barnes,[22] or what Scott Herring calls her "commitment to antirepresentation."[23] According to Herring, Barnes promises to deliver a certain kind of narrative — a sort of slumming exposé on the Parisian nightworld — but constantly defers.

> It is this capacity to toy with reader expectations — to tantalize with the sexual or ethnic type but to refuse to deliver — that prompts a minor crisis in sensational underworld

---

19 Barnes, *Nightwood*, 43.
20 On modernism's view of sentimentality see Caselli, *Improper Modernism*, 175.
21 Greenblatt, "Resonance and Wonder," 49.
22 Caselli, *Improper Modernism*, 175.
23 Herring, *Queering the Underworld*, 165.

representation. The refusal to represent properly what the audience expects will develop into a commitment to antirepresentation, a dedication that owed a great deal to her impersonal modernist counterparts: Joyce, Eliot, and Eugene Jolas. Promising insight, she undoes her slumming narratives even as these stories seem to grant geographic and cultural specificity. Within this epistemological uncertainty, ethnic and sexual freaks vanish as soon as they are found.[24]

Even though Barnes positions her characters neatly in her museum-text, her framing of them rejects any sort of representation that would permit her readers truly to possess, to acquire or consume, them.[25] If Barnes's characters are dispossessed, we, too, become dispossessed in the act of reading. Barnes compels us to wander the halls of the text with wonder and to return home having been transformed by the experience — even if it has also left us empty-handed. Although it is true that this commitment reflects the influence of her modernist counterparts, Barnes's stance also, as we shall see, is profoundly shaped by the rich and alienating experience of modernity itself.

Modernism and the Rise of the Museum

As numerous scholars in museum, cultural, and literary studies have observed, the turn of the twentieth century was a period of expansion and transition for museums on both sides of the Atlantic. Although the term *musaeum* dates back to the ancient Greeks and the famous library at Alexandria, both the word and the concept fell out of use during the Middle Ages.[26] Museums were revived during the Renaissance as private and royal collections called "wonder rooms" or curiosity cabinets, and the

---

24 Ibid.
25 On this see Erin G. Carlston, *Thinking Fascism: Sapphic Modernism and Fascist Modernity* (Stanford: Stanford University Press, 1998), 85.
26 Paula Findlen, "The Museum: Its Classical Etymology and Renaissance Genealogy," in *Museum Studies: An Anthology of Contexts,* ed. Bettina Messias Carbonell (Malden: Blackwell Publishing, 2003), 26.

concept was expanded to include textual compendia such as encyclopedia. Throughout the eighteenth century, collections were converted from private to public. Due to their new prominence in the public sphere, by the nineteenth century (the so-called "age of history") museums were rapidly expanding their collections and drawing both high praise and intense criticism from artists and social theorists.[27] In "Museum or Picture Gallery: Its Functions and Formations," (1880) John Ruskin — champion of the power of the museum to reverse what he saw as a dangerous decline in art and appreciation — writes that the institution showcases what is lovely in nature and heroic in men.[28] On the other side were art theorists like Quatremere de Quincy, who argued that when objects are taken out of context, they lose their vitality — what Greenblatt calls their wonder — and their ability to teach us anything. De Quincy was writing around the time of the French revolution, but his concerns about the museum resonated with subsequent philosophers such as Friedrich Nietzsche (*The Use and Abuse of History*, 1874) and Paul Valéry ("Le problème des musées," 1934).

Whether critics liked it or not, museums continued to flourish. In Britain alone the number of public museums grew from fewer than 60 in 1850, to 240 in 1887, and then to more than 500 by 1920.[29] Confronted with the growing prominence of the public museum, the modernists responded with widely varying degrees of enthusiasm. The most outspoken detractor by far was

---

[27] See Michel Foucault, *The Order of Things* (New York: Random House, 1970). As Foucault writes, in the nineteenth century "History" becomes our preferred means of ordering and categorizing our experience as a civilization; "History, from the nineteenth century, defines the birthplace of the empirical" (219). For Barnes, the orders and categories of the official historical record are subjective, exclusive, and incomplete.

[28] John Ruskin as quoted in Edward T. Cook, *The Life of John Ruskin*, Vol. II(New York: Haskell House Publishers, 1911), 345. The use of the phrase "simple person" reveals the classism and prejudice evident in the early history of public museums — a problematic inheritance that postmodern museums have had to confront.

[29] Susan Pearce, *Museums, Objects, and Collections: A Cultural Study* (Washington, DC: Smithsonian Institution, 1992), 107.

F.T. Marinetti, leader of the Futurist movement in Italy, who in his 1909 Futurist Manifesto called for the urgent destruction of museums, libraries, and academies.[30] For Marinetti, the museum was indeed a mausoleum, representing not only art that is already dead but also the death of the imagination of artists who dare seek inspiration there. Other writers engaged with the institution of the museum in more subtle ways, as John Pedro Schwartz demonstrates in his analysis of representations of national and cultural identity in the works of Virginia Woolf and James Joyce. Along similar lines, Catherine E. Paul contends that W.B. Yeats, Ezra Pound, Marianne Moore, and Gertrude Stein all enrich the writing and presentation of their poetry by drawing upon a museological framework that conveys meaning by juxtaposing objects and texts.[31] Although Paul's focus is on poets, Barnes's poetic novel functions in a very similar way.

Significantly, many of Barnes's contemporaries share her interest in the more general idea of collecting. Jeremy Braddock opens *Collecting as Modernist Practice* (2013) by observing that many modernist works themselves resemble collections: the quotations of Pound's *Cantos* or Eliot's *The Waste Land*; the "collage aesthetics" of futurism, cubism, Dada; the work of Langston Hughes or Zora Neale Hurston as "assemblages of folk songs and folklore."[32] As Braddock sees it, the modernist collection became a "provisional institution" that suggested new modes of public, potentially democratic engagement between artists and their audiences.[33] On the other hand, Lawrence Rainey argues, in *Institutions of Modernism* (1998), that the modernist collection constituted an "institutional counterspace" allowing for a

---

30 F.T. Marinetti, "The Futurist Manifesto," in James Joll, *Three Intellectuals in Politics* (New York: Pantheon Books, 1961), 183.
31 Catherine E. Paul, *Poetry in the Museums of Modernism* (Ann Arbor: University of Michigan Press, 2002), 6.
32 Jeremy Braddock, *Collecting as Modernist Practice* (Baltimore: Johns Hopkins University Press, 2012), 1.
33 Ibid., 3.

"tactical retreat" from popular mass culture.[34] The juxtaposition of these two interpretations exposes one of the many contradictions at the heart of the museum: is the institution inherently exclusive, catering to the cultural elite, or is it rather a "colossal mirror" (as George Bataille calls it) for all mankind, in which the aristocrat and the proletariat alike can come to encounter their own humanity as "an object of wonder?"[35] In their conclusion to *The Love of Art,* Pierre Bourdieu and Alain Darbel suggest that the actual function of museums is to emphasize for the participants the feeling either of belonging or of exclusion.[36] As we shall see, it is this very dynamic between inclusion and exclusion, insiders and outsiders, that motivates Barnes's use of the museum in *Nightwood.*

Museums of their Encounter

For Barnes, the museum cannot be disassociated from the people who selected and arranged its objects. When the museum appears, it is always "a museum of their encounter" — Guido's and Hedvig's, and Robin's and Nora's. In the first chapter, "Bow Down," we meet Felix Volkbein, the orphaned son of a Jew (Guido) who had hidden his ancestry from his wife (Hedvig) and her family. In the second chapter, "La Somnambule," Felix falls in love with Robin Vote, an American who produces a son (Guido) before leaving him. Chapters three and four, "Night Watch" and "The Squatter," relate the doomed love affair of Robin with Nora Flood, at the end of which Robin leaves Nora for Jenny Petherbridge. In chapter five, "Watchman, What of the Night?" Nora turns in her despair to Dr. Matthew-Mighty-Grain-of-

---

34 Lawrence Rainey, *Institutions of Modernism: Literary Elites and Public Culture* (New Haven: Yale University Press, 1998), 5.

35 George Bataille, "Museum," in *Museum Studies: An Anthology of Contexts,* ed. Bettina Messias Carbonell (Malden: Blackwell Publishing, 2004), 430.

36 Pierre Bourdieu and Alain Darbel, "Conclusion to The Love of Art: European Art Museums and Their Public," in *Museum Studies: An Anthology of Contexts,* ed. Bettina Messias Carbonell (Malden: Blackwell Publishing, 2004), 434.

Salt-O'Connor (finding him in bed in a woman's nightgown), a transsexual and sometimes-gynecologist who is prone to rambling philosophical narratives. The Doctor continues to talk (to Felix) in "Where the Tree Falls" and (to Nora) in "Go Down, Matthew." The novel ends with a chapter titled "The Possessed," in which Robin and Jenny have moved to America. In the final scene, Nora comes across Robin in a church, where Robin gets down on all fours, crying and barking and crawling after Nora's dog. This ultimate encounter, like every other encounter in the novel, is enigmatic and complex, seeming rife with a meaning held just beyond the reader's grasp.

What we learn from *Nightwood* is that the museum — like the text — is always an encounter, always predicated on the inhabitants' relationships to each other, to history, and to the material world. Within the museum, each object and each visitor has its set and proper place; but the relationships between what is viewed and the person viewing, between the visitors and the collection, as well as among the visitors themselves, is what sets the modern museum apart from its Renaissance predecessors. According to Bataille, the physical walls and artifacts of the museum constitute the container for the true content of the institution: the visitors.[37] In *Nightwood*, the concept of the museum's content, including the visitors, the people themselves, takes on a more literal significance. The first time we are introduced to Robin, as noted above, she is described "like a painting by the douanier Rousseau."[38] A few pages later Felix feels, while looking at her, as if he were "looking upon a figurehead in a museum."[39] She has "the look of cherubs in Renaissance theaters" and the "fading grace" of "an old statue in a garden."[40] Later we witness Jenny and Robin sitting across the table from one another like a "sculpture" of "Greek runners [...] eternally angry, eternally separated, in a cataleptic frozen gesture of abandon."[41] Here we

---
37 Bataille, "Museum," 430.
38 Barnes, *Nightwood*, 38.
39 Ibid., 41.
40 Ibid., 75
41 Ibid.

see that Robin's lovers, in addition to viewing her as a fixed piece of art, become fixed figures themselves in the act of loving her.

Indeed, in *Nightwood* love becomes an act of preservation: a testament to the fragility and ephemerality of a shared life. Every object and every word in Robin and Nora's house was a testament to their love. They collect furniture from circuses, a horse from a merry-go-round, statues and hangings from churches, music boxes and chandeliers from across Europe. This is "the museum of their encounter, as Felix's hearsay house had been testimony of the age when his father had lived with his mother."[42] The objects are fantastical and the house full of personality; the trouble is that the objects last long after the lover has gone. When Robin leaves, Nora is tortured by the collection they have amassed together. She treads lightly through the empty rooms, "disturbing nothing" out of fear that if she rearranges any of their shared objects, Robin "might lose the sense of home" and never return to her.[43] Thus, the objects of the house-as-museum become a stand-in for the person who arranged them there, and the desire to preserve those objects is simply the displacement of Nora's desire to keep Robin as a lover — to preserve Robin's love for her. Her possession of those artifacts signifies her inability to possess Robin herself.

Robin leaves Nora for Jenny, whose chapter is entitled "The Squatter" and whose house, while not described in precisely the same terms as Nora's, reinforces the pervading sense of dispossession. Jenny's houseful of objects is also a place of encounter — only this time the encounter is that of Jenny with other lives. "Her walls, her cupboards, her bureaux," we are told, "were teeming with second-hand dealings with life"[44]: she wears someone else's wedding ring, displays a photo of Robin that was taken for Nora, collects books that others have suggested but which she has not read. The objects in a museum might also be called "second-hand dealings": we stroll through the gallery in order to

---

42 Ibid., 61.
43 Ibid.
44 Ibid., 74.

view someone else's jewelry, or the portrait that an artist painted for someone else. The narrator describes Jenny moving through her own home like a visitor would move through a museum, stopping to examine every object. The experience of stealing, or borrowing, extends beyond her objects to even her mannerisms: she borrows words and facts from others.[45] Because she was incapable of possessing a great love of her own, Jenny appropriated Nora's love for Robin.[46] Interestingly, although Jenny's home is the only one described as packed with "second-hand dealings," the objects chosen by the other characters for their living spaces — old shields, false family portraits, Roman fragments, circus chairs, merry-go-round horses — are all things that have been appropriated from someone or someplace else. Felix, for example, frequents antique shops; it is there that he sees Robin dressed in a second-hand, vintage gown that will be added to her collection of clothes that seem "newly ancient."[47] The "museum of their encounter," we find, contains objects that belong more to history than to the current occupants who live among them.

This borrowing of history is even more evident in the home of Guido and Hedvig Volkbein, which is also the first use of "museum of their encounter" in the novel. In an effort to hide — or erase — his Jewish ancestry, Guido marries a Christian woman and never tells her the truth about his background. Instead he adopts the trappings of her religion, tells her that he is an Austrian of noble lineage, and produces a false coat of arms along with a family tree. Since, as a Jew, he has been excluded from the official record of history, he must borrow someone else's history in order to make a place for himself. The most salient instance of this is his purchase of two life-size portraits of strangers (two actors, aptly enough) who he claims as his mother and father. Because Guido dies before Felix is born, Felix comes into the world without a true sense of his own history, able to claim only

---

45 Ibid.
46 Ibid., 75.
47 Ibid., 46.

the heritage that his father borrowed from others. Felix Volkbein's shame over this lack of a past, the narrator tells us, takes "the form of an obsession for what he termed 'Old Europe.'"[48] This obsession is made manifest in a number of ways: in restaurants "he bowed slightly to anyone who might be someone," for example. He chooses his home because a Bourbon had lived in those rooms before him; he selects his valet because the man looks like Louis the Fourteenth and his cook because the woman "resemble[s] Queen Victoria, Victoria in another cheaper material, cut to the poor man's purse."[49]

Felix's behaviors are, if we recall Greenblatt's definition, museum-like: they are demonstration of the fragility of culture. Museums present objects that have been emptied of their original significance — much like Felix's mannerisms. Just as his father borrowed coats of arms, titles, and family portraits, so Felix borrows historical behaviors and characters: the act of bowing in restaurants, the servants who resemble royal historical personages. Dispossessed of his own history, he is forced to look elsewhere for his sense of identity and his place in the world.

Outside of History

When Felix falls in love with Robin, his attraction is in keeping with his characteristic pursuit of history. He first sees Robin passed out on a bed, arranged in a tableau as though she already belongs in a gallery. He felt, the narrator goes on, "that he was looking upon a figurehead in a museum, which, though static [...] seemed yet to be going against the wind; as if this girl were the converging halves of a broken fate."[50] Felix's sense of Robin as his fate underscores the degree to which his desire for history is also, simultaneously, a quest for his purpose. He finds that his love for her is not a choice, but something predetermined. While on the surface these lines sound like something out of a

---

48 Ibid., 11.
49 Ibid., 12.
50 Ibid., 41.

clichéd romance, for Barnes, the sentiment is darker and more complex. Robin provides Felix with the identity he craves because he has been stripped of his history; yet, although he cannot help but fall for a woman who is a "carrier of the past,"[51] she is an "*infected* carrier of the past" (emphasis mine) who, like history itself, is unattainable, incomprehensible, unbound, and even savage. We might easily describe Robin as Victoria Smith describes history: as a forever-desired yet always-unattainable object.[52] The narrator tells us that she "carried the quality of the 'way back' as animals do," that she had the air of a statue that "is not so much the work of man as the work of wind and rain and the herd of the seasons."[53] She is more animal than human, more natural than urban; and in *Nightwood*'s modern era of cities and machines, she stands as both an object of (nostalgic) desire and a threat to the new order. As a "figure of doom," she gives Felix the son that he wants — although the small, sickly boy is not what he had hoped for — and then she abandons them both.[54]

Robin reappears in the company of Nora Flood, a woman who represents history in a very different sense: her history is not wild or cold, but rather devoted and utterly human. For those who attend her salon in America, she encapsulates historical narratives. Foreigners who look at her face recall stories of presidents, Civil War battles, and the great western migration.[55] And yet, for all her connection to history, Nora does not feel certain of her place in it, and in this feeling, she is like Felix. To Nora, "The world and its history were [...] like a ship in a bottle; she herself was outside and unidentified [...]."[56] The sentence immediately after this one is, "Then she met Robin" — suggest-

---

51 Ibid.
52 Victoria L. Smith, "A Story beside(s) Itself: The Language of Loss in Djuna Barnes's *Nightwood*," PMLA 114, no. 2 (1999): 197. The idea of an object as simultaneously desired and unpossessable recalls Lacan's distinction between plaisir and jouissance: the former can be satisfied or obtained, while the latter cannot.
53 Barnes, *Nightwood*, 44, 45.
54 Ibid., 45.
55 Ibid., 56.
56 Ibid., 59.

ing that her relationship with Robin provided her (or so she hoped) with a place inside that bottle, in history. Once she finds that place, she is made to feel as Felix does when he loves Robin: "that I would not only be able to achieve immortality, but be free to choose my own kind."[57] The idea of being able to choose one's own kind of immortality is unusual and compelling, and the freedom of choice, that sense of individual agency, is especially important for marginal figures like Felix and Nora, who understand that the grand narrative of history is likely to leave them out entirely. Therefore, if they are to be remembered, they bear the responsibility of carving out a place for themselves.

According to Victoria Smith, for Barnes, the figure of the Jew becomes a means of representing who is and who is not inscribed in history.[58] If Felix and his family are considered marginal by a society still suspicious of their status as Jews, then Robin, Nora, Jenny, and the doctor are similarly excised from history because of their sexuality, the desires and the love that place them outside the bounds of the social rules and conventions. In the insightful essay "Woman, Remember You," Julie L. Abraham highlights the connections Barnes draws between personal memory and the "official record of history," pointing out the ways in which Barnes's characters must rely on living in each other's memories since — due to race, gender, and sexuality — they have already been excluded from the overarching historical narrative.[59] As such, the text itself becomes a type of museum, gathering fragments of individual subjectivities, arranging and juxtaposing them so that out of those fragments and out of those relationships, a new narrative is born. Abraham emphasizes the double meaning of history for Barnes, which is simultaneously "fixed" and "fragmentary," perpetually being constructed.[60] *Nightwood*'s mode of challenging the official his-

---

57 Ibid., 120.
58 Smith, "A Story beside(s) Itself," 197.
59 Julie L. Abraham, "Woman, Remember You: Djuna Barnes and History," in *Silence and Power: A Reevaluation of Djuna Barnes,* ed. Mary Lynn Broe (Carbondale: Southern Illinois University Press, 1991), 253.
60 Ibid.

torical record is through memory, a source of "alternative stories" and subjective perspectives.

Felix explains his obsession with history in a crucial passage where he expounds upon the significance of memory. He tells the doctor that his family is preserved because his whole lineage comes from the memory of one woman, his aunt, which makes it clear and unalterable. For Felix, this sense of constancy is "the motivation of a marriage. No man really wants his freedom. He gets a habit as quickly as possible — it is a form of immortality."[61] Memory and marriage are interrelated: one is a sense of immortality, and the other is a form of it. Both are a means of preservation, ways to protect what Greenblatt calls the precariousness of objects and what *Nightwood* shows to be the vulnerability of the human heart. The connection Felix establishes between relationships and history recalls the "museum of their encounter." A relationship — here, with Robin — and a museum both function in the same way: they offer a space in which history can be collected and transcended, a place where a person can establish a sense of immortality by linking her existence to someone or something else; someone or something who will memorialize her, who will remember her when she is gone. This is why memory is such a powerful motif in the text, something that all the characters attempt to grasp in their own particular way. Nora is devastated over the loss of Robin not just because love has departed, but also because she has ceased to exist in her lover's memory. Nora's tragedy is not to have loved and lost, but to have loved and then been forgotten. When it comes to both individual memory and the official record of history, whatever lies outside of or beyond them "might as well not exist."[62] If the motivation behind a marriage, behind a relationship, is to establish a "museum of encounter" and thereby insulate oneself and one's love from the ravages of time, then it is not the lover who leaves but the lover who *forgets* that strikes the awful blow.

---

61 Barnes, *Nightwood*, 119–20.
62 Abraham, "Woman, Remember You," 261.

Human Heterotopias

Plenty has been written on the qualities that make Robin a carrier of the past, but what has not been explored in great depth is the Doctor's unusual representation of history. A person who functions as a museum all on his own, the Doctor is someone who stands outside of all time, who contains epochs and eras piled on top of one another in his soul. I'd like to suggest that the Doctor is what Foucault calls a "heterotopia," a term Foucault proposes to describe the opposite of a utopia. Where a utopia exists nowhere, the heterotopia is a place "outside of all place," a place "capable of juxtaposing in a single real place several spaces, several sites that are in themselves incompatible."[63] One of his primary examples of heterotopic space — along with theaters, cinemas, and gardens — are museums.[64] In "Of Other Spaces," he observes that contemporary space has yet to be "de-sanctified" — unlike contemporary time, which, he claims, was, in the nineteenth century, removed from the sacred.[65] Foucault argues that our age is one defined by space rather than by time, and that the spaces that we occupy are heterogeneous rather than voids.

Like a heterotopia or a museum, the Doctor, too, possesses "the curious property of being in relation with all the other sites, but in such a way as to suspect, neutralize, or invert the set of relations that they happen to designate, mirror, or reflect," a space which is "linked with all the others."[66] A female trapped in a male's body, someone who suffers from socially forbidden desires, a person who has existed in several bodies across multiple generations, the Doctor does indeed invert and make suspect our ideas of bodies, sexualities, and histories. When the Doctor reminisces about the time that Catherine the Great sent for him to bleed her, the ex-priest who is listening to him exclaims: "For Heaven's sake! Remember your century at least!"[67] The irony,

---

63 Michel Foucault, "Of Other Spaces," *Diacritics* 16, no. 1 (1986): 24–25.
64 Ibid., 26,
65 Ibid., 23.
66 Ibid., 24.
67 Barnes, *Nightwood*, 173.

of course, is that in addition to remembering his own century, the Doctor — like a museum — remembers all of them. "What an autopsy I'll make," he declares, "with everything all which ways in my bowels! A kidney and a shoe cast of Roman races; a liver and a long-spent whisper; a gall and a wrack of scolds from Milano, and my heart that will be weeping still."[68] Here the doctor claims that within his very body are the artifacts of history, objects that attest to different times and places but which also confirm the universal sorrow and suffering that unites them all. In this description of his own dismemberment, the Doctor transforms his body into a sacred space and himself into a saint whose relics are scattered and whose limbs and organs belong not to himself, but to the Church, to its followers, and to history. If in life he felt dispossessed of his proper body — he should have been born a woman, but instead is trapped inside the body of a man — then in death that dispossession becomes even more acute. There is nothing left to him in death; there is nothing that he owns. Even his bowels will be swept up into history, into the space of the museum.[69] As a novel that emphasizes the body in the museum, as well as outside of it, and particularly the body *as part* of the museum, *Nightwood* underscores the extent to which, especially for marginal figures such as the Doctor or Nora, even one's body is not one's own.

The Possessed

The final chapter of *Nightwood*, entitled "The Possessed," uses Robin to underscore the impossibility of possession. The title is enigmatic, although Robin's strange and inhuman actions (getting down on all fours, barking and crying at the dog) in the setting of the chapel seem to imply the religious meaning of the term: one who is possessed by an evil spirit. Yet, because this

---

[68] Ibid., 107

[69] For a discussion of the disembodied in turn-of-the-century literature see Ruth Hoberman, *Museum Trouble: Edwardian Fiction and the Emergence of Modernism* (Charlottesville: University of Virginia Press, 2011), 26.

chapter ends with Robin alone — Nora is there, but has passed out on the floor, and Jenny does not know where Robin is — it demonstrates how futile were the efforts of all those lovers (Felix, Nora, and Jenny) who tried to possess her, to make her their possessed. All the characters who fall in love with Robin attempt to place her in their museum-homes, but all fail at the task of securing Robin, "the 'figurehead,' the prize piece," among their collections.[70] I suggested at the beginning of this essay that at the heart of the novel is this sense of dispossession — an experience that is, I contend, intimately associated with the museum of the twentieth century. The concept of *not* possessing an object on display is relevant only to the modern iteration of the museum.[71] The modern museum marks an important transition from the viewer's marvel at the *possessor* of the object to her marvel at some wondrous aspect of the object itself that makes it unable to be possessed. The power of an object in a museum has shifted from that of "proprietorship" to that of "mystique."[72]

I contend that it is precisely this shift from possession to wonder that makes *Nightwood* one of the most remarkable texts of high modernism. Where other critics have pointed to her politics of representation or called her commitment to anti-representation, I see, more specifically, her *representation of dispossession*. Her novel frustrates our expectations, as Herring has observed: when she promises to reveal she only obscures, leaving deliberately unresolved what Frances Doughty calls the "powerful and conflicting desires to tell and not to tell."[73] The reader's inability to possess the text is not a failure of interpretation, but rather the only logical outcome for Barnes's project. Furthermore, the inability to possess is not necessarily an undesirable state of affairs. Although she exposes the dispossession of her characters from society, from history, from their loved

---

70 Wilson, "No Place Like Home," 442.

71 See Greenblatt, "Resonance and Wonder," 50.

72 Ibid., 52.

73 Frances M. Doughty, "Gilt on Cardboard: Djuna Barnes as Illustrator of her Life and Work," in *Silence and Power: A Reevaluation of Djuna Barnes*, ed. Mary Lynn Broe (Carbondale: Southern Illinois University Press, 1991), 137.

ones, and even from their own bodies, Barnes also refuses to let them *be* possessed by her readers — an experience that is at once disconcerting and oddly exhilarating. If the reader, too, is able to see herself reflected in the novel, if she is able to understand herself as both dispossessed and unable to be possessed by others, she becomes liberated from the constraints of history and of society. She becomes, in the words of Felix, free to choose her own kind of immortality, free to transcend the alienation and isolation so characteristic of modernity. Indeed, the experience of *Nightwood*, the experience of the museum, is a way of coping with the modern individual's sense of fragmentation and her disconnection from her group identity — or what Émile Durkheim labeled anomie. What *Nightwood* offers is a space in which to house of our scattered pieces, to forge new meaning out of the juxtaposition of disparate experiences and the proliferation of modern identities.

This is, in fact, the project of *Nightwood*. Its poetry and its complexity arise, as Joseph Frank explains in "Spatial Form in Modern Literature," from its dreamlike state, from the connections drawn between symbols and themes across space rather than through linear time. It is a novel of juxtapositions, a series of relationships established between art objects as well as between individuals in heterotopic space. We understand the characters in *Nightwood* as they understand each other: by studying their encounters with each other, by looking for the ways in which one impacts or is impacted by another. This reading experience parallels Greenblatt's experience of resonance within the gallery of the museum. The characters of *Nightwood* resonate in and through one another, and just as importantly, *Nightwood* itself resonates with the other cultural productions and inventions of its era. The aim of New Historicism is to locate the text in relation to other forms of representation operating within the culture of a certain moment.[74] For *Nightwood*, I contend, that key other representational practice is the modern museum.

---

74 See Greenblatt, "Resonance and Wonder," 43.

It is no coincidence, I believe, that Barnes wrote the bulk of the novel while staying with her friend Peggy Guggenheim — an art appreciator and collector who established the modern art museum on the Grand Canal in Venice. Two decades earlier, in 1929, Abby Rockefeller spearheaded the effort to found the Museum of Modern Art in New York. Thus, modernism saw not only the shift in representational practices within art, but also drastic changes in how that art was represented to the public. Proving herself to be a true "maker of the marvelous," Barnes expresses this change by creating an object of wonder with *Nightwood* — an object that both defies possession and reflects our own experience of dispossession in the modern world.[75] Like any visitor to a museum, readers of *Nightwood* experience the simultaneous sense of inclusion and exclusion, which is troubling, liberating, and highly modern. We may not be able to fully grasp the text, which slips time and again — as Carlston has written — through our "hermeneutic nets,"[76] but we walk away from the novel as we walk out of the museum: transformed. As Paul writes of William Carlos Williams's poem "History," the speaker leaving the museum "brings with him his changed vision [...] and the objects that at the beginning of the poem were ordinary and unappealing have become magical because of the way he perceives them."[77] Similarly, Barnes's representation of dispossession in the modern world reminds us of the poetry, the vulnerability, and the terrible wonder of human beings and of the works that we create.

---

75 Francesco Patrizi, as quoted in Greenblatt, "Resonance and Wonder," 51.
76 Carlston, *Thinking Fascism*, 85.
77 Paul, *Poetry in the Museums of Modernism*, 34.

Bibliography

Abraham, Julie L. "Woman, Remember You: Djuna Barnes and History." In *Silence and Power: A Reevaluation of Djuna Barnes,* edited by Mary Lynn Broe, 252–70. Carbondale: Southern Illinois University Press, 1991.

Adorno, Theodor. "Valéry Proust Museum." In *Prisms,* translated by Samuel and Shierry Weber, 173–86. Cambridge: MIT Press, 1981.

Barnes, Djuna. *Nightwood.* New York: New Directions, 1937.

———. *Nightwood.* New York: New Directions, 2006.

Bataille, George. "Museum." In *Museum Studies: An Anthology of Contexts,* edited by Bettina Messias Carbonell, 430–31. Malden: Blackwell Publishing, 2004.

Benstock, Shari. *Women of the Left Bank: Paris, 1900–1940.* Austin: University of Texas Press, 1987.

Bourdieu, Pierre, and Alain Darbel. "Conclusion to The Love of Art: European Art Museums and Their Public." In *Museum Studies: An Anthology of Contexts,* edited by Bettina Messias Carbonell, 453–56. Malden: Blackwell Publishing, 2004.

Braddock, Jeremy. *Collecting as Modernist Practice.* Baltimore: Johns Hopkins University Press, 2012.

Carlston, Erin G. *Thinking Fascism: Sapphic Modernism and Fascist Modernity.* Stanford: Stanford University Press, 1998.

Caselli, Daniela. *Improper Modernism: Djuna Barnes's Bewildering Corpus.* Burlington: Ashgate Publishing Company, 2009.

Findlen, Paula. "The Museum: Its Classical Etymology and Renaissance Genealogy." In *Museum Studies: An Anthology of Contexts,* edited by Bettina Messias Carbonell, 23–50. Malden: Blackwell Publishing, 2004.

Foucault, Michel. "Of Other Spaces." *Diacritics* 16, no. 1 (1986): 22–27. DOI: 10.2307/464648.

———. *The Order of Things.* New York: Random House, 1970.

Frank, Joseph. "Spatial Form in Modern Literature." In *The Widening Gyre: Crisis and Mastery in Modern Literature*, 3–49. New Brunswick: Rutgers University Press, 1963.

Goethe, Johann Wolfgang. *The Autobiography of Johann Wolfgang von Goethe*. Translated by John Oxenford. New York: Horizon Press, 1969.

Greenblatt, Stephen. "Resonance and Wonder." In *Exhibiting Cultures: The Poetics and Politics of Museum Display*, edited by Ivan Karp and Steven D. Lavine, 42–56. Washington, D.C.: Smithsonian Institution Press, 1991.

Grobbel, Michaela. *Enacting Past and Present: The Memory Theaters of Djuna Barnes, Ingeborg Bachmann, and Marguerite Duras*. Lanham: Lexington Books, 2004.

Herring, Scott. *Queering the Underworld: Slumming, Literature, and the Undoing of Lesbian and Gay History*. Chicago: University of Chicago Press, 2007.

Hoberman, Ruth. *Museum Trouble: Edwardian Fiction and the Emergence of Modernism*. Charlottesville: University of Virginia Press, 2011.

Kaup, Monika. "The Neobaroque in Djuna Barnes." *Modernism/modernity* 12, no. 1 (2005): 85–110. DOI: 10.1353/mod.2005.0043.

Marinetti, F. T. "The Futurist Manifesto." In James Joll, *Three Intellectuals in Politics*, 133–84 (New York: Pantheon Books, 1961).

McShine, Kynaston. *Museum as Muse: Artists Reflect*. New York: The Museum of Modern Art, 1999.

O'Doherty, Brian. *Inside the White Cube: The Ideology of Gallery Space*. Santa Monica: The Lapis Press, 1986.

Paul, Catherine E. *Poetry in the Museums of Modernism*. Ann Arbor: University of Michigan Press, 2002.

Pearce, Susan. *Museums, Objects, and Collections: A Cultural Study*. Washington, DC: Smithsonian Institution, 1992.

Pollock, Griselda. "Un-Framing the Modern: Critical Space/Public Possibility." In Museums *after Modernism: Strategies of Engagement*, edited by Griselda Pollock and Joyce Zemans, 1–39. Malden: Blackwell Publishing, 2007.

Preziosi, Donald. "Brain of the Earth's Body: Museums and the Framing of Modernity." In *Museum Studies: An Anthology of Contexts,* edited by Bettina Messias Carbonell, 71–84. Malden: Blackwell Publishing, 2004.

Rainey, Lawrence. *Institutions of Modernism: Literary Elites and Public Culture.* New Haven: Yale University Press, 1998.

Setz, Carolyn. "'The Great Djuna:' Two Decades of Barnes Studies, 1993–2013." *Literature Compass* 11, no. 6 (2014): 367–87. DOI: 10.1111/lic3.12143.

Smith, Victoria L. "A Story beside(s) Itself: The Language of Loss in Djuna Barnes's *Nightwood*." PMLA 114, no. 2 (1999): 194–206. DOI: 10.2307/463391.

Schwartz, John Pedro. "Between the Muses and the Mausoleum: Museums, Modernism, and Modernity." PhD dissertation, University of Texas at Austin, 2006.

Taylor, Julie. *Djuna Barnes and Affective Modernism.* Edinburgh: Edinburgh University Press, 2012.

Taylor, Kathryn Rose. "Exhibiting Domesticity: The Home, The Museum, and Queer Space in American Literature, 1914–1937." Ph.D. dissertation, University of California Los Angeles, 2006.

Cook, E.T., and Alexander Wedderburn, eds. *The Works of John Ruskin.* Vol. 34. New York: Longmans, Green, and Co., 1903–12.

Wilson, Mary. "No Place Like Home: *Nightwood*'s Unhoused Fictions." *Studies in the Novel* 43, no. 4 (2011): 428–48. DOI: 10.1353/sdn.2011.0053.

9

Interior Spaces in Literature: A Sociological and Historical Perspective

Álvaro Santana-Acuña

Despite the important contributions of the spatial turn — one of the most fecund turns that followed the linguistic turn — reflections on interior spaces in literature remain scanty and barely interdisciplinary. Arguably, an explanation for the scarce attention to the interior space in literature by spatial-turn research has to do with the tendency to frame such a space as located either outside the individual or inside of her (especially in her consciousness). Hence, this volume's main contribution is, rightly, to provide an understanding of the interior space in literature as a liminal but well-defined area between the outside and the inside. Rather than framing literary space in dyadic terms (public versus private or outside versus inside), I argue that this volume suggests conceiving it as a triad, which includes the subjective inside, the interior space, and the non-subjective outside.

The sociological significance of triadic relationships was first highlighted by Georg Simmel, who built on the distinguished tradition of German dialectics as formulated by Johann Gottlieb Fichte and Georg Wilhelm Friedrich Hegel. In "The Triad" (1908), Simmel defined the dyad as a two-person group or a social relationship of two, and the triad as a three-person group or a social relationship of three, in which the third element appears. He argued in favor of the sociological significance of the third element, whose "existence [...] may directly start or strengthen the union of the two."[1] For instance, the birth of a child should increase the mutual love of spouses. Yet, the third element can also harm the group as a whole. For instance, parents going through a divorce might use the child as a weapon to attack a group: the family.

Building on Simmel's views on the triad, in this Postscript I contend that the ambivalent nature of the third element appears also in interior spaces in literature. Let me begin with two cases analyzed in this volume. (1) In William Faulkner's novel *Absalom, Absalom!* (1936) the house and plantation, called Hundred, is the inner space that Civil War veteran Thomas Sutpen uses to restore his self from damage he suffered during the war. The restoration of Hundred channels the restoration of Sutpen's subjectivity from social harm. (2) In Robert Musil's novel *The Man without Qualities* (1930–1943) the main character, Ulrich, observes street traffic in Vienna behind a window. From this space, he reflects on the moral shock caused by the modern city. This shock becomes a larger reflection on modernity's negative dimensions during the last days of the Austro-Hungarian monarchy, before the outbreak of World War I.

As these and other cases studied in this volume show, the interior space in literature can be defined as a third space, namely, as a liminal location between individual subjectivity and the social outside. My definition does not imply that subjectivity is a realm outside the social. (This claim would most likely be endorsed by an orthodox practitioner of rational choice theory, for whom non-social constraints ultimately inform an individual's rational choices.) On the contrary, the understanding of subjectivity I endorse here regards it as *social, spatial,* and *historical.* As it is well known among those familiar with the history of so-

---

[1] Georg Simmel, "The Triad," in *The Sociology of Georg Simmel,* ed. Kurt Wolff (New York and London: Free Press and MacMillan, 1964), 146.

cial theory, this formulation of subjectivity is not entirely new. Readers, for example, can think of sociologist George Herbert Mead's notions of "I," "Me," and self. Mead defined the "I" as the unpredictable part of our subjectivity and the "Me" as the socialized subjectivity, which belongs to the "conventional, habitual individual."[2] According to Mead, the unpredictable "I" introduces novelty in social life, while the "Me" tries to discipline the "I" by adapting it to social conventions. The self results from the combination of the "I" and the "Me." Mead's contemporary, Sigmund Freud, understood subjectivity as a psychological structure that functioned as a triad. He divided it into Ego, Id, and Super-Ego. Unlike Freud, Mead understood subjectivity as "a social structure [that] arises in social experience."[3] Hence, contra Freud too, Mead argued that the human "mind is essentially a social phenomenon; even its biological functions are primarily social."[4]

However, taken together, Freud's and Mead's approaches to human subjectivity are inadequate on a particular dimension. They view subjectivity ahistorically, as if it exists universally and as if its study is scientifically viable. For this reason, although not entirely new, my formulation contains an often-overlooked point: subjectivity has a history. One of the earliest and most successful attempts to theorize modern subjectivity appears in the work of Adam Smith. He is a theorist traditionally portrayed as a supporter of self-interest (although he was more fond of the term "self-love," among others) and as a founding figure of utilitarian individualism or rational choice theory. In this Postscript, I do not intend to revisit the Adam Smith problem, namely, how to reconcile the moral-philosophical Smith (who argued in *The Theory of Moral Sentiments* (1759) that fellow-feeling must inform an individual's actions) with the political-economic Smith (who claimed in *The Wealth of Nations* (1776) that an individu-

---

2   George Herbert Mead, *Mind, Self, and Society: From the Standpoint of a Social Behaviorist* (Chicago: University of Chicago Press, 1967), 197.
3   Ibid., 473.
4   Ibid., 472.

al's pursuit of his own interests benefits "the society").[5] In fact, I claimed elsewhere that this problem does not really exist.[6] My point here is a different one. In *The Theory of Moral Sentiments,* Smith contended that subjectivity is not only unthinkable without "sociality," as he called it, but also without taking into account the space in which subjectivity occurs.[7] For Smith, subjectivity emerges in the social space created by individuals' interactions. Hence, the meaning that individuals attribute to their sentiments arises not so much from the view of the sentiment "as from that of the situation which excites it."[8] In short, a spatially-driven sociality is at the center of subjectivity in *The Theory of Moral Sentiments.* Two decades later, in *The Wealth of Nations,* Smith applied the same framework to a key interior space of modernity: the nation.

Smith developed this framework at a moment of four major transitions in the organization of secular knowledge.[9] (1) The transition from the moral sciences of Jean-Jacques Rousseau and David Hume to the social sciences of Auguste Comte and Herbert Spencer. This transition made it possible to transform "society" into a new realm of human affairs. Accordingly, society would now be fully autonomous from the providential

---

5   Adam Smith, *An Inquiry into the Nature and Causes of the Wealth of Nations* (Chicago: University of Chicago Press, 1976), 475.
6   Álvaro Santana-Acuña, "Outside Structures: Smithian Sentiments and Tardian Monads," *The American Sociologist* 46, no. 2 (2015): 194–218.
7   Adam Smith, *The Theory of Moral Sentiments* (Indianapolis: Liberty Classics, 1982), VI.i.9. "Sociability" is an eighteenth-century neologism. See Daniel Gordon, *Citizens without Sovereignty: Equality and Sociability in French Thought, 1670–1789* (Princeton: Princeton University Press, 1994). This neologism is absent in Smith's book. He opted for "sociality" and other terms. See Santana-Acuña, "Outside Structures."
8   Smith, *The Theory of Moral Sentiments,* I.i.1.10.
9   I elaborate further on these eighteenth-century transitions in my review essay of Charles Taylor's *Modern Social Imaginaries.* See Álvaro Santana-Acuña, "El imaginario social moderno y la génesis de la modernidad occidental," in *Cátedra Edmundo O'Gorman: Teoría de la historia,* eds. Alfonso Mendiola and Luis Vergara (Mexico City: Universidad Iberoamericana and Universidad Nacional Autónoma de México, 2011).

realm.[10] (2) The transition from *belles lettres* (which encompassed the practice of history, rhetoric, poetry, and grammar) to literature.[11] This transition attracted the attention of Smith's contemporaries such as historian Edward Gibbon.[12] As readers of *Don Quixote* (1605 and 1615) might recall, for early modern European writers, such as Miguel de Cervantes, "literary" referred to what belonged to letters, sciences, or studies.[13] This usage of "literary" remained customary and widespread until the eighteenth century among major European languages.[14] As late as the 1730s, literature meant primarily "the knowledge and science of letters."[15] Since literature referred to learning acquired through reading a wide range of books, occupations such as judge required men of "superior talent and endowed with literature and science."[16] In short, until the 1750s, literature's semantic field was closer to law, science, learning, and scholarship than to art, imagination, creativity, and aesthetic writing, as it has been for the past three centuries. In Smith's times, literature started to

---

10 Keith Baker, "Enlightenment and the Institution of Society: Notes for a Conceptual History," in *Main Trends in Cultural History: Ten Essays*, eds. Willem Melching and Wyger Velema (Amsterdam: Rodopi, 1994); Miguel Cabrera and Álvaro Santana-Acuña, "De la historia social a la historia de lo social," *Ayer: Revista de historia contemporánea* 62 (2006).

11 Philippe Caron, *Des "Belles Lettres" à la "Littérature": Une archéologie des signes du savoir profane en langue française (1680–1760)* (Paris: Société pour l'information grammaticale, 1992); Raymond Williams, *Keywords: A Vocabulary of Culture and Society* (New York: Oxford University Press, 1983), 150–54.

12 Edward Gibbon, *Essai sur l'étude de la littérature* (London: T. Becket & P.A. de Hondt, 1762).

13 For instance, in Chapter 18 of the Second Part, Don Quixote challenges Don Lorenzo, an aspiring poet, to a "literary jousting" (*justa literaria*).

14 Real Academia Española, *Diccionario de la lengua castellana*, vol. IV (Madrid: Francisco del Hierro, 1734), s.vv. "literario" and "literatura"; *Oxford English Dictionary Online*, http://www.oed.com/, s.vv. "literature" and "literary"; Accademia della Crusca, *Vocabolari degli Accademici della Crusca*, 4th edn. (Florence: Domenico Maria Manni, 1729–1738), s.vv. "letteratura" and "litteratura"; Antoine Furetière, *Dictionnaire universel* (Paris: Veuve Delaune, 1743), Vol. 2, s.v. "littérature."

15 Real Academia Española, *Diccionario de la lengua castellana*, IV, 417.

16 Ibid.

become a domain different from that of *belles lettres*, that is, an independent, secular domain of knowledge about fictionalized human subjectivity. For the success of this transition, the rise of the novel was central.[17] (3) As Reinhart Koselleck investigated, another transition was the diffusion of the collective concept of "History."[18] This diffusion entailed a new way of experiencing the present (marked by an increasing acceleration of time) and a new way of distinguishing past from future. And (4) the concept of "subjectivity" (a nineteenth-century neologism) began to acquire its primary meaning as a space differentiated from the providential realm and the social realm.[19] Taken together, these four transitions brought about the emergence of three key domains of secular knowledge: literature, history, and sociology.[20] Yet the boundaries between the three remained fuzzy for most of the nineteenth century (and until the twentieth century in regions like Latin America) as these domains struggled to become disciplines.[21]

Auguste Comte's positivism is among the earliest examples of boundary fuzziness between literature, history, and sociology. He popularized but did not coin the word "sociology" (the

---

17 Álvaro Santana-Acuña, "How a Literary Work Becomes a Classic: The Case of *One Hundred Years of Solitude*," *American Journal of Cultural Sociology* 2, no. 1 (2014); Robert Escarpit, *Sociologie de la littérature* (Paris: Presses Universitaires de France, 1986); Franco Moretti, ed., *The Novel* (Princeton: Princeton University Press, 2006).

18 Reinhart Koselleck, *Futures Past: On the Semantics of Historical Time* (New York: Columbia University Press, 2004).

19 Dror Wahrman, *The Making of the Modern Self: Identity and Culture in Eighteenth-Century England* (New Haven: Yale University Press, 2004); Jan Goldstein, *The Post-Revolutionary Self: Politics and Psyche in France, 1750–1850* (Cambridge: Harvard University Press, 2005); Cabrera and Santana-Acuña, "De la historia social."

20 Like literature, "fine arts" and "classical music" became popular terms in the same period. See William Weber, "The Rise of Classical Repertoire in Nineteenth-Century Orchestral Concerts," in *The Orchestra: Origins and Transformations*, ed. Joan Peyser (New York: Scribner, 1986); Nathalie Heinich, "De l'apparition de l'«artiste» a l'invention des 'Beaux-Arts,'" *Revue d'histoire moderne et contemporaine* 37 (1990).

21 Santana-Acuña, "El imaginario social moderno."

abbé Sieyès first coined it on the eve of the French Revolution).[22] Like sociology, he claimed that history was part of positive science. His project in that direction was *Course of Positive Philosophy* (1830–1842), which consisted of six volumes of Balzacian proportions and influenced writers Thomas Hardy and Harriet Martineau, among others. The latter became the first female sociologist and one of the discipline's first methodologists. In *How to Observe Morals and Manners* (1838), Martineau understood the observer as a hybrid between the literary traveler and the social ethnographer. Karl Marx's historical materialism and critique of capitalism was inseparable from the now-separated disciplines of history and sociology. For him, literature also served as a window into the ills of capitalism. Marx, who was an avid reader of Honoré de Balzac, indicated that writing *Das Kapital* (1867) and other economic works was preventing him from devoting time to a book project on Balzac's portrayal of a rising bourgeois society in *La comédie humaine* (1830–1856).[23] The founding figure of modern academic history, Leopold von Ranke, wrote narrative, literary history with a sociological (organicist) taste.[24] A founding figure of sociology, Herbert Spencer, imported ideas from literature. He did so from Samuel Taylor Coleridge's essay "The Theory of Life" (1848) as part of his effort to offer a theory of social evolution. Spencer's efforts first came into fruition in the essay "Progress: Its Law and Cause" (1857).[25]

---

22 Comte continues to be wrongly credited for inventing the word sociology. On Sieyès's neologism, see Jacques Guilhaumou, "L'avènement de la 'métaphysique politique': Sieyès et le nominalisme politique," in *L'invention de la société: Nominalisme politique et science sociale au XVIIIe siècle*, eds. L. Kaufmann and J. Guilhaumou (Paris: EHESS, 2003).

23 Sandy Petrey, "The Reality of Representation: Between Marx and Balzac," *Critical Inquiry* 14, no. 3 (1988).

24 Georg Iggers and James Powell, eds., *Leopold von Ranke and the Shaping of the Historical Discipline* (Syracuse: Syracuse University Press, 1990).

25 For additional evidence of boundary fuzziness between these domains of knowledge, see Wolf Lepenies, *Between Literature and Science: The Rise of Sociology* (Cambridge: Cambridge University Press, 1988) and Lewis Coser, *Sociology through Literature: An Introductory Reader* (Englewood Cliffs: Prentice-Hall, 1963).

What about writers at work in the rising domain of literature? For most of the nineteenth century, rather than being impervious to the influence of other domains, writers mixed literary inquiry with sociological and historical insights. Wolfgang von Goethe, Charles Dickens, Leo Tolstoy, Balzac, Émile Zola, Benito Pérez Galdós and others conceived literature (especially the novel sequence) as a holistic and scientific discourse about society. For them, the literary was not simply an aesthetic, fictional description of society, but more ambitiously it was supposed to offer a program to understand and reform society. Far from merely narrating social life, these writers sought to advance theories that explained how their societies functioned. Taking into account the international impact of their writing on contemporary readers, their theories rivaled those produced by rising social scientists. To build and support a theory, the literary researcher had to get his facts right and prove it in his texts. (Long textual forms such as the novel sequence became preferred vehicles of theory building in nineteenth-century literature.) Three decades before a founding figure of sociology, Émile Durkheim, placed "social facts" at the center of the discipline's agenda, Dickens put "facts" at the center of one of his most successful literary enterprises, *Hard Times* (1854). As the character Thomas Gradgrind stated in the opening paragraph:

> NOW, what I want is, Facts. Teach these boys and girls nothing but Facts. Facts alone are wanted in life. Plant nothing else, and root out everything else. You can only form the minds of reasoning animals upon Facts: nothing else will ever be of any service to them. This is the principle on which I bring up my own children, and this is the principle on which I bring up these children. Stick to Facts, sir![26]

---

26 Charles Dickens, *Hard Times for These Times* (New York: Hurd and Houghton, 1869), 1.

Modernity's obsession with "facts" disembarked in literature before it did in sociology and history.[27] Given the long trajectory of these three domains and their common roots, the study of interior spaces in literature should not be dissociated from the sociological and the historical.[28] Most of the contributions in this volume prove this to be the case. Several among them address the issue of the outsider *versus* the insider. In *The Man without Qualities*, Robert Musil explored the tension between the individual's inside and the social outside. Musil was a contemporary of sociologists Simmel and Max Weber, who also addressed that tension in their work. For Simmel, the stranger stands as the quintessential outsider. Yet a social actor (whether an individual or a nation) needs the stranger in order to better define and strengthen her own identity. Thus, each definition of the outsider implies a definition of what an insider is in a particular social context.[29] In a similar vein, Weber argued that society consists of an endless mixture of "open and closed [social] relationships."[30] The protagonist of Musil's novel, Ulrich, encounters similar social relationships in pre-World War I Vienna. Musil describes him as an outsider who reflects about modernity and especially about urban life and who is resigned to accept the individual's incapacity to absorb all stimuli existing in a modern city. This realization also lies at the heart of Simmel's classic essay "The Metropolis and Mental Life" (1903).[31]

In Elsa Morante's works, the interaction between the inside and the outside becomes the encounter of arts, illness, and secret stories, as Gabriele Orsi shows in her contribution. Morante's last novel, *Aracoeli* (1982), is quite meaningful because in

---

27 Mary Poovey, *A History of the Modern Fact: Problems of Knowledge in the Sciences of Wealth and Society* (Chicago: University of Chicago Press, 1998).
28 See Lepenies, *Between Literature and Science*.
29 Georg Simmel, "The Stranger," in *Georg Simmel on Individuality and Social Forms*, ed. Donald Levine (Chicago: University of Chicago Press, 1971).
30 Max Weber, *Economy and Society: An Outline of Interpretive Sociology*, 2 vols. (Berkeley: University of California Press, 1978), 43.
31 Georg Simmel, "The Metropolis and Mental Life," in *Georg Simmel on Individuality and Social Forms*, ed. Donald Levine (Chicago: University of Chicago Press, 1971).

it her view of interior spaces as prisons of subjectivity becomes more apparent. In William Faulkner, on the contrary, interior spaces function as locations to reanimate subjectivity, as Stefanie Sobelle contends. Interior spaces in Faulkner's Yoknapatawpha County express owners' subjectivity, and interior space and subjectivity are intertwined historically. For instance, in *Absalom, Absalom!*, Hundred, the main house of a plantation, behaves like a real character (Gabriel García Márquez, a devout reader of Faulkner, incorporated this technique in several of his novels; more on this below).

The interior space in literature can enable a process of self-representation. This process is evident in Joris-Karl Huysmans's novel *À rebours* (1884). Its main character, Jean des Esseintes, locked himself up in his house. Its interior — full of things — recreates many objects found in the social outside. Yet the interior also represents his subjectivity. Rather than a late nineteenth-century version of Molière's misanthrope, I would argue that des Esseintes's outlook shares more similarities with the current social problem of cocooning.[32] In an age of rapidly growing home delivery services, cocoons are people who voluntarily retreat from social life. They live inside their homes to obtain peace of mind and personal welfare. Hence, they avidly consume merchandise that allows them to practice a stay-at-home lifestyle.[33] Cocoons, like des Esseintes, end up turning their homes into museums of subjectivity.

Like the museum, the interior space cannot just be full of objects but also it needs people interacting among themselves. As actor-network and material culture researchers claim, an important type of interaction occurs between people and objects. Furthermore, these bodies of research contend that one of the ways in which people can achieve their sense of subjectivity is through interactions with objects. This contention is especially suitable to interior spaces in literature, which are hardly thinkable without object-human interactions. Lindsay Starck confirms

---

32 Álvaro Santana-Acuña, "¿Eres un cocoon?," *Truman Factor* (2010).

33 See, for instance, *Cocoon Zone*, http://www.cocoonzone.com.

this contention in analyzing the connection between museum and mausoleum in Djuna Barnes's novel *Nightwood* (1936) and Erin Edgington does the same in her study of the nineteenth-century bourgeois interior described by Edmond de Goncourt in *La maison d'un artiste* (1881).[34] Like Gustave Flaubert's unfinished novel *Bouvard et Pécuchet* (1881) and Huysmans's *À Rebours*, Goncourt's *catalogue novel* reads as an extensive spatial description of the writer's possessions; a literary version of Marx's fetishism of the commodity, I would argue.

The boundaries between interior and exterior, between private and public, change constantly. Our modern understanding of these boundaries comes mostly from eighteenth-century Europe. As Jürgen Habermas explained in his classic book *The Structural Transformation of the Public Sphere* (1962), this sphere emerged as a new domain of political action. A particular component of this transformation was material and spatial. For instance, commodities such as umbrellas displayed in streets and promenades became more common among the middle classes, as did glass windows in their houses.[35] As Sandy Isenstaadt documented for the United States and as Sobelle reminds us in Faulkner's case, "glass allowed the outside to come in." Glass windows create the illusion of an interior space that expands beyond the frame of the window into the social outside, into the public sphere.

The expansion of Paris in Haussmann's times required the construction of thousands of brand new houses equipped with glass windows. Furthermore, the glasshouse emerged as a new material space for women, as Campmas states in her analysis of the violation of interior spaces in Émile Zola's *La curée* (1871). This is the second novel of *Les Rougon-Macquart* (1871–1893), Zola's twenty-novel sequence on France's Second Empire. Ar-

---

34 This novel deals with the themes of alienation and isolation, which were central to the founders of sociology (e.g., Marx and Durkheim).

35 William Sewell, "The Empire of Fashion and the Rise of Capitalism in Eighteenth-Century France," *Past and Present* 206, no. 1 (2010); Daniel Roche, *Histoire des choses banales: Naissance de la consommation dans les sociétés traditionnelles (XVIIe-XIXe siècle)* (Paris: Fayard, 1997).

guably, this sequence remains a pioneering work of what I call "literary historical sociology," as well as the best example of boundary fuzziness between literature, history, and sociology in nineteenth-century Europe.

Zola's naturalism left its mark in literary history. Other movements did not. This happened to Jules Romains's *unanisme,* which presents reality as floating, organic, unstable, and unfixed. According to *unanisme,* the individual loses its subjective isolation and becomes a simultaneous consciousness, while the city becomes an organic, unified, and self-aware consciousness. Unanimism marked a change in the literary imagery of big cities after the Second Industrial Revolution. In *La vie unanime* (1907), the city of Paris functions for Romains as a second skin. How is his unanimist strategy similar to Pérez Galdós's and Dostoyevsky's contemporary approaches to Madrid and St. Petersburg, respectively? Dominique Bauer does not address this question in her contribution, but she points out the connection between unanimism and trends in the plastic arts in the early twentieth century, especially futurism. By conceiving reality as an uninterrupted flow, futurism proclaimed the instantaneity of the present. Yet, I would also argue that unanimism shared similarities with philosophical Bergsonism, which, among other aspects, emphasized the importance of *durée* (duration), intuition, and instantaneity.[36] Furthermore, literature, history, and sociology parted ways in Romains's times. He embraced an understanding of literary temporality anchored in the idea of an actual present and immediacy. This understanding collided with an understanding of social temporality supported by early sociologists such as Durkheim. Rather than in simultaneity and actual present, Durkheim insisted on the importance of history and historical development for sociological analysis.

Finally, I want to add an important twentieth-century case to the interior spaces in literature studied in this volume: *One*

---

36 Jimena Canales, *The Physicist and the Philosopher: Einstein, Bergson, and the Debate that Changed Our Understanding of Time* (Princeton: Princeton University Press, 2015).

Hundred Years of Solitude (1967). García Márquez's classic novel consists of a series of concentric interior spaces. The first one surrounds the main character, colonel Aureliano Buendía, who in the midst of his deepest episode of solitude traced a ten-foot circle on the floor of his military tent to prevent people from approaching him. The second circle is the Buendía's house, which expands as the family grows. The third circle contains the Buendía family, with its seven generations. The fourth circle comprises the town of Macondo, removed from civilization and yet a space that contains all places. An untranslatable manuscript creates the fifth and final circle. As the novel approaches its end, the undecipherable manuscript suddenly becomes readable. As a result, readers discover that the manuscript happens to be the text of the actual novel, which they see coming to its conclusion as a hurricane of apocalyptical proportions destroys every concentric interior space: Macondo, the house, the last of the Buendías, and the manuscript itself.

The theme of interior spaces falling apart is at the center of this novel, as I explain elsewhere.[37] Arguably, García Márquez imported this theme from Faulkner's novels, Nathaniel Hawthorne's *The House of the Seven Gables* (1851), and Álvaro Cepeda Samudio's *La casa grande* (1962). My research with little-known primary sources revealed that the Buendía's house started to silently fall apart shortly after its construction in Chapter 1. But in the last version of *One Hundred Years of Solitude,* García Márquez removed all references to the house's decay and saved them for the last three chapters.[38] In his next novel, *The Autumn of the Patriarch* (1975), he changed the approach to interior spaces. As the novel opens, an interior space collapses. The vultures get into the patriarch's presidential palace and, while flapping their wings, they stir up the stagnant time inside. Interior space

---

[37] Álvaro Santana-Acuña, *Ascent to Glory: The Transformation of* One Hundred Years of Solitude *into a Global Classic* (New York: Columbia University Press, forthcoming).
[38] Álvaro Santana-Acuña, "Los siete capítulos olvidados de *Cien años de soledad,*" *El País* (May 28, 2017): 36–37.

and static time are set in motion backwards to tell the story of a dictator's fall from grace.

Interior spaces in literature have a history. Contributors to this volume rightly point out that the interior space in literature constitutes a hermeneutical field in its own right. But as I argued in this Postscript, understanding this particular space as a liminal and yet well-defined area between exterior and subjective spaces calls for the use of the tools not only of literary analysis but also of sociological and historical analysis. Once the study of the interior space in literature is framed historically and sociologically, it becomes apparent that the heart of modern literary fiction beats strongly in interior spaces located in between individual subjectivity and the social outside.

Bibliography

Accademia della Crusca. *Vocabolari degli Accademici della Crusca*. 4th Edition. Florence: Domenico Maria Manni, 1729–1738.

Baker, Keith. "Enlightenment and the Institution of Society: Notes for a Conceptual History." In *Main Trends in Cultural History: Ten Essays*, edited by Willem Melching and Wyger Velema, 96–120. Amsterdam: Rodopi, 1994.

Cabrera, Miguel, and Álvaro Santana-Acuña. "De la historia social a la historia de lo social." *Ayer: Revista de historia contemporánea* 62 (2006): 165–92.

Canales, Jimena. *The Physicist and the Philosopher: Einstein, Bergson, and the Debate That Changed Our Understanding of Time*. Princeton: Princeton University Press, 2015.

Caron, Philippe. *Des "Belles Lettres" à la "Littérature": Une archéologie des signes du savoir profane en langue française (1680–1760)*. Paris: Société pour l'information grammaticale, 1992.

Coser, Lewis. *Sociology through Literature: An Introductory Reader*. Englewood Cliffs: Prentice-Hall, 1963.

Dickens, Charles. *Hard Times for These Times*. New York: Hurd and Houghton, 1869.

Escarpit, Robert. *Sociologie de la littérature*. Paris: Presses Universitaires de France, 1986.

Furetière, Antoine. *Dictionnaire universel*. Paris: Veuve Delaune, 1743.

Gibbon, Edward. *Essai sur l'étude de la littérature*. London: T. Becket & P.A. de Hondt, 1762.

Goldstein, Jan. *The Post-Revolutionary Self: Politics and Psyche in France, 1750–1850*. Cambridge: Harvard University Press, 2005.

Gordon, Daniel. *Citizens without Sovereignty: Equality and Sociability in French Thought, 1670–1789*. Princeton: Princeton University Press, 1994.

Guilhaumou, Jacques. "L'avènement de la 'métaphysique politique': Sieyès et le nominalisme politique." In *L'invention de la société: Nominalisme politique et science sociale au XVIIIe siècle,* edited by L. Kaufmann and J. Guilhaumou, 201–26. Paris: EHESS, 2003.

Heinich, Nathalie. "De l'apparition de l'' artiste' a l'invention des 'Beaux-Arts.'" *Revue d'histoire moderne et contemporaine* 37 (1990): 3–35.

Iggers, Georg, and James Powel, eds. *Leopold von Ranke and the Shaping of the Historical Discipline.* Syracuse: Syracuse University Press, 1990.

Koselleck, Reinhart. *Futures Past: On the Semantics of Historical Time.* New York: Columbia University Press, 2004.

Lepenies, Wolf. *Between Literature and Science: The Rise of Sociology.* Cambridge: Cambridge University Press, 1988.

Mead, George Herbert. *Mind, Self, and Society: From the Standpoint of a Social Behaviorist.* Chicago: University of Chicago Press, 1967.

Moretti, Franco, ed. *The Novel.* Princeton: Princeton University Press, 2006.

Petrey, Sandy. "The Reality of Representation: Between Marx and Balzac." *Critical Inquiry* 14, no. 3 (1988): 448–68. DOI: 10.1086/448450.

Poovey, Mary. *A History of the Modern Fact: Problems of Knowledge in the Sciences of Wealth and Society.* Chicago: University of Chicago Press, 1998.

Real Academia Española. *Diccionario de la lengua castellana,* vol. IV. Madrid: Francisco del Hierro, 1734.

Roche, Daniel. *Histoire des choses banales: Naissance de la consommation dans les sociétés traditionnelles (XVIIe–XIXe siècle).* Paris: Fayard, 1997.

Santana-Acuña, Álvaro. *Ascent to Glory: The Transformation of* One Hundred Years of Solitude *into a Global Classic* (New York: Columbia University Press, forthcoming).

———. "¿Eres un cocoon?" *Truman Factor* (2010).

———. "El imaginario social moderno y la génesis de la modernidad occidental." In *Cátedra Edmundo O'Gorman: Teoría de la historia,* vol. I, edited by Alfonso Mendiola and Luis

Vergara, 193–213. Mexico City: Universidad Iberoamericana and Universidad Nacional Autónoma de México, 2011.

———. "How a Literary Work Becomes a Classic: The Case of *One Hundred Years of Solitude*." *American Journal of Cultural Sociology* 2, no. 1 (2014): 97–149. DOI: 10.1057/ajcs.2013.16.

———. "Outside Structures: Smithian Sentiments and Tardian Monads." *The American Sociologist* 46, no. 2 (2015): 194–218. DOI: 10.1007/s12108-015-9264-y.

———. "Los siete capítulos olvidados de *Cien años de soledad*." *El País,* May 28, 2017, 36–37.

Sewell, William. "The Empire of Fashion and the Rise of Capitalism in Eighteenth-Century France." *Past and Present* 206, no. 1 (2010): 81–120. DOI: 10.1093/pastj/gtp044.

Simmel, Georg. "The Triad." In *The Sociology of Georg Simmel,* edited by Kurt Wolff, 145–69. New York: Free Press, 1964.

———. "The Metropolis and Mental Life." In *Georg Simmel on Individuality and Social Forms,* edited by Donald Levine, 324–39. Chicago: University of Chicago Press, 1971.

———. "The Stranger." In *Georg Simmel on Individuality and Social Forms,* edited by Donald Levine, 143–49. Chicago: University of Chicago Press, 1971.

Smith, Adam. *An Inquiry into the Nature and Causes of the Wealth of Nations.* Chicago: University of Chicago Press, 1976.

———. *The Theory of Moral Sentiments.* Indianapolis: Liberty Classics, 1982.

Spencer, Herbert. "The Social Organism." In *Essays: Scientific, Political and Speculative,* Vol. 1, 265–307. London: Williams and Norgate, 1891.

Wahrman, Dror. *The Making of the Modern Self: Identity and Culture in Eighteenth-Century England.* New Haven: Yale University Press, 2004.

Weber, Max. *Economy and Society: An Outline of Interpretive Sociology.* Berkeley: University of California Press, 1978.

Weber, William. "The Rise of Classical Repertoire in Nineteenth-Century Orchestral Concerts." In *The Orchestra:*

Origins and Transformations, edited by Joan Peyser, 361–86. New York: Scribner, 1986.

Williams, Raymond. *Keywords: A Vocabulary of Culture and Society.* New York: Oxford University Press, 1983.

Contributors

Dominique Bauer is a professor at the Faculty of Architecture and a research fellow at the Faculty of Canon Law at the Catholic University of Leuven. She has a background in cultural and legal history and philosophy and did her Ph.D. on proceduralism, the subject and historicity in the legal thought of the early twelfth-century canonist Ivo of Chartres. Expanding this research into early modern contexts, she has published with Brill Academic, and with other publishers, a number of book chapters on law and historicity in the legal philosophy of Francisco Suárez. At the Faculty of Architecture her research focuses on the same and related notions of the subject, history and simultaneity as an intellectual concept in the imagery of interior spaces in the research groups "Interiority, Inhabitation and Architecture," and "Perspectives on Architecture from the distant past." She published articles on this theme as well as a monograph *Beyond the Frame: Case Studies* in 2016 with Academic and Scientific Publishers in Brussels.

Marcus Breyer received his Ph.D. from the Department of Germanic Languages and Literatures at The Ohio State University in 2017. His research addresses the role of language and the ways in which it shapes the human environment. He is particularly interested in metaphors of existence and their epistemic as well as experiential implications for human ecology. This is also the focus of his dissertation, as well as his current book project, in which he is conducting a metaphorological investigation into late-nineteenth-century sea metaphors in literature, early psychology, and in the emerging ecological sciences.

Aude Campmas is Lecturer in French Studies at Southampton University. Her current research interests include the relation between science and literature, and the representation of "the monstrous family" in Francophone literature. She is finishing a book based on her Ph.D., *Fleurs monstrueuses: histoire d'une métamorphose, Littérature, femmes et botanique,* describing the links between visual and textual representations of flowers, and the monstrous representation of women during the late nineteenth century. At the same time, she is working on the contemporary Lebanese-born Canadian playwright, painter and director Wajdi Mouawad and how he explores the family as a metaphor and origin of the Lebanese civil war.

Stijn De Cauwer is a postdoctoral researcher in Literary Theory and Cultural Studies at the University of Leuven. He completed his Ph.D. in 2012 at the University of Utrecht. The dissertation titled *A Diagnosis of Modern Life: Robert Musil's* Der Mann ohne Eigenschaften *as a Critical-Utopian Project* was published in 2014 by P.I.E. Peter Lang in Brussels. He is the editor of the volume *Critical Theory at a Crossroads: Conversations on Resistance in Times of Crisis* (New York: Columbia University Press, 2018) and co-editor of *50 Key Terms in Contemporary Cultural Theory* (Kalmthout: Pelckmans, 2017). He has co-edited special issues of *Configurations, Orbis Litterarum,* and *De Uil Van Minerva* and he is currently co-editing a special issue of *Angelaki*.

Erin E. Edgington is Assistant Director of the Honors Program at the University of Nevada, Reno. She earned her Ph.D. in French Literature from Indiana University-Bloomington in 2013. Since then, she has taught French language, literature, and culture at Queen's University Belfast and the University of

Michigan. A specialist of nineteenth-century French literature and art, she is the author of *Fashioned Texts and Painted Books: Nineteenth-Century French Fan Poetry* (Chapel Hill: University of North Carolina Press, 2017) as well as articles on the works of Stéphane Mallarmé, Théophile Gautier, Edmond de Goncourt, Octave Uzanne, and language pedagogy. Her research in the field of Honors education includes book chapters on internationalizing the Honors curriculum and the role of contract courses in the Honors experience.

Michael J. Kelly is Visiting Assistant Professor in Comparative Literature at Binghamton University (SUNY). He is an interdisciplinary scholar who specializes in Continental Thought, Historical Theory and the pre-Modern History of the Mediterranean. Michael received his Ph.D. in History from the University of Leeds, where he was twice awarded the annual extraordinary research prize. Michael is Director of the international, open-access project *Networks and Neighbours,* co-Editor, with Dolores Castro, of the *Visigothic Symposia* and co-Editor, with Paulo Pachá, of *Capitalism's Past.* He has published articles and books in philosophy, literary theory and history, including, with Arthur Rose, *Theories of History: History Read Across the Humanities* (New York & London: Bloomsbury, 2018).

Gabrielle Elissa Orsi earned her Ph.D. in Italian at the Department of Italian of Columbia University in New York in 2008 and has held fellowships at The Graduate Center, City University of New York, Northwestern University, and the Getty Research Institute of Los Angeles. She has served as a Discipline Peer Reviewer for the Council for International Exchange of Scholars (CIES), Language and Literature (Non-US) Fulbright Scholar committee since 2014. In 2014, she was a Visiting Scholar at the American Academy in Rome. Her academic interests include contemporary Italian literature, Italian Judaism and Holocaust studies. She is presently employed in the Office of Effectiveness and Strategic Planning at Bellevue College in Bellevue, Washington, where she also teaches Italian in the World Languages

Institute. Her most recent publication is "Battle Lines: Elsa Morante's War Writing," in the volume *Resistance, Heroism, Loss: World War II in Italian Literature and Film* published in 2018 by Fairleigh Dickinson University Press.

Álvaro Santana-Acuña is an Assistant Professor of Sociology at Whitman College. He holds a B.A. in History from the University of La Laguna, M.A. in Social Sciences from the University of Chicago, M.A. and Ph.D. in Sociology from Harvard University. He studies political and cultural objects, their role in producing collectively shared meanings, and their contribution to the maintenance of long-lasting social orders. He is the co-editor of *La nueva sociología de las artes* (Barcelona Gedisa, 2017) and author of *Ascent to Glory* (New York: Columbia University Press, forthcoming) in which he analyzes how the novel *One Hundred Years of Solitude* became a global classic. His research has been featured in *The New York Times, The Atlantic,* TIME, and *El País,* among other media. He is the recipient of multiple awards; most recently the 2017 Distinguished Scholarly Publication Award from the American Sociological Association.

Stefanie Sobelle is an Associate Professor of contemporary American literature and culture at Gettysburg College and the Art & Architecture Editor at the *Los Angeles Review of Books*. She is the author of *A Building is a Book: The Architectural Novel in America, 1865–2015* (forthcoming from Oxford University Press) and the dramaturg for HOME, a work of physical theater commissioned by the Brooklyn Academy of Music (where it premiered in 2017), which one a Bessie Award for Outstanding Production in 2018.

Lindsay Starck is an Assistant Professor of English at Augsburg College in Minneapolis, Minnesota. She completed her Ph.D. at the University of North Carolina at Chapel Hill and her M.F.A. at the University of Notre Dame. Her articles on modernist gossip have recently appeared or are forthcoming in *The Journal of Modern Periodical Studies* and *Modern Fiction Studies*. Her first novel was published by G.P. Putnam's Sons in 2016, and her short fiction has been published in *Ploughshares* and *The Cincinnati Review.*

www.ingramcontent.com/pod-product-compliance
Lightning Source LLC
Chambersburg PA
CBHW071001160426
43193CB00012B/1873